AMAZING GRACE

Embracing God's Empowering Presence

ROBERT GRIFFITH

GRACE AND TRUTH PUBLISHING
PO Box 338, Gunnedah NSW 2380 Australia
www.graceandtruthpublishing.com.au

Edited by Susan Pierotti - Creative Text Solutions
www.creativetext.com.au

Quotes in square brackets are the author's comment.

ISBN 978-0-646-88589-6

TABLE OF CONTENTS

PREFACE

I remember my Sunday School days with great fondness. The Bible stories and all the fun songs about Jesus provided a foundation for my spiritual life. However, by the time I reached high school, the church no longer seemed relevant or engaging for me, and so I drifted away. I am sure my basic worldview was still Christian, but a personal faith and a genuine encounter with God still eluded me.

That all changed at the age of fourteen when a school friend invited me to a youth Bible Study at his church. Within a few weeks, all of those Sunday School lessons morphed into a very real experience with God. I firmly embraced God's gift of salvation in Christ, and I was baptised in February 1973.

As I rose from the water at my baptism, I discerned a crystal-clear call from God into full time ministry. Of course, like Moses and David, I learned that the call of God rarely comes with a detailed schedule. It was not until fifteen years later when I finally entered Bible college and commenced my journey into full time ministry. Twenty years after that call from God at my baptism, I was ordained as a pastor in the Baptist church. In that same year I was appointed Senior Pastor of the local church I had been attending before entering college.

Only weeks after commencing my ministry in this new church, my wife and I had the privilege of spending three weeks at an intensive equipping retreat for pastors. One of those weeks was spent sitting under the teaching of Dr Ken Blue, then Pastor of Foothills Church in San Diego, California. He had already authored several books and had an established international teaching ministry. Ken spent the first two days of that week completely demolishing the theological foundation of my life and ministry. He knew we were pastors and preachers holding positions of leadership, teaching the people of God every week, yet Ken pulled no punches. He was quite brutal.

The theme of the week was grace. God had called Ken to present the message of God's amazing grace to the church in a way that most of us had never heard before. I am pleased to say that I finished that week in a different place to where I started. That was thirty years ago but I can still remember how my entire understanding of the gospel, the church and the kingdom of God changed that week. I was never the same again.

Within weeks of returning from that retreat, I began a teaching series titled *Setting the Captives Free*, in which I spent months exploring the centrality of grace in the Christian faith. I recall that the response from many people in my congregation was similar to my response when Ken Blue first undid most of what I had been taught, so it was a wild ride for a while. I didn't stop there – I was determined to lead my congregation through this 'grace awakening.' I followed with another teaching series which built on those foundations. I then preached through the book of Galatians, a letter which talks about grace on every page! For over a year, I hammered home the message of grace, and to my delight, God brought the vast majority of people with me on that transformational journey. Thirty years later, many of those dear brothers and sisters still talk about how life-changing that time was for them and for our church.

I served that congregation for over fifteen years. I often thank God for the miracle He performed in our midst and for the lessons He taught me which have defined my life and my ministry. All this began because one man was brave enough to tell it like it is, and if you have encountered Ken Blue's ministry, you may hear him speaking throughout this book.

Now before you read on, I want to encourage you to be prepared to read this book more than once. This is not a novel. Being exposed to this teaching once is usually not enough. I recall when I began expounding God's grace years ago, so many brothers and sisters told me that the full revelation came later after they had gone back and listened to all my sermons or read the manuscripts again. It was on the second and even third time through when the Lord fully opened their eyes, changed their lives and deepened their understanding of the gospel.

I must admit that even though I have been preaching about God's grace for decades now, I was confronted once again with the power of the gospel as I was writing this book. As you may know, when the Holy Spirit is involved, even truths which you have known for many years can slap you in the face like you have only just heard them for the first time! So, for me, writing this book has been confronting, but also very affirming.

My prayer is that God will richly bless you and empower you as you explore and embrace His amazing grace, and that you will allow God's spirit to transform you and revitalise your faith as the Holy Spirit prepares you for the next chapter of your kingdom journey. We have been given the greatest story in history to tell the whole world. This book was written to ensure that we tell the right story!

Robert Griffith

CHAPTER ONE
The Priority of Grace

What immediately comes into your mind when you read or hear the word 'grace'? Given that you are reading a Christian book, the field of possible definitions is probably narrowed. In the English language, there are seventeen different ways that 'grace' can be used as a noun and a few ways as a verb. In the face of those many definitions, which one should we choose if we are talking about God and the gospel? I don't think I would pick any of the dictionary definitions we would find today. To complicate matters even further, if I was to look up the word 'grace' in a Bible dictionary, I would most probably not be happy with most of the definitions there either, given what I now know and understand about God's amazing grace. Herein lies a significant problem.

Of all the words in our language; of all the concepts in the Bible and in our understanding of the Christian faith; I would have no hesitation in saying that 'grace' is by far the most important word for us to understand, embrace and embody as disciples of Christ who are committed to His mission. In fact, I would suggest that if we drilled down beneath all the heresies and false teaching, every theological error ever postulated and every church ministry which ever failed over the past two thousand years, we would find the root cause would be the same: a flawed or inadequate understanding of grace. I know that's a bold assertion, but it's one I believe you will agree with when you have finished reading this book.

Millions of people all over the world, who have struggled with those multiple definitions and tried to mine the depths of this simple but powerful word, will testify to a 'grace awakening' in recent years. Some of these people are new believers but many of them have been dedicated followers of Christ for many years and yet they have never really understood or fully embraced the radical message of grace.

It is those people to whom God called me to minister many years ago. What a privilege it has been to see captives set free within the church – to witness the Spirit of God opening people's hearts and minds across a church community – bringing a renewal which takes them into a very different place in their journey with God.

In June 1993, while serving as Senior Pastor in a Baptist congregation, I began to teach about God's grace and continued to do so in a focused and concentrated way for more than a year. During that time, many people experienced a radical 'awakening' as the Spirit of God moved with power through our local church. People who had been walking with God for most of their lives confessed that they had never heard teaching like that before. (I think they may have sat under similar teaching but may not have been ready to receive it.) When their eyes were finally opened to the heart of the gospel and the central truth of God's amazing grace, so many of them testified that it changed everything else they thought about God, themselves and the mission of Christ.

Grace is not just one of many beliefs or doctrines we need to embrace. Grace is not part of the gospel; grace *is* the gospel, and the gospel is grace! In fact, grace is to the Christian faith what oxygen is to us all. If we do not have a firm grasp of grace, if grace has not had its effect within us, then all we have is a facade, a shell, a Christian 'religion' with no power, no motivation and no real ability to fulfil our true purpose as God's children. Unless we have a firm understanding of God's amazing grace, unless His grace permeates everything we think, say and do each day, then our Christian lives will lack substance, vitality, truth and power. We need to get to the point of saying (and understanding) with Paul,

> But by the grace of God, I am what I am, and his grace to me was not without effect. No, I worked harder than all of them – yet not I, but the grace of God that was with me. (1 Corinthians 15:10)

You may think you already know all about God's amazing grace. Prior to my 'grace awakening', I probably thought that too. That is also what our brothers and sisters in Galatia thought all those years ago. We read in Galatians chapter 3 what happened to them when they lost sight of grace. That's why the apostle Paul preached about grace over and over again. He said it was a safeguard for his hearers (Philippians 3:1).

However, before we begin this journey together, I have a few warnings. Be prepared to think. Be prepared to have some of your views about God and your faith challenged. Be prepared for a spiritual battle. Satan and his religious spirits will fight against the message of grace with all their might. Therefore, you need to be as alert as you are excited. You need to be on guard, but full of faith and anticipation of what God will do in you and through you as you journey through this book.

For many years now, people have been asking me why I place such a heavy emphasis on grace in all my preaching. There are many reasons but allow me to share just a few. I emphasise the grace of God because that's what Jesus and Paul did, so I'm just following their lead. They both emphasised the grace, goodness and love of God and the fact that God has taken the initiative in our salvation. God has spoken to us, called us, forgiven us, saved us, redeemed us and transformed us. He does all this unconditionally, by His grace, before we are even born! Then we show up and have our eyes and ears opened by the Holy Spirit and we believe that truth; we step into that reality and participate in His grace.

Another reason why I emphasis grace is because it releases joy in people. If you want to sum up Paul's own personal ministry, it was to increase the joy of his followers (Philippians 1:25–26). We only have one life to live, and I would like to live that life with as much joy as possible, and so would you, I'm sure. I'd also like those who are part of the church to be happy and to personally experience the inexpressible joy of the Lord. So, I will preach and teach grace in order that your joy may increase and that will make church a joyful place to be. Only then will people outside the church be attracted to us and want to know the source of our joy.

When the ministry of Jesus began on earth, He confronted the 'senior pastors,' scholars and teachers of His day and exposed the heavy burden of legalism they had dumped on God's people. He stood against anything which contradicted the message of God's grace and the truth of the gospel. An important part of His mission on earth was to lift the burden of expectation off the back of God's people, a burden which the religious leaders had placed there over hundreds of years. A spirit of religion had enslaved the people of God and Jesus came to demolish those strongholds as He preached, demonstrated and lived God's amazing grace.

Jesus came to set the captives free, and I've been called by God to do the same: to expose the religious spirits which have enslaved God's people by false teaching and to lift the crushing burden of religion from His disciples. I want people to bear the rich fruit they were created and called to bear. Trees in an orchard bear fruit because the life is in the tree to produce that kind of fruit. It just happens – the tree doesn't need to grunt and groan and strain to bear fruit; it simply needs to be fed and watered and the rest comes naturally.

So too with Christians who know the truth and are filled with the joy of the Lord. They will produce the fruit of the life of Christ within them and it will take very little effort on their part. They just need to be fed the right spiritual food and immersed in the living water Christ promised to give them. When you understand the grace of God in all its truth, before long you'll just overflow with fruit. Then people who are starved for joy are going to look at you and say, 'Where did you get that? I want some too!' You will then be able to say with great enthusiasm, 'I got it from the Lord Jesus Christ as a free gift. Let me tell you about it …'

Grace permeates my teaching because of the radical healing that it brings to people's lives and the fruit it produces. I have had the joy of seeing thousands of people set radically free in so many ways when they finally understand grace. It's like they have met God for the first time! Their joy has become mine as I've read letters and emails from around the world and spoken to many whom God has touched in the depth of their being as I have unpacked the central truth of the gospel: God's amazing grace.

When people believe the truth of the gospel and then embrace it personally, profound changes occur in them. I'm not talking about unbelievers here – I'm talking about Christians. There is an urgent need for the people of God to be reintroduced to the radically free grace of God and the power which His grace brings to our lives.

I have seen people, some having wasted countless hours and thousands of dollars on clinical counselling, set free in one glorious moment as the power of the living gospel of God's grace transforms their hearts and their lives. Perhaps the main reason why I continue to preach the gospel of grace is summed up beautifully by the apostle Paul:

> ... the gospel [of grace] which has come to you, as indeed in the whole world it is bearing fruit and growing [spontaneously and habitually] – so among yourselves, from the day you [first] heard and [then] understood the grace of God in truth ... (Colossians 1:5b–6, RSV)

Hearing and understanding God's grace in all its truth produces more than just joy. It produces *all* the fruit of the gospel, the fruit of the Spirit – love, joy, peace, patience, kindness etc. Everything you want in life, everything that makes life worth living as an authentic human being, everything that makes the gospel attractive, everything that we love and appreciate about the personality of Jesus Christ – that is what's birthed within us when we understand grace in all its truth.

I don't just want people to be joyful and happy. I really want to play a significant part in advancing the kingdom of God on earth, and to help others do the same. I want to understand God's grace in all its truth and lead others to fully embrace that truth because it's the power of God for the salvation of everyone who believes. Grace is the power that releases fruit-bearing energy in Christians and in fellowships.

That's why I don't put my efforts into church growth or counselling techniques, although they may have their place. I don't rely on exhortation, manipulation, wrenching money out of people, self-promotion or even church promotion! There are a dozen different ways we might grow the church numerically; none of them interest me and I am sure they don't interest God either. As Paul reminds us in Romans 1:16, the gospel is itself the power of God for the salvation of everyone who believes. I want to help build and be part of a *real* church. If it's a little smaller than some, then so be it, as long as it's real. However, I believe that if it's real, it will not be small for long.

In this book, which I have been writing for over twenty years, I am going to explore the heart of the gospel and talk about God's amazing grace from lots of different angles, knowing that in time it will bear fruit on a large scale in your church, in your community and across your whole nation. But before you begin this grace marathon, I need to warn you again – this teaching is dangerous. It produced many enemies for the apostle Paul. His preaching split synagogues all over Asia Minor. Believe it or not, his life was in constant danger because of the liberating message contained in the pages of this book – the message of God's free, radical grace.

What you are going to read here is what landed Paul in hot water over and over again and eventually got him killed. That same message is even more dangerous today because the church has had a very long time to become even more steeped in legalism and performance-based religion than it was in Paul's day.

If you believe what (or rather, Who) you encounter in this book, then your life will change – radically. I don't care how long you have been a disciple of Christ, how knowledgeable you are in the Scriptures or what Bible teaching you have enjoyed – God's grace is always transformative. Regardless of where you are in your spiritual journey, your life will change as you embrace the grace of God fully. As that happens, be prepared for some opposition. The enemy will not back off when he sees his captives being set free. He will fight hard and dirty, and more often than not, he will use those closest to you to drag you back under his bondage.

Whenever I have taught the truths in this book, there has been a wide variety of reactions in people. I don't expect it will be any different as I travel this road with those who read this book. Some will receive what they read here without questioning; some will question it and even be a little confused for a while as I unpack the gospel chapter by chapter; and some may reject it completely. In their hearts, some will feel the liberating power and presence of the Spirit of God releasing them and giving them a new hunger and thirst for the gospel.

Some others will feel uncomfortable and find what they read here to be foreign to what they currently understand; others may wonder how anyone could have the audacity to write or teach such heresy!

I want you to know that all of those reactions are perfectly normal. I have encountered them all at various times in my journey into grace, so I know exactly how it feels. But this is the gospel. This is what Jesus died for. This is what got Stephen stoned to death while Saul of Tarsus watched on and laughed. This is what then turned Saul on his head, transformed him into the apostle Paul and put him in jail for preaching what he used to denounce. This is what got all of the apostles except one killed! This is the heart and soul of the Bible message, and it possesses the life-changing, mind-blowing power of God. That is why I must write this, why I must teach this. But you don't have to receive it.

All I ask of you is this: if you encounter any teaching here that is new to you, please be patient, because many of your questions and concerns will be answered within this book. Don't let the enemy close your mind and harden your heart before you get a chance to find those answers. As tempting as it may be, don't dismiss a statement until you have read the whole book. As I said earlier, I have letters from people for whom the lights didn't go on until months or years later as they revisited this teaching and God opened their eyes.

So, what's it going to be? Are you going to press on like Paul and search for the treasures that are yours in Christ? Are you going to find the freedom that Christ promised and let Him make it a reality in your life? Are you going to come out from under any bondage of religion and evil religious spirits that may have infiltrated the church and robbed you of the fullness and reality of Christianity? Is your Christian faith real? Be honest, how much of it has made it from your head to your heart? Is the Holy Spirit as real to you as He was to Jesus, the early disciples and the apostles in the book of Acts? Are you prepared to stand before God right now and say:

> 'Lord, I want more! I'm not satisfied with my life and my relationship with you as it us. I want to keep growing and maturing in Christ. I want to press on and receive all that You have for me. I want it all Lord, by Your grace, for Your glory, through Your Spirit!'

If the Holy Spirit has placed that desire in your heart, I want to encourage you to press on with this book and take all the time you need to embrace the truths which will be unpacked page by page and make the most of the opportunity God is giving you here.

This book will challenge you, confront you, excite you and, I trust, transform you from the inside out. You may well meet a God that you never knew existed – a God of grace and mercy and power; a God Who still speaks and moves in powerful ways; a God Who desires desperately to be in relationship with you and Who will take ninety-nine out of every hundred steps to achieve that for you.

Will you take that one step towards Him?

CHAPTER TWO
A Prison Without Doors

Can you remember your early days as a Christian? Can you remember the joy, the excitement and the wonder that gripped your heart? Can you remember that powerful desire to know God and the longing to receive all that He has for you? How long did that last? Do you still feel that way now? Do you desire to know God more than anything else in the world? If you do, then I rejoice with you!

Sadly, as I've rubbed shoulders with my brothers and sisters in Christ over many years across the church, I have been grieved to observe that many of them have lost a lot of that deep, passionate yearning for God. They no longer have that reckless abandon and desire to be an explorer and adventurer in the kingdom of God. I also know this from personal experience because that's exactly what happened to me many years ago.

As new believers, we become part of the only community in this broken world where our new-found joy and excitement should be encouraged and fed (the church), only to find that we are a square peg in a round hole. When we begin with the Lord, we are bursting with love for Jesus and love for others; we are involved in every ministry we can and this new-found relationship with God is wonderful and all-consuming.

Then, more often than not, something happens over time and the fire starts to lose its heat. Before long, the inevitable happens – the square pegs start to lose their edges, and very soon they conform to the round holes and now fit in very well. The fact that this happens is sad, but the fact that most Christians are unaware of it is tragic. It's a gradual process that most of us are not even aware of; our passion and zeal for God Himself is slowly replaced with programs, ministries, meetings and events. For many in the church, their once-vibrant relationship with God is subtly overtaken by exhausting, life-draining, religious activity.

We may not know it at the time, but we are allowing Satan to take God's people captive in the prison of religion. The apostle Paul knew all about religion and the deceptive work of the enemy who always wants to hold God's people back through false teaching and deception. As 'Saul the persecutor', he was an expert on religion. His religious qualifications, experience and performance were second to none prior to meeting Jesus on the road to Damascus. But once his eyes were opened by the Spirit of God, Paul declared (in Philippians 3:8) that he considered his entire religious pedigree to be rubbish, and his primary desire was that he might gain Christ.

From the day when the church was born, and thousands of people were set free from the chains of religion and brought into the freedom of a relationship with God through Jesus Christ, the enemy of God, Satan, has been running a relentless campaign to drag God's people back under the bondage of the law. He has blinded so many believers to the spiritual reality that lies beneath much of the religious activity that can consume our time, energy and focus.

What grieves me most is that most of those believers who were taken captive again are no longer engaging with teaching like this – because they have already gone. I am writing this book primarily for those still in the church because it is vitally important for us to stay alert and remain free from the chains of legalism and religion, but my heart is breaking for the thousands of people who used to be part of the church.

In every community across our nation, there are more ex-church members than those currently involved in the church. I believe that if we could round up all those people who were once part of a church community, we would not have an auditorium large enough to fit them in. We can mourn that reality and wish it were different, or we can find out why this has occurred and change it. There are lots of reasons given by those who have left the church and by those who may have willingly or unknowingly helped them out the door. They didn't like the pastor or the music or the theology or the leadership direction – and the list goes on. I believe that's all a smoke screen for what ultimately made it easy for them to walk away.

In my opinion, and from observing this dynamic in the church for fifty years now, the main reason why such people chose to break fellowship with the family of God is far less complicated and far more serious. I believe they were no longer hearing or receiving the good news. The gospel of God's amazing grace was not being role-modelled, preached, taught and lived. Consequently, the living, reigning Christ was no longer observably present and central. A community of faith which encounters the true gospel and understands grace in all its truth will always encounter God in their midst and when God is truly present in a community of faith, people are usually drawn to that community, not pushed away or given a reason to leave.

As I have observed this dynamic over many years, I now understand why Jesus spoke out so strongly against religion – He knew who was behind it. We may think that Satan does his best work in the world. We

11

may look at the sin, moral decay and desperation in the world around us and think that's Satan's best efforts at work. I don't believe that's true. The devil doesn't have to work very hard at all to keep the world from encountering God. His greatest goal is to keep believers from truly understanding, embracing and living the gospel. If he can replace new covenant, Christ-centred, Spirit-empowered Christianity with religion, then he has effectively disempowered all that Jesus did in the life of the believer and all that His Spirit desires to do in the church. Jesus tore off the doors of the prison of sin, death and religion, but so many believers are still living as captives, oblivious to their true freedom.

I recall one Sunday many years ago when we had a visitor in our church, a Baptist pastor from Victoria. At the end of the service, he came to me and asked if he could share a vision with me which he believed the Lord had given him in the middle of my sermon. I was happy to listen. The picture he described was as simple as it was confronting, and I have never forgotten it. He saw a group of people in a prison cell. It looked like they had been there for some time and were very familiar with their surroundings. They were not stressed or trying to get out or protesting their lot in life. They actually seemed resigned to their fate. But when he looked closer into this vision, he could not believe what he saw – this prison had no doors! They had been ripped from their hinges and there was a huge gaping hole where there used to be locked doors. Everyone in this prison was free to leave and yet they were so used to life inside the prison, they either didn't notice there were no longer any doors, or they were just too afraid to step into the unknown and embrace their freedom.

I have never forgotten that vision, and over the following several years in that congregation, I had the incredible privilege of seeing hundreds of people finally venture out of that prison into the freedom which Christ died to give them. That prison is religion. That prison is what the visible church will always become when God is not given free rein.

I believe Satan has worked in two major ways to rob the church of our experience of God. Firstly, by convincing believers that their current experience of God is as good as it gets and to pursue more would make them fanatical. As a result, they embrace complacency and disappointment as normal. Secondly, the way the enemy works within the church is by loading us with heavy burdens of religious expectation to exhaust us, discourage us and rob us of our energy and enthusiasm. Both strategies work equally well for his purposes and there is a body of false teaching to support each view. This leads people further away from a personal experience of God and His amazing, empowering grace.

A deadly mist of deception has settled over parts of the church which has caused too many Christians to forget that they are on a spiritual pilgrimage. All of the riches of heaven are in Christ, and as Christians, we are in Christ, so those riches are all available to every Christian from day one. However, we do not automatically experience them. That's why Paul encouraged believers to 'press on' into the heart of God and embrace those riches one by one.

Many teachers today deny this necessity, teaching that to seek more is unbelieving or fanatical. In so doing, they either leave a trail of frustrated, unfulfilled and hopeless Christians behind them; or they develop a breed of satisfied, self-assured Christians who are blinded to the possibility of a deeper, more vibrant and more fruitful encounter with God.

The apostle Paul amazes and humbles me as I read his words in the third chapter of his letter to the Philippians. His earnest desire was to press forward and become all that a disciple of Jesus can become in this life. He had no desire to be average or mediocre. He detested the very idea. Paul humbly but intensely breathed his great desire, with passion and longing with words like: 'that I may gain Christ', 'that I may be found in Him', 'that I may know Him'. His Christian faith was an ongoing, exciting journey with God, as he testified, 'I follow after; I press on toward the mark ... I have not obtained ... I am striving to lay hold of that for which Christ laid hold of me'.

An alarming number of people who identify as Christians across the world are complete strangers to the desire, the longing and the Spirit which drove Paul forward each day. Many are content to believe that their current experience is as good as it gets in this life and that we should just be thankful and cultivate what we already have. Why are so many Christians deaf to the clear appeals in the Bible concerning spiritual desire, longing and progression in our walk with God?

Why are we so quick to accept the view that we have arrived at some spiritual plateau and that we just need to maintain what we have in Christ? Some days it feels like the church is in a holding pattern just waiting to land in heaven, going round and round in circles waiting for their homecoming. Have we forgotten that Jesus brought heaven here over two thousand years ago and commissioned us to tell the world that the kingdom of heaven is *here*?

There also exists a strange view in the church, which has been with us from the very beginning, that assumes because we know chapter and verse and may even be privileged to understand the original Greek or Hebrew, we also possess the content, the experience and the powerful reality embodied in those words. The spirit of the Pharisees is still with us today and I think this is one of the deadliest, most chilling breezes ever to blow across the church.

There has never been a time in the history of Christianity when believers have known so much about God. We have dozens of different translations of the Bible at our fingertips, thousands of Bible commentaries and books, computer programs that can search every word in the Bible in two seconds, devotional books written by people who have had very special experiences with God. We have so many wonderful teaching institutions where we can absorb more information about God and ministry in a few years than most people will in a lifetime. In fact, if spiritual vitality were judged by the amount we know about God, we should be seeing an unprecedented movement of God's Spirit right across the world.

The reason we are not seeing such a revival is clear. The Bible, and all of history, tells us that the only thing that will bring about revival is the fire of God being ignited deep in our souls. When that happens, all that wonderful knowledge about God is supernaturally transformed into something that is truly ours. We no longer have to just believe it because it's in the Bible or because some respected author or preacher says so. We know it's true because the Spirit of the living God has burned it into our experience. When we have become convinced that our experience of God is complete, our spiritual life stalls. When we forget that our journey into the heart of God is progressive and dynamic, we will not grow in our relationship with the God, and we will fail to fully embrace the mission of Christ.

We may have heard truth that we are just not willing to act upon. As a result, we are brought to a dead halt in our spiritual journey. We dry up on the vine. If there's something that we will not do for Him, some confession we will not make, something we refuse to straighten out – something we lack the courage to do for God's glory –we might still be saved, we might still be heaven-bound, but we will come to a sudden stop in our spiritual journey this side of heaven.

People are sitting in church buildings all over the world each week having made no significant spiritual progress for years. Many have been rendered useless by accepting a chronic state of discouragement. As a result, they've become resigned. They have rationalised their situation and are convinced that this condition is normal for all Christians. If we are in this category, we are believers but we're not believers for ourselves. We say we believe in this progressive, victorious, abundant Christian pilgrimage, but we are forced to concede it's for others, not for us. We've gone forward at every altar, we've been to all the seminars and conferences, we've read all the latest books, but the blessings, the joy, the wonder, the power and the effectiveness of kingdom living seems to be for someone else – not us.

What Jesus is saying to such people is exactly what He said to the man lying by the pool at Bethesda: 'Do you want to be made whole?' Jesus made that man whole and raised him up because he *wanted* to be healed and delivered more than anything else in the world. If Jesus had found in that man the same attitude as He finds in too many Christians today, I believe He may have passed him by!

Another reason why many of us make no progress with God is that we've joined the 'Respectability Club.' We've learned the art of 'becoming adjusted'. We've chosen to be cool and proper, poised, self-controlled and well-rounded. We would never want anyone to think that we've taken an extreme position, particularly in spiritual matters. For many years, I accepted just an average spiritual state, and I had no deep desire for God.

So many Christians are living like that today: 'going to church' week in and week out and rarely feeling an extra heartbeat, rarely feeling any kindling of godly desire or passion. God made it clear to me years ago that unless I was willing to surrender to Him absolutely and allow Him to move in and have His way, I was never going to have the spiritual adventures like those who have been explorers in His kingdom. *God will light the fire when we lie on the altar!*

There is so much more for us. We don't think often enough about those who have been the prospectors in the hills of God's kingdom, the spiritual adventurers, the trailblazers. God wrote about them in the Bible because they were seeking a better land, a better life, a better tomorrow, and we should thank God for their example. Why did Abraham pack up and leave his hometown of Ur? Because God promised him spiritual adventures and he moved out at God's bidding. But that didn't make Abraham a hero at home. Just think of what the contented people of Ur must have said to Abraham. 'What are you doing, Abe? What's the matter with you? Everyone else is satisfied with their current religion (they actually worshipped the moon god), but you talk about hearing a voice that told you to 'go into the land which I will show you'. You're a fool,

Abraham, a demented fool!' But Abraham would have simply said, 'I heard the voice of God, plain and clear. I'm moving out!' Abraham was no hero – he was the laughingstock of his hometown, I'm sure. But you know the rest of his story, don't you? God blessed that man and all believers since, because of his willingness to step out of his comfort zone and follow God. All of the heroes in God's 'hall of fame' had something happen deep inside them. An internal fire had to be lit before anything happened externally.

Far too many Christians still believe that outward changes in life and character and behaviour is what God expects. Many have made decisions to enter full-time ministry or to go to work on some foreign mission field because of advice and pressures from the outside. That's religion – that's what Jesus condemned – that's what real Christianity was supposed to replace! This is a journey that must begin in the heart. But some of God's dear children have not embarked upon such a journey, or they started and got scared and pulled back. So now they lack that deep longing for His best pastures because they've not found the delight of experiencing for themselves the glorious riches of Christ!

I recall a statement made by an old Hindu writer: 'You, who are busy learning texts and not living them, are like the man counting other people's cattle without having a single heifer of his own.' Translated for our context: a lot of professing Christians are busy 'counting other people's cattle' – studying theology, reading lots of other people's books, even studying the Bible for hours – but they have very little from God which is truly their own. They have this enormous amount of acquired knowledge about God which really belongs to somebody else.

Another way the enemy deceives us is by leading us to trust in our own performance. The zeal of those who want it all and want it now can cause these enthusiastic believers to run ahead of God and not realise how they have been led astray from the gospel that saved them. This is the essence of religious behaviour, and it totally distorts our love relationship with God. One line of this kind of thinking is that God saves us and forgives us – He gets us into the race by His free love and grace – but then we have to run the race ourselves.

This idea of two stages in our Christian walk is a common error which has been taught in the church for centuries. This is a lie perpetrated by the enemy and one that has caused more burn-out and pain in believers' lives than any other. When people believe it is their responsibility alone to make their lives work, they punish themselves when the work goes slowly, or when they fall back into sin, or don't seem to get a grip on their emotional or spiritual life or those disciplines – as if this work was waiting for them to get their act together.

We need to understand one thing here: *what God starts, God promises to finish.* That's what God's amazing grace does; it frees people to tell it like it is and not feel condemned. People have been surprised when they have come to me over the years and felt comfortable to confess things they've been carrying around for years and I have not reacted in shock. I certainly hope I was sympathetic, but my calm response to their confession was because I never trusted them with their life anyway! I don't trust you to get it right any more than I trust myself. If I had faith in your commitment to the Lord or in your resolution to follow the Lord, or if I put faith in your disciplines, then I would be distressed, but I will never do that. I trust the Holy Spirit within you, and I need you to trust the Holy Spirit within me and not place your trust in any fallible human being.

The New Testament tells me that God decided a long time ago that He would take charge of our lives, and He would take final responsibility to save us, to go on saving us and to perfect us in the end. From the first to the last, building on grace is God's building project, not ours. Let me illustrate this with another clear statement from the apostle Paul:

> *Therefore, my dear friends, as you have always obeyed – not only in my presence, but now much more in my absence – continue to work out your salvation with fear and trembling, for it is God who works in you to will and to act in order to fulfill his good purpose. (Philippians 2:12–13)*

Paul is not saying, 'Work out your salvation because God has begun a good work in you and now it's your turn to shine.' He tells us to work out our salvation, believing with the faith God has given us, that God has decided to continue working in us. God doesn't just get us started and then hand the reins to us. We see this nailed down even more here:

> *… being confident of this, that he who began a good work in you will carry it on to completion until the day of Christ Jesus. (Philippians 1:6)*

God will not stop carrying it on until it's completed. When we work out our Christian lives in the midst of a fallen world – with all its temptations and all its opposition – we have confidence that God, Who by His grace began a good work in us, has taken personal responsibility for completing that work.

So, when someone says, 'Things are really happening. My life is being transformed by God's grace. I can't believe how great I feel', I thank God for continuing His work in that person. When someone comes to me

17

broken and upset and overwhelmed by sin past or present, I thank God for continuing His work in that person too. The mere fact that they even desire to struggle against this sin is evidence that God is at work. If He was not at work, they would simply submit to the sin and relax. It is God Who builds on His grace in you. Your responsibility is to cooperate with Him, and very often. Just get out of His way and submit to His Spirit's work in you. Our faith must be in God's work, never in our own work. Our job is to believe and receive, believe and receive, believe and receive. It's all by grace alone.

The experience of exhaustion, discouragement or quiet despair, which is the outcome of both of these errors, has produced a further misunderstanding, which the enemy uses to keep Christians bound by guilt and shame. I am talking about the idea that there are 'first-class' and 'second-class' Christians. The first-class Christians are those without any observable serious sin; they are victorious or fully committed or Spirit-filled or powerful or whatever. The second-class Christians are the strugglers, the ones who can't quite get it together, who have not yet yielded to God or died to self or 'ticked the right box' to reach the 'higher levels' of Christian life and experience.

We can start off with this false assumption of two classes of Christians; from that have come thousands of books, videos, podcasts and teaching on the deeper Spirit-filled life. We have been bombarded with thousands of seminars, sermons and talks aimed at getting us to 'qualify' for God's 'higher purposes'. From this teaching comes the terms 'carnal' or 'worldly' Christian. These teachers would tell us that if we can just pull these carnal and worldly Christians into line, everything will be fine. I don't believe we have a problem with 'carnal' Christians because I don't believe they exist, and nor does the Bible.

It's my belief that when you're looking at the church and see who you think are worldly or carnal Christians, what you're actually looking at are either non-Christians who think they are Christians, or Christians who have become discouraged and disempowered, largely by bad teaching. There is only one kind of Christian, and that is one who is in Christ. There is no two-stage Christian life! It's that simple. That is the clear teaching of the New Testament. You can't be a little bit pregnant – you either have a life within you, or you don't. The same is true for us: you either have Christ in you – or you don't.

Let me be very specific and practical. As I wrote earlier, many people have said to me, or implied, 'I've blown it big time. I guess I'm not a first-class victorious Christian after all, and now I wonder if I ever will be.'

Those may not be their actual words, but the hopelessness that comes into their eyes tells me that such people have bought into this lie. They believe that because they've stumbled or fallen, they are now somehow relegated to a second-class status and that they may never get out of that rut. There is no such thing as a second-class Christian! You are simply a Christian who has stumbled. The reason I know this is because you were knocked down and got up again; that's what happens to true believers. Unbelievers get knocked down and stay down. The desire to deal with that sin or that problem is evidence that God is working out His purposes in you. He's completing that which He decided a long time ago to begin in you by His grace.

God will not allow you to completely sabotage your life. Look at the entire flow of your life. Do you keep coming back to God? If you don't, then you're not a Christian. Your heart has not yet been regenerated by the Holy Spirit, and we need to share the gospel with you; it's that simple. But let's never say that if you don't keep coming back to God, you're a backslidden or 'carnal' Christian. No, you're not – you're not a Christian!

Some people may not appreciate this, but when dear old Grandpa Joe comes to me and says, 'Pastor, I'm really worried about my little Billy. He's not walking with the Lord, but when he was eight years old, he made a profession of faith. He hasn't been with the Lord since, but I know that God honours that profession.' No, He doesn't! This kid isn't a Christian. Look at his life. Christianity isn't some theory that you need to guess at. You just need to look at a person's life– not today, not tomorrow, not even over the stretch of a year, but over the long haul – and you will see who is a Christian and who is not.

Those who are true believers will keep returning to God and will keep working out their salvation, because God is at work within them. When they fall, they get up. Maybe not immediately, but sooner or later they are drawn back because there is a hunger and thirst for God. He has a hook in their heart, and they can't deny it. You have to look at the whole thrust and direction of a person's life to determine if they are in Christ or not. The authentic Christian life is characterised by a hunger for God and a desire for righteousness, yet it is marred by sin.

Until the new heaven and new earth comes, that statement is true of every one of us. If God has begun a work in us, there will be a hunger for Him within us and it will keep bringing us back to Him. This is not a do-it-yourself project. God is doing it, in us. Now if we want to speed up that process, there are some things we can do to cooperate with God's work in us. If you want to cooperate with the grace-building that God is doing within you:

- Read the Bible – it will inform you and give you faith.
- Pray – it will bring power into your life.
- Worship – it will release you and heal you.
- Give – it will set your priorities straight.

There are certain Christian disciplines that you can embrace, not in order to be a good Christian, but as a response to what God is doing in you and so that you can cooperate with the life that God is building in you. God is the builder, but you should throw Him a few bricks occasionally!

When you believe in Jesus Christ, you believe into a great, broad, fast-flowing river of redemptive power. You are caught in its grip, being carried along, and it's easier to swim with it than to swim against it or to deny its reality. So, when you ask, 'When will I conquer my sins?' and 'When will I have joy?' and 'When will I really experience the power and presence of God?', the answer is, 'When you start to believe God, when you relax and cheer up in light of His promises and His faithfulness, when you take seriously what He has said and what you can observe all around you.' That is when these burdens and barriers will begin to disappear at an increasingly faster rate. So, cheer up, take heart, have faith in God, practice His presence and rejoice in His provision, because His grace is sufficient to complete what He has started.

What's the very first thing you did when you became a Christian? You had faith in the work of Jesus, right? Well, why stop? You need the same faith in the work of Jesus today as you did back then. The entire Christian life is making a choice to believe God every day, in every way. The entire Christian life from your end is lived by faith; that is, making a choice to believe something that may be very radical for some, but entirely reasonable. God is trustworthy; we've seen enough of His character to know that He can be trusted. If you can say that, then you can have a happy Christian life, despite your inconsistencies and occasional sins.

Jesus Christ came to set the captives free. He tore the doors off that prison cell over two thousand years ago. Thousands upon thousands of those early converts were freed from the religion of the Pharisees. Two thousand years later, the visible church has once again allowed itself to be imprisoned by the law and religion in spite of our freedom in Christ. Do you want to experience the fullness of the radical freedom which is yours in Christ? Do you want to become one of the adventurers, an explorer in the hills of God's kingdom, one who will do anything possible to find the treasures that God has for those who are prepared to look away from themselves and look to Him? Are you fed up with being average, mediocre, frustrated, depressed or defeated, wishing you had something real in your relationship with God? Do you want to know God personally – not just know about Him? How strong is that desire really? How badly do you want to be close to God and set free from the physical, emotional or spiritual torment that you are enduring?

Many of us say that we want something more in our life, but we are reluctant to admit it and face it head-on. Are you prepared to admit your need to God, to yourself and to others? Are you prepared to swallow the pride that the enemy will put there, and confess that you haven't got it all together, that you're struggling, that you want something real from God? If you are, then that desire has come from Him.

As we journey together through this book, I want us to explore the wide-open spaces of God's freedom and the grace He has given us in Christ, and I want to encourage you to pursue Him with all the energy and passion you have and not let anything or anyone get in your way – especially not your pride. The enemy of God would try to catch us in the traps and snares of religion to destroy that freedom, render grace ineffective in our lives and bring us under bondage again, so we must learn to recognise his work in us and around us.

'It is for freedom that Christ has set us free!' (Galatians 5:1). So, don't stop. Press on! Jesus Christ came to set captives completely free and destroy the work of the enemy. From beginning to end, our journey is by His grace, for His glory and through His Spirit. God has committed Himself to you totally, completely and forever. He has promised to bring you safely home. Understand that, and you will understand God's amazing grace in all its truth.

CHAPTER THREE
Relationship vs. Religion

You may have grown up in the church or you may have come to faith later in your life. You heard the message of forgiveness of sin, the love and acceptance of God, eternal life in a new relationship with Him, and your heart was pierced by the Holy Spirit as you responded to what God had already done for you. You knew without any doubt that God was real. He was powerful. He was your gracious, loving, heavenly Father. You were filled with joy and everyone around you knew it.

Then maybe you were taught (or it was implied) that if you wanted to go on from there, if you wanted to be a 'first-class' Christian and really see the blessings of God, you needed to start adding disciplines to your life. Soon, these disciplines became standards or rules by which you judged yourself and others. You were told that Jesus is the only way to the Father, but you need to also do your bit. If you don't think you were exposed to that kind of teaching, praise God! But I can assure you that hundreds of thousands of others have been and many of them are no longer with us in this journey, and they need us to bring them back to the true gospel message of 'Jesus plus nothing.'

Let me make it clear right at the outset. If you hear 'Jesus plus something', you are not hearing an improvement on the gospel. You are not hearing a new version of the gospel, or even a distortion of the gospel. You are hearing the absolute destruction of the gospel, along with its integrity and its power. When, by the revelation and power of the Holy Spirit, those 'extras' are removed as requirements, then the beauty, purity and power of the gospel will return to our hearts and lives.

That is the whole focus of this book. That is God's calling on my life. That's why I am here, more than any other reason – to speak the truth of the gospel into a needy church and a needy world. This is what all those brothers and sisters who have walked away from God and the church desperately need to hear: the true gospel. When it comes to our basic understanding of God and our relationship with Him, most of us don't need to hear something new, we just need to believe what we may have heard the first time: *Jesus plus nothing is our salvation and our life!*

We need to experience afresh the life of God that is already in us, that never left us and will continue to hold us fast and bring repentance, holiness and godly fruit. The gospel is the power of God for the salvation of everyone who believes. (Romans 1:16). The gospel contains God's power to bring about radical and lifelong change. As I have already made clear, I don't have confidence in my ability to communicate these truths or in your ability to discern them, but I do have absolute confidence in the Holy Spirit within all believers Who will energise God's Word and produce the changed lives that we all want. The grace of God will have its own effect; of that, I am sure. That is why it *must* be preached and taught over, and over, and over again.

Many years ago, the apostle Paul wrote a scathing letter to the Galatian believers after he learned that they had accepted this 'Jesus plus' teaching. This is some of what he wrote:

> *I am astonished that you are so quickly deserting the One who called you in the grace of Christ and are turning to a different gospel – which is really no gospel at all. Evidently some people are throwing you into confusion and are trying to pervert the gospel of Christ. (Galatians 1:6–7)*

Paul can't believe the report he has been given: these brothers and sisters, whose lives were changed through his preaching of the gospel of God's amazing grace, have thrown their freedom away and accepted something so much less than the full and free life they received through Christ. Paul is wondering whether he completely wasted his time with these people. The Galatians had allowed well-meaning but false teachers to come among them and cut the heart and soul out of the message of Jesus Christ. The gospel message was simple: *God loves you and has saved you in Jesus Christ, and He gives you an ongoing relationship at His expense, with His power – and it's all free to you upon your believing.*

Why does that simple, beautiful message upset anyone? It only upsets those who have been taken captive by religion – it is a breath of fresh air to everyone else! Jesus and Paul taught that the people who struggle with sin but keep looking to God for forgiveness and relationship, depending on Him to put them right, are closer to the power of the kingdom of God than those who seem to have it all together. The person filled with the Spirit of God looks to Him for mercy and always finds it. Then God throws in His empowering presence, spiritual gifts and all the blessings of heaven as a bonus! Whereas the person who appears to be strong says:

> *'Thanks for giving me a start, God. I was lost without You, but I can take it from here. I am going to get my act together; I'm going to memorise the New Testament and really pay my way. I'll earn my status in the kingdom of heaven, so You won't be ashamed of me ...'*

That person has shifted their focus to their own performance, and their heart is full of pride. They have fallen away from grace. The awful thing is that when their life dries up, they will work harder and harder to please God, and the more they perform to please God, the more they will suppress the life of Christ within them. Just like the Galatians, they 'have turned to a different gospel, which is really no gospel at all'.

The true gospel says that God loves us and accepts us just the way we are through the perfect life of Jesus. His perfect performance against the holy law of God is credited to us and that becomes our experience when we believe, accept and embrace that good news. The gospel says that God has already fully and forever taken care of sin. The punishment for the sins of the world fell on Jesus on the cross and killed Him.

The gospel says that God has assured us of abundant life before death, and promised eternal life after death, because of the resurrection of Jesus. Everything has come to us who believe through Him. The gospel is not a set of beliefs and practices – the gospel is a person, Jesus Christ. Everything He is, everything He has ever done and everything He has ever promised to do is yours and mine and it's all radically *free*! We just have to believe it and accept it as our own. When we do, all the experience of the gospel will explode within us as we move out in faith and act on what we believe.

Paul is not getting angry because the Galatians turned away from an idea, or a concept, or a set of principles for life. He's upset because they are deserting the One Who called them. When we believe something other than the gospel of God's amazing grace, we don't turn from a belief system; we turn away from Jesus. No wonder our lives don't work! The nature of God's grace in Christ is so radical that you get it for free by receiving it, or you don't get it at all. Like any parent, God is looking for our love and a close, intimate relationship. The only way for that to happen is for Him to cleanse us and set us free, to love Him (or not), and with no strings attached. He refuses to deal with us on the basis of our performance.

So, when we turn away from Him, and all that He's provided for us in Christ, we sabotage the substance and the power of the Christian faith. Why would anyone turn away from such a relationship and substitute religious works? There are many reasons. Grace is risky. Freedom is scary. We might get it wrong. Church leaders who don't understand the basis of grace in our relationship with God may place rules and regulations on us to keep things neat and tidy and controlled in the church.

We've been taught that we have to work to get on in this life; so we're suspicious of anything we haven't done ourselves. It is difficult for us to believe that our acceptance by God, together with His gifts, power and enabling, does not depend on our performance. Everything of value in this world costs us something, or so we believe. So, to be offered the most valuable gift imaginable – for free – causes many of us to reject it outright. It sounds too good to be true, and that we don't deserve it! I guess that is why it's called the *good* news! In our fallen, broken world the gospel is too good to be true, but in God's eternal kingdom, it is the only truth and the power of God for the salvation of everyone who believes!

We can also seek affirmation from our brothers and sisters by our performance, so we end up trapped on the 'do-more-try-harder' treadmill, and we can't get off. We are happy if we do well, and in despair if we fail. It's only in God that we receive affirmation which is independent of our performance. He gives us the same affirmation He gave His only Son at His baptism. Before Jesus did any miracles or began 'performing' in any way, His heavenly Father said, 'This is my beloved Son in whom I am well pleased.' This is not only a possibility for us, but also our birthright, and the single greatest threat to us embracing that birthright fully and experiencing the wonder of our relationship with God in Christ is *religion*.

Unfortunately, the word religion has been used in a positive or descriptive sense all throughout history to describe the Christian faith. People still refer to that which you and I believe in and live as the 'Christian Religion'. But when you look up the definitions of religion in all the secular dictionaries, you will not find one description which contains the word 'relationship'. That is very interesting and significant, because even a quick browse through the Bible will reveal to the most unenlightened, sin-impaired mind that the Christian faith is <u>all</u> about relationship! From Genesis to Revelation, we have the story of God creating us to be in relationship with Himself and with each other. The whole Bible is about relationships – where they went wrong, what God did to fix that and what we are meant to do (and not do) to participate in His global campaign to re-establish close, intimate, eternal relationships with His lost children.

I am not talking about man's relationship to God in some abstract philosophical sense here. That is what religion does; that is what philosophy does. I am talking about man's relationship with God – personal, one-to-one, an intimate communion. That concept is foreign to religion, and yet that is what the Bible is all about.

That's what the Great Commission is about. That's what the Golden Rule is about. That's what the Ten Commandments are all about, and every teaching and instruction from Jesus and Paul and all the other biblical writers. It's all about *relationship,* and none of it is about religion. Religion is our feeble attempt to establish and maintain a relationship with God through every means possible other than that which He ordained, provides and empowers.

Some of the most powerful and effective demonic spirits in Satan's army are religious spirits. They are the ones who spend all their time working on Christians like you and me, the ones who went after the believers we read about in Galatians. Those believers were totally and powerfully set free in the Spirit, and they knew what it was to have a dynamic, personal, life-changing relationship with a living God. Yet within a few short years, they had been bewitched by religious spirits and were trying to relate to God through dead religious works again.

You were included in Christ when you heard the truth about your salvation and believed it. At that point, the Holy Spirit of God was released in you to make it all real and introduce you to the risen living Lord. In Ephesians 1:3–14, Paul states emphatically that everything you could possibly want or imagine, and even things that you can't imagine, are yours for free. It's all part of the salvation package, but that package is all or nothing.

Therefore, you have the following assurance from God in Christ: God chose you and adopted you as a son or daughter and lavished His grace upon you in Christ. Your salvation and eternal life with God is a free gift with no strings attached. Nothing you do or don't do could ever save you or cause you to lose your salvation. Your eternal relationship with God was secured on the cross by Jesus before you were even born, before you could say yes or no, before you could sin or rebel. You have been totally and wonderfully set free by the grace of God to love and serve. There is no other name under heaven by which you can be saved, except the name of Jesus.

The only way into a relationship with the Father is through Jesus and by accepting your salvation as a free gift – not just once but every day of your life. To know Him at all is to know Him as a free gift. To participate in His life, ministry and fellowship, you have to understand His grace, because nothing in the kingdom of God is bought, sold or traded. It's all given and received, received and given – *free*!

It can be hard to learn to receive love from God and others, but it is so important. We also need to learn to give love to God freely in worship, obedience and service, and to love one another in acceptance and kindness. We need that assurance so we can discern the religious traps that would make us slaves to performance again. We need the empowering presence of God in our lives to be able to rest in that assurance, revel in our relationship and be kept free from those influences. The trouble is, they can look so plausible.

I'm sure the Galatians would not have chosen to desert the gospel if they had realised that was what they were doing, and nor would we. But well-meaning Christian brothers and sisters, many of them teachers in the church, would say (or imply):

> *'So, you've accepted Jesus? Great start! But now, you need to press on into the higher things of God, by having a daily quiet time, reading and memorising the Bible, praying, fasting etc. You get in for free, but you get on at your own expense!'*

Now these disciplines are all great, but they are never a basis for being accepted or not by God. Instead of looking to Jesus and being blown away by His love and grace and empowering presence in our life, we are encouraged by religion to look at ourselves. That personal relationship is traded for our performance, and that is so deadly in our walk with God.

The great thing about freedom is that when you know you're free, law, religion, people and even the devil himself can no longer manipulate you. My highest goal for each believer is that you become so secure in God's love and acceptance nobody can manipulate you or obligate you or make you feel guilty or oppressed in any way ever again. That is my prayer. That is God's will.

One of the reasons that the spirit of religion does not want this transforming, liberating grace of God to get out is because people in the church may do whatever they want to do! Leaders will not be able to crack the legalistic whip and lay a little guilt on people anymore. God wants you free; He wants you to respond to Him out of love and gratitude, not obligation or guilt. Those are the devil's tactics, the world's tactics. That's the flesh, that's religion, and God hates religion. Jesus died to save us from that whole world of manipulation and guilt. That's what Jesus meant when He said this:

> *The Spirit of the Lord is on me, because he has anointed me to proclaim good news to the poor. He has sent me to proclaim freedom for the prisoners and recovery of sight for the blind, to set the oppressed free ... (Luke 4:18)*

When you embrace that freedom, when you allow this teaching to get past any barriers in your mind and take root in your heart, you will find joy like you've never experienced before. You'll find freedom, spontaneity and a sense of confidence because you know it ultimately all depends on God, not you. You will even sleep well at night because the guilt and sense of not measuring up will be gone. You'll also sleep well at night because you will have worked so hard that day for the Lord for the sheer joy of it: *'Lord, You've done everything for me. Now what can I do for you?'*

It won't take God long to show you what you can do to help fulfil the mission of Christ. It will be hard but wonderful work, all done without a shred of guilt, manipulation or a sense of duty. It will be the natural response of a grateful heart overwhelmed by God's love and grace. God produces this life in us and impregnates us with the ministry of the kingdom of God. Through the intimacy of prayer, Bible reading, worship, listening and responding to good teaching, obedience, service etc., this life is released in us more and more. That is the purpose of those disciplines in our lives, never to gain acceptance or make God pleased with us.

Under the law, prayer, Bible reading, worship, service and obedience all become legal requirements. Under grace in Christ, the exact same activities are transformed in the context of a love relationship and flow from our free love response to a loving God Who has saved us, redeemed us and reconciled us to Him forever. The Bible is not a book of answers and rules for life. It is the revelation of God's love and a sharing of His thoughts and His heart with His much-loved children.

There will be a lot that we may never understand and appreciate about our Lord in this life, but the Holy Spirit has preserved some of His most intimate and revealing thoughts on paper for us. That's how we should approach the Bible and prayer and worship – from the point of a relationship. Loving God will then be our only motivation for any and all of those activities and spiritual disciplines. Jesus and Jesus alone, is the gospel and our salvation. Whenever we add anything as an 'improvement', we have removed ourselves from the power of the gospel and seek once again to save ourselves by our self-righteousness. This is the essence of religious behaviour, which despises God's grace and His free gift of salvation. Religion is an ugly and deadly distortion of relationship.

We experience the freedom we have in Christ when we look to Him alone, not just for our salvation, but for our ongoing walk in the Christian life, depending on Him in all things. Our response is love and gratitude for all He has done for us. He is enough. God wants us to live freely in His love and grace, free from sin, free from shame, free from religious expectations and rule keeping. He wants us to return His love freely as we learn to know Him more. Relationship or religion – which will it be for you? Let me remind you of the stark difference between the two:

- Relationship causes us to be dependent.
  Religion drowns us in our own strength.

- Relationship produces fire and passion in our lives.
  Religion produces complacency.

- Relationship compels us to serve.
  Religion drives us to apathy.

- Relationship draws us towards what's risky.
  Religion draws us to something safe.

- Relationship drives us to our knees.
  Religion drives us to our platforms.

- Relationship births love for the lost.
  Religion births love of our rules.

- Relationship brings change.
  Religion forces conformity.

- Relationship brings forth life and fruit.
  Religion brings spiritual death and decay.

I want to plead with you to not move on from this chapter too soon. Take some time here and reflect on what you believe God may be saying to you at this point. Understanding the difference between relationship and religion is paramount to understanding the difference between spiritual life and spiritual death. The implications of this truth will be unpacked more in further chapters, but a firm grasp of the foundational nature of what I have shared thus far is vitally important.

As your awareness of God's amazing grace continues to grow, 'I will keep asking that the God of our Lord Jesus Christ, the glorious Father, may give you the Spirit of wisdom and revelation, so that you may know him better. I pray that the eyes of your heart may be enlightened in order that you may know the hope to which he has called you, the riches of his glorious inheritance in his holy people, and his incomparably great power for us who believe (Ephesians 1:17–19).'

May it be so, Lord, may it be so!

CHAPTER FOUR
Knowing God

How do we know God? How do we comprehend Him? How do we relate to God? How are all those wonderful stories about God in the Bible, spanning thousands of years, converted today into His supernatural, life-changing presence in our life? How do we experience divine things? How do we know Jesus is alive and real today? How do we know we have eternal life?

I believe the Lord would have us face those questions honestly at this point in our examination of God's amazing grace. That process may confirm that we really do know God in the deepest sense, or we may have to admit that our faith and belief in God has been more a belief in some teaching *about* God, and that we are yet to encounter God Himself in a rich, personal, supernatural way.

Perhaps we have not yet experienced that real relationship with God which Jesus died to secure for us. God may show us that we have been trying to relate to Him through religious activity. By that I mean we 'go to' church, read our Bible;, pray, give of our time, talent and resources, read books, go to conferences, get involved in ministries within the church and community, pray a certain way, believe certain things, do all sorts of things for all sorts of reasons – but underlying all that activity is a deep desire in us to really know and experience God as a person. Well, that's God's desire too!

The Lord wants to remind us today that doing our religious duty just won't cut it with Him. It never will. None of those activities are wrong in themselves, but if we do them in order to please God or get blessings from Him, the Bible calls them dead religious works and they lead to spiritual stagnation, not the abundant Christian life. We must never forget that all those activities are things you and I can do in our own strength as human beings, and therefore can be largely devoid of any real meaning or power. As spiritual as they may appear, unless they are the fruit of something else, they are dead works!

Worse still, religious activity can effectively replace God Himself in our lives. The Bible calls that idolatry. We may not burn incense and bow before a golden calf, but our religious deeds can become idols in the same way as anything can which takes the place of God.

We are actually pretty clever. We can achieve an enormous amount in our own strength. We may even do it all in God's name. We can fill church buildings with people; we can get thousands of them to jump through religious hoops and get their name on a membership roll; we can get people to believe what we believe. In fact, we can run a Christian organisation extremely well with all the technology and skills at our disposal today. We can even call it a church and get away with it for a long time. However, in reality, all we may have is a group of well-meaning people who spend their time acting out a role, singing *about* God, hearing *about* God and knowing all there is to know *about* God, yet still not knowing God Himself.

Let me explain it this way. If you tell me all there is to know about a friend of yours, I still don't know that person, do I? You might spend years talking to me about your friend, but I still haven't met them personally. I don't know the touch of their hand, the look in their eyes, the smile on their face or the sound of their voice. I only know a lot of things about them. We can know about God in the same way. We can know about Christ's death for us, we can write songs and books, or be the head of a Christian organisation and hold an important position in the church, and yet still never have experienced a vital, personal, intimate relationship with the God about whom we know so much.

The things of God can never be known by our physical senses; they are revealed by His Holy Spirit. We can never know God fully with our minds – never! The Bible does talk about our mind being renewed, and our mind has a vitally important role to play in living the Christian life. In fact, I believe we need to use our mind far more than we do when learning about God and His ways. Every heresy and all bad theology that has ever risen up in the church has been the result of sloppy thinking and a failure to wrestle with the practical outworking of the truth which God reveals to us.

However, our mind is not all that needs to be engaged if we are to have an intimate relationship with God. It's really not that difficult to understand why this may be the case. Our spirit is the agency by which we embrace spiritual things, and the human spirit has died; it is dead because of sin and has to be made alive again before we can comprehend spiritual things. So, when I say that we are not able to apprehend God through our intellect, I'm not saying anything new or profound. It just makes sense.

When musical instruments are played, we don't hear them with our eyes, do we? When there is a beautiful sunset, we don't enjoy it with our ears. God gave us ears to hear and eyes to see, and it would be ridiculous to confuse the two. It's just as ridiculous to try and relate to and experience a spiritual, infinite God with our fallen, finite minds. Now don't get me wrong – understanding God with our minds is vitally important. Our thoughts run our lives, and if you think the wrong things about God, it will most certainly hinder your ability to relate to Him. So, our minds are vitally important. Our minds can inform our spirit, but that is all they do; they do not fulfil the function of our spirit. The truth I am highlighting here is simply that our minds are not what we use to relate to God as a person. Intellectual knowledge does not equate to or guarantee a relationship.

As a result of the ignorance of this truth, the church now appears to have two Christs. We have the Christ of history – the bearded, sandalled man from the Middle East, the Christ about Whom we know a great deal from the records we have been given. We then have the living, risen Christ as revealed to our spirit by the Spirit of God. We have never met the bearded, sandalled Christ from two thousand years ago, although we know a lot about Him. Yet we do get to meet the risen, living Christ Who is present today.

Now there is only one Christ, whether He has skin on or not, but can you see the difference between the two manifestations of Christ in how we relate to God? Can you see how it might be possible that the only Christ we know (or think we know) is the one who lived in the flesh on the other side of the world and died before we were born?

Just think about this for a moment. You can read the whole New Testament and not encounter the living Christ on one single page! You may be convinced that He is the Son of God, and still not find Him as the living Person He is. No man knows the things of God, but only the Holy Spirit (1 Corinthians 2:11). One glorious flash of revelation from the Holy Spirit can teach you more about our Lord Jesus as a person than ten years in a Bible college! You can learn so much about Jesus, but it will mean nothing until the Holy Spirit shines His light into your heart.

We take beliefs, texts of Scripture, creeds and theology and build them up like a wall, but we can't find the door. We stand in the darkness and all about us is this intellectual knowledge of God, but we don't have true knowledge of God at all. The only true knowledge of God is that which His Spirit reveals supernaturally. If we don't experience God as a person, we really don't experience Him at all.

Now that I have your attention, let's take a look at what the apostle Paul said about this:

When I came to you, I did not come with eloquence or human wisdom as I proclaimed to you the testimony about God. For I resolved to know nothing while I was with you except Jesus Christ and him crucified. I came to you in weakness with great fear and trembling. My message and my preaching were not with wise and persuasive words, but with a demonstration of the Spirit's power, so that your faith might not rest on human wisdom, but on God's power.

We do, however, speak a message of wisdom among the mature, but not the wisdom of this age or of the rulers of this age, who are coming to nothing. No, we declare God's wisdom, a mystery that has been hidden and that God destined for our glory before time began. None of the rulers of this age understood it, for if they had, they would not have crucified the Lord of glory. However, as it is written:

"What no eye has seen, what no ear has heard, and what no human mind has conceived" – the things God has prepared for those who love him – these are the things God has revealed to us by his Spirit.

The Spirit searches all things, even the deep things of God. For who knows a person's thoughts except their own spirit within them? In the same way no one knows the thoughts of God except the Spirit of God. What we have received is not the spirit of the world, but the Spirit who is from God, so that we may understand what God has freely given us. This is what we speak, not in words taught us by human wisdom but in words taught by the Spirit, explaining spiritual realities with Spirit-taught words. The person without the Spirit does not accept the things that come from the Spirit of God but considers them foolishness, and cannot understand them because they are discerned only through the Spirit. The person with the Spirit makes judgments about all things, but such a person is not subject to merely human judgments, for,

"Who has known the mind of the Lord so as to instruct him?"

But we have the mind of Christ. (1 Corinthians 2:1–16)

Two things are made very clear in this incredibly important passage. Firstly, fallen human beings do not have the ability to comprehend divine things, and secondly, God can give us that ability. The Bible makes it very clear that spiritual things are hidden behind a veil and within our fallen human nature we do not have the ability to comprehend them. We come up against a blank wall in our understanding of God in verse 14:

The man without the Spirit does not accept the things that come from the Spirit of God, but considers them foolishness, and cannot understand them because they are discerned only through the Spirit.

Isaiah confirmed this centuries before Christ came to earth:

"For my thoughts are not your thoughts, neither are your ways my ways," declares the LORD. "As the heavens are higher than the earth, so are my ways higher than your ways and my thoughts than your thoughts." (Isaiah 55: 8–9)

In our natural human state, we cannot understand or receive the things of the Spirit of God. They are foolishness to us. God gave us a spirit to engage with Him personally, and an intellect to apprehend truth or knowledge about Him – there is a huge difference. The verse does not say, 'No man knows the things of God except the man who studies his Bible!' It says that no man knows the things of God *except by the Holy Spirit.* Jesus did not say we should worship Him in truth: He said we should worship Him *in spirit* and in truth (John 4:24).

We believe the Holy Spirit inspired the writing of the Bible; therefore, the Holy Spirit must also inspire its reading and understanding. I believe that to understand a Bible verse, it takes an act of the Holy Spirit equal to the act which inspired that verse to be written in the first place.

All Scripture is God-breathed and is useful for teaching, rebuking, correcting and training in righteousness. (2 Timothy 3:16)

... a person can receive only what is given them from heaven. (John 3:27)

I have much more to say to you, more than you can now bear. But when he, the Spirit of truth, comes, he will guide you into all the truth. He will not speak on his own; he will speak only what he hears, and he will tell you what is yet to come. He will glorify me because it is from me that he will receive what he will make known to you. (John 16:12–14)

Now that is perfectly plain, isn't it? The One who reveals God to us, the one who reveals Christ to us, is the Spirit of God. That's what Paul says in this passage:

We do, however, speak a message of wisdom among the mature, but not the wisdom of this age or of the rulers of this age, who are coming to nothing. No, we speak of God's secret wisdom, a mystery that has been hidden and that God destined for our glory before time began. None of the rulers of this age understood it, for if they had, they would not have crucified the Lord of glory. However, as it is written: "What no eye has seen, what no ear has heard, and what no human mind has conceived – the things God has prepared for those who love him." (1 Corinthians 2:6–9)

Isn't it strange how often we quote a passage and stop where we shouldn't stop? Most people stop at this point because that accurately describes where we are in relation to God – ignorant and distant – but everything changes when we read one more verse:

> *… these are the things God has revealed it to us by His Spirit. (1 Corinthians 2:10)*

Now there is nothing wrong with our mind; it is good. (God created it so it must be good!) He gave us our intellect and it has an important job to do. However, that job is not the apprehending of divine things; that is only possible through our spirit as it is touched by the Holy Spirit. Some scholars included Paul among the six greatest intellects that ever lived, but this intellectual giant said this:

> *… When I came to you, I did not come with eloquence or superior wisdom as I proclaimed to you the testimony about God … My message and my preaching were not with wise and persuasive words, but with a demonstration of the Spirit's power. (1 Corinthians 2:1, 4)*

Paul had confidence in this gospel because it was personally revealed to him (Galatians 1:11–12). He had a graphic, first-hand experience of the saving grace of his Lord. He knew that salvation was all from God and to His glory because he had come face to face with it and was radically impacted and transformed by it. The other apostles confirmed it (Galatians 2:1–2, 6–8). Paul was sure that God had chosen him from his birth, forgiven his sins and saved him by grace. Paul had done nothing to earn it, nor could he pay it back. However, he submitted this revelation to those who had been apostles before him. Nothing was added to his message of the absolute, amazing grace of God.

When a clear contradiction of that gospel arose, Paul confronted Peter about it and showed him his error. The fact that Peter was in a position of authority in the church in Jerusalem didn't influence Paul; he stood firmly on the truth of the gospel (Galatians 2:11–14). Paul's confidence did not come from his profound scholarship. It was a direct result of the revelation of the Holy Spirit and was proved by subsequent events.

In Jesus' name, understand this: if you have been reasoned into Christianity through your intellect, sooner or later some wise philosopher or smart thinker is going to come along and reason you right out again! But if the Holy Spirit has turned your spiritual lights on and given you that inner conviction and special relationship with God, then no one can ever reason you out of your faith, because its roots are not in your mind but in the depths of your spirit, the place where nobody has access except God. Christianity stands or falls on the illumination of the Holy Spirit.

When Jesus asked the disciples who people thought He was, they began to reason with their minds. Some of them said, 'John the Baptist'; others said, 'Elijah'. Now, they could have reasoned all day long – they loved religious debates, just as much as some of us do! – but the Holy Spirit ended that useless debate when He came upon Peter and revealed something that Peter didn't know beforehand. Peter said, 'You are the Christ, the Son of the living God!' Jesus then acknowledged that the Spirit of God had revealed this to Peter. It's really simple – it's the Holy Spirit or it's darkness.

If our faith is to be New Testament faith, if Christ is to be the living, communicating Christ of God rather than the Christ of our intellect or the Christ of history, we must enter beyond the veil. We must press in until the illumination of the Holy Spirit fills our heart and we are learning at the feet of Jesus Himself, not at the feet of man. The apostle John understood this very well:

> As for you, the anointing you received from him remains in you, and you do not need anyone to teach you. But as his anointing teaches you about all things and as that anointing is real, not counterfeit - just as it has taught you, remain in him. (1 John 2:27)

The man who wrote those words was a teacher, so how could he write that we do not need anyone to teach us? One of the gifts of the Spirit is teaching, so he couldn't mean that we do away with teachers in the church. What he did mean is this: your knowledge of God is not taught to you from outside; it is received inside by an inner illumination of the Holy Spirit. The Spirit of the living God eliminates any dependency we have on ourselves. He does not allow us to depend on human wisdom, human intelligence, human effort, human ability, efficiency or personality.

A genuine Christian faith is totally dependent, every second of every day, on a perpetual miracle of God. If you are a true, Spirit-filled believer, you are a miracle of God! The world cannot understand you at all. You are an alien, a stranger, a pilgrim *en route* to your promised land. You have been born again into an entirely different realm, a different kingdom. The Spirit of God has touched your spirit and God has become a real person to you, living and working within you.

God wants to pour out His unconditional love on everyone and let them know that they are accepted by Him in Christ, and that they can do nothing at all to change that! Satan is the accuser – that is what his name

36

means – and he wants to do all he can to remind us of our weaknesses and sins (especially past sins because he knows we can't do anything about them). Now when God's unconditional love and acceptance takes root in our hearts, Satan knows that he has lost his grip on us.

As we have already seen, God wants to release us from a purely intellectual faith (if such a thing even exists) and He often has to offend our minds to open our hearts. Satan will keep bringing up reason and logic, and other people's bad experiences, to keep our understanding of God in our heads. He has deceived a large section of the church into thinking that God can be understood and comprehended in just our minds, leaving many with no real experience of God at all.

God wants a relationship, not intellectual assent and religious activity. He wants us to be released from the prison of human wisdom and expectation. He wants us to relate to Him spirit to Spirit, not through a set of man-made pharisaic rules, requirements and dry doctrines. He wants our service, devotion and obedience to flow from an overwhelming sense of His love, not out of guilt, shame, manipulation, obligation or Christian duty. Satan wants to bring Christians back under the Old Covenant law. He wants to fill us with guilt and shame and a sense of failure as he constantly reminds us of those areas that are not up to scratch in God's eyes. You know that little niggling voice we have in our conscience – 'How's your quiet time going? You missed church today. Now that wasn't 10%, was it? You call that a prayer life? If you want to be a first-class Christian, you'd better get your act together'? That's not God! God is never the accuser.

I believe there are many people in the church who have been under constant attack from the enemy and don't even know it. Worse still, they have been deceived into thinking that their guilt and shame and feelings of inadequacy have come from God. Nothing could be further from the truth! Jesus hung on a cross, His heart and body and soul crushed by the enormous weight of the sins of all mankind, as He cried out in anguish, 'My God, my God why have you forsaken me?' At that very moment, He was bearing all your guilt, all your shame and all your inadequacy so that you would never have to carry any of that stuff again.

In fact, when you allow the enemy to accuse you and drag you down, when you take on board old sins and guilt, when you read some clever pop psychology book that takes you back into your past and tells you all the problems you have and why you are the way you are – when you take that garbage on board, you are turning your face away from Jesus on that cross. You are literally denying what He has done for you. You have fallen away from grace and are once again carrying the guilt and sin and pain and rejection that Jesus already carried for you once and for all time.

Paul says there is no condemnation for those who are in Christ. All that condemnation fell on Jesus, and it is an offence to the cross of Christ for us to pick any of it back up again! God wants to set all captives free from this bondage. He wants to restore New Testament Christianity to His church. He wants the book of Acts to be a commentary on the life of the church *today*, not just the first-century church. He wants to release the full ministry of Jesus in this nation. Yet before He can do that, He must release us once and for all from the notion that we can truly know God via any means other than the revelation and illumination of the Holy Spirit to our spirit.

The 'religion' of Christianity is on notice; it's an offence to God. He wants *real* Christianity, which is a personal, vibrant, powerful relationship with the living God through the indwelling of His Holy Spirit. Jesus, the Lord of the church, is confronting the religious leaders of today just as He did the Pharisees all those years ago. He is calling on those who bind up His children to step aside and let His Holy Spirit take up His rightful place in the church. God is at work among His people and those believers who are prepared to be stretched, to grow and to have old ways, thoughts and judgements challenged by the Word of God will experience the love, power and strength of God in a new and dynamic way.

Those who are prepared to expose all they think, believe, say and do to the light of the Holy Spirit as He shines afresh on the Word of God, who are prepared to hunger and thirst after God – they shall be filled! Any real relationship must be based on truth, which is why it is vital that we truly know God so we can relate to Him the way He desires.

The good news is that God has revealed Himself to us and enabled us to be in relationship with Him. He has done all that is required, and He continues to do that in us.

> *"What no eye has seen, what no ear has heard, and what no human mind has conceived" - the things God has prepared for those who love him – these are the things God has revealed to us by his Spirit. (1 Corinthians 2:9–10)*

CHAPTER FIVE
The Power of the Gospel

The entire foundation of our Christian life and the foundation of the church is grace. Literally speaking, the word 'grace' means 'free gift', and the name of that free gift is Jesus Christ. Jesus lived His life perfectly for us as one of us, completely obeying the law of God and now His performance is credited to us. God's free gift to us is not only the life but also the death of Jesus Christ. Our sins are punishable by death and that punishment was endured by Jesus when He died on the cross. His death is also credited to us as if we had suffered the punishment for our sins. Jesus' resurrection is also a gift to us. In Him we have risen above the power and penalty of sin. In Christ we have conquered death. Then after His resurrection, the Lord Jesus poured out His Holy Spirit Who made all this real to us and continues to do so today.

The free gift of God's grace is that Jesus lived a life pleasing to God and He now empowers us to live a life pleasing to God after Him, or more accurately, in Him. Another way of saying it is that Jesus lived His life for us, and now He lives His life through us by the power of His Spirit. All of this is free. The great Baptist preacher Charles Spurgeon put it best when he said, 'You stand before God as if you were Christ, because Christ stood before God as if He were you'.

So now we are no longer subject to sin and the laws governing sin. We are no longer necessarily subject to the results of sin. Sickness can be healed, demons can be driven off, depression can be cured, relationships can be reconciled and offences can be forgiven. It's not guaranteed because we are still broken, but it is all now possible. What Satan has sought to do since the fall can be undone, by the free gift of God's grace – His empowering presence. It's a gift in the beginning; it's a gift in the end; it's a gift all the way through.

Not only is this grace radically free to us, but it is also radically different to the way things once were. The difference between the way things were and the way things are, after the giving of that gift, produces in us gratitude that motivates us to live the lives that we are meant to live. Why is this truth so important for our relationship with God? Well, part of that answer comes when we see what happens in our lives and relationship without it. Unless we know the truth of who we are in Christ, the foundation of His grace in our salvation and sanctification, what God has done and how we are supposed to live out that salvation, any exhortations to holy living will result in works of the flesh, our feeble attempts to do in our own power and strength what only God can and has done.

It is so important we understand that there is nothing that we can do to save ourselves or pay for our sins. The Bible says, '… there is none righteous, no, not one … For all have sinned and fallen short of the glory of God, and all are justified freely by his grace through the redemption that came by Christ Jesus' (Romans 3:10, 23–24). So, since we could not come to God, God came to us. Let's look some words of the apostle Paul:

> … it is by free grace (God's unmerited favour) that you are saved (delivered from judgment and made partakers of Christ's salvation) through [your] faith. And this [salvation] is not of yourselves [of your own doing, it came not through your own striving] but it is the gift of God; Not because of works [not the fulfilment of the Law's demands], lest any man should boast. [It is not the result of what anyone can possibly do, so no one can pride himself in it or take glory to himself.] (Ephesians 2:8–9, AMP)

And in his letter to the church in Rome, Paul wrote this:

> For I am not ashamed of the gospel, because it is the power of God that brings salvation to everyone who believes: first to the Jew, then to the Gentile. For in the gospel the righteousness of God is revealed – a righteousness that is by faith from first to last, just as it is written: "The righteous will live by faith." (Romans 1:16–17)

Religion says the righteous will live by keeping the law. Paul says very clearly the righteous are not only saved by grace, through faith, but that is also how they must live each day. Now I am sure that you have heard 'I'm not ashamed of the gospel' sermons before. The most common way I have heard these verses preached is something like this: if you're afraid to go knock on doors and witness, if you're afraid to preach on street corners, if you're afraid to share your faith in Christ with every non-believer the Lord leads your way, then you're ashamed of the gospel. And you should not be ashamed of the gospel because it's the power of God unto salvation.

What's so incredulous about that nonsense is not what Paul is trying to say but that it undermines the very thing that Paul is trying to accomplish! Paul is saying, 'What I'm about to tell you is going to free you from shame.' So, what do we do? We heap shame on ourselves and others with the very verse that is supposed to free us from shame! Does that make sense to you? Religion is so powerful in its brain-fogged, spirit-deceived ways of doing things that it takes liberating Bible verses and turns them into guilt, oppression and heavy burdens.

If you understand the gospel of God's amazing grace, like Paul did, you will never be ashamed of it. Let me go further and say that when that happens, you will never again experience shame about anything at all. If you know shame, there is still a lot you can learn about the gospel of Jesus Christ, and when you do – when it comes to you not just in your mind but by revelation from His Spirit to your spirit –you will be free from all shame for all time. The gospel delivers you from shame of every description.

The key is found in verse 17: Paul says he is not ashamed of the gospel, because in the gospel 'the righteousness of God is revealed'. When you look at your own righteousness, you're ashamed, right? When you see how it measures up to God's standards, you *should* be ashamed. Shame says, 'You don't measure up. There's something wrong with you.' Now if that could be taken away completely, you would never have any shame, would you? Well, that is what the gospel does.

Paul says, 'I'm set free from shame because a righteousness has been given to me from God. I don't depend on my righteousness for how I feel about myself. I have a new standard by which to judge.' So, understand at the outset that if there's any shame in your life, you still haven't fully understood or embraced the gospel.

In the gospel, we discover a righteousness from God, a goodness and an acceptability from God that is not dependent upon our personal performance. It is dependent upon the performance of Jesus Christ. It is a righteousness that is by faith from first to last. You start off with the gift of God; you end with the gift of God. The righteous shall live (not just get born again) by grace. We are meant to live each and every day by the good news which says, 'You don't measure up, but God has made you measure up through this free gift.'

I am not ashamed of the gospel for it is the power of God that brings salvation to everyone who believes. (Romans 1:16)

The power of God is a free gift of His grace to every single believer. It is part and parcel of the gospel. You don't have to get saved and then do something to get the power of God. The gospel is the power of God for those who do only one thing – *believe!*

There has been a line of teaching around for many years now that says that God is ready to pour out His end-times power, and if we just pray harder and clean up our lives more and become holy enough, then

God will 'award' it to us. If we 'pay the price', we will 'qualify for God's higher purposes.' That is to say, God's power is available to those who are 'spiritually affluent' enough to 'buy' it.

First of all, that kind of teaching is totally inconsistent with the everything the Bible tells us, especially Romans 1:16 which we are considering here. Secondly, it is totally inconsistent with our own experience. Some of the most powerful ministers of God in this world have, at the very peak of their effective ministry, been caught in adultery or some other moral failure. Now we may jump in and say they must have been evil all the time; they must have been operating under a different spirit to the Spirit of God; they must not have even been Christians. Why do we deduce that? Simple, really; we think that nonsense because we have believed the lie which says God can't use unholy people and He only pours His anointing and power into 'clean' vessels.

In spite of all the evidence from church history and in the Bible, in spite of the clear message of the New Testament and the experience of millions of people, so many in the church believe that the power of God is waiting for us to clean up our act and get holy! In case you have any doubts, look at what Paul said:

> Oh, the depth of the riches of the wisdom and knowledge of God! How unsearchable his judgments, and his paths beyond tracing out! Who has known the mind of the Lord? Or who has been his counselor? Who has ever given to God, that God should repay him? (Romans 11:33–36)

That is to say, God will not 'sell' you anything and He will not 'buy' anything from you. He gives freely and He invites us to give back to Him freely. 'I am not ashamed of the gospel because it is the power of God for salvation to all who believe.' All who *believe* have the power of God in the gospel. Not some who qualify or work the hardest, but *all* who believe.

Many people cannot understand how God would give spiritual power to morally defective people. This is a real problem for some people. It certainly is a pastoral problem, because it can get very messy, but it's not a logical problem; it's not a theological problem; it's not a spiritual problem; it's not a biblical problem! I would suggest it's only a problem for those who don't understand the gospel, who don't understand that it's *all free* and we are *all unholy*. It's free for anyone who wants to believe it and act on it. It doesn't depend on whether you're good or not. We are quite happy to accept that God loves us whether we are good or not, but why do we stumble on the next bit, that God also gives His gifts and power to us whether we are good or not? The only possible conclusion you can draw from the Bible and from the evidence all around us throughout history is it's all free. That's just the way God is, and we need to deal with it.

In one of the greatest parables Jesus told, that of the Prodigal Son, the father gives his son everything when he returns, even though he has just proven himself to be incompetent in every respect. Why? Because that's Who God is and that's what God does. There isn't any other reason, and you and I are stuck with the way God is. So rather than asking why God would act so differently to us, we should just get on with life and believe what He says, act on it and enjoy the transformation which follows.

When we stop worrying about our righteousness – feeling bad because we're not good enough or feeling good because we're not bad enough – we will share the gospel with everything that moves. We won't be ashamed of the gospel. When we believe that spiritual power is a gift of God, which does not depend on our prayer or our righteousness or our holiness or our personal performance in any way, we are going to experience the presence and power of God in an unprecedented way!

God wants to free us all from the bondage of works. Most of us don't even know we are under that bondage. Jesus said that the truth will set us free (John 8:32). Well, the opposite is true too: if you do not possess the truth, you will not be free; you will be in bondage like so many millions of Christians. We are not under a contract with God; we are under a covenant, the New Covenant. God says, 'I've given everything to you free. Now believe into it, act upon it, and it will become your experience. But you can't buy anything from Me. I already gave it all to you in the gospel. I gave it all to you in Jesus Christ, and it is completely free.' Everything we receive from God, from salvation to sanctification, comes to us by grace and through faith.

Let's get back to the text: 'I am not ashamed of the gospel, because it is the power of God for the salvation of everyone who believes.' What are we saved from? Do you think Jesus saved you from your sins? Let's think this through. When you were still an unbeliever, were you a drunk? Did you do drugs? Did you lie? Did you steal? Did you cheat? Were you immoral or dishonest in some way? Were you selfish and refused to honour God? Everyone can probably identify with that list at one point or another. Most people also agree that those sins were separating you from the experience of God and His kingdom. So now let me ask you this: if you had stopped all those sins, would you have been propelled into God's presence? No? So, it wasn't your sins that were the problem! Well, that was easy, wasn't it?

Your behaviour doesn't condemn you any more than changing your behaviour sends you to heaven. So, Jesus didn't save you from your behaviour or your sins in the way you might think He did. The ultimate problem is not your sins; in fact, it isn't anything you do. Your ultimate problem lies somewhere else. Let me explain this from a different angle. Now that you're saved, have you stopped sinning? No. Are you still going to heaven, even though you keep on sinning? Yes, you are. Wow! Isn't that radical? Therefore, if we are not saved from our sins, what *are* we saved from then? Paul tells us clearly.

The wrath of God is being revealed from heaven against all the godlessness and wickedness of people, who suppress the truth by their wickedness. (Romans 1:18)

But because of your stubbornness and your unrepentant heart, you are storing up wrath against yourself for the day of God's wrath, when his righteous judgment will be revealed. (Romans 2:5)

What are you saved from? You are saved from God! You are saved from God's holy wrath against the wickedness you were born into, because you were born into a fallen humanity. Your problem is not your sin, your problem is you were born!

Everyone who is born into the fallen family of mankind is born under the judgement of God. Now that doesn't mean God has a mean streak. It just means that a holy God must judge sin. There are certain things that just can't happen at the same time. You can't go up and down at the same time. You can't say 'yes' and mean yes, and say 'no' and mean no, at the same time. God is holy, and He can't be anything but holy, one hundred per cent of the time. His holiness means that His unbending, pure, moral perfection must burn against all imperfection of every kind. That's just the way God is. Anything that falls short of His holiness and perfection comes under His judgement, His purging and His wrath.

We are therefore saved first and foremost from God's wrath. Now you may be thinking, 'His wrath is still against sin, so sin is still our problem, isn't it?' How much sin do you need to get rid of before it's no longer a problem? One hundred per cent! Any chance of that happening in this life? No. So your problem still isn't sin. Your problem is the judgement of God on all sin, any sin, every sin. The problem is that *all* have sinned and fall short of the glory of God and the righteousness of God. The solution to that problem is the atoning death of Jesus and God's gift of salvation to us. Paul sums it up powerfully further on in his letter to the Romans.

44

Now we know that whatever the law says, it says to those who are under the law, so that every mouth may be silenced and the whole world held accountable to God. Therefore no one will be declared righteous in God's sight by the works of the law; rather, through the law we become conscious of our sin [our unrighteousness]. (Romans 3:19–20)

The gospel tells us something about our righteousness; that is, we don't have any. That's clear.

But now apart from law the righteousness of God has been made known, to which the Law and the Prophets testify. This righteousness [from God, not from you] is given through faith in Jesus Christ [not works] to all [not some] who believe [not work for it]. There is no difference between Jew and Gentile, for all have sinned and fall short of the glory of God, and all are justified freely by his grace through the redemption that came by Christ Jesus. God presented Christ as a sacrifice of atonement, through the shedding of his blood – to be received by faith. He did this to demonstrate his righteousness. (Romans 3:21–25)

According to this passage, the last human being on earth has fallen short of God's righteousness. We have all failed the test. What's more, we failed the test even before we were born!

I love the law of God, not just in principle. I really love the law of God because it puts me out of my moral misery! I don't have to worry about trying to be a little bit better. I don't have to work on cleaning up a few of my sins to earn God's favour. I don't have to do more and try harder in the hope that one day I'll measure up. I'm dead before I start! All have fallen short. Mother Theresa fell short. Billy Graham fell short. John the Baptist fell short. The apostle Paul fell short. They *all* fell short. Every human being except One has fallen short. You were born under God's judgement. Face the truth and thank Him. The law is so merciful because it puts tortured men and women out of their misery.

Isn't that good news? The Bible says even the things that we do well are as filthy rags in God's eyes (Isaiah 64:6). We don't just need forgiveness for the things we do wrong; we need forgiveness for the things we think we do right! Thank the Lord for the law of God. Read the Ten Commandments and listen to Jesus summing them up when He says, 'Love the Lord your God with all your heart, soul, mind and strength and love your neighbour as yourself'. When are you ever going to get good enough to do that? Never! The law demands one hundred per cent perfection, yet we can't give it and never will be able to this side of heaven. We therefore have to look somewhere other than our performance for our attitude to ourselves. When we look totally away from ourselves and the law, what do we see in the opposite direction? Let's look at that Romans passage again, and unpack it some more:

> But now apart from the law [looking away from the law and my performance in relation to the law], the righteousness of God [and apart from me] has been made known, to which the Law and the Prophets testify. This righteousness [from God, not from you] is given through faith [not by doing but by believing] in Jesus Christ to all [not the ones we think qualify but to all] who believe. There is no difference between Jew and Gentile [we're all dead], for all have sinned and fall short of the glory of God [all fall short of the standard] and are justified freely by his grace through the redemption that came by Christ Jesus. God presented Christ as a sacrifice of atonement, through the shedding of his blood – to be received by faith. [God presented Him as payment for everything we came up short on. Jesus scored all A's on His report card and then put our name on the top of that report].

You see the problem of our sin is not *our* problem; it's *God's* problem. How is He going to get those precious children, whom He created, back into a right relationship with Himself while they are still sinning, without compromising His holiness? Let's move on and see.

The whole problem facing humanity from the beginning comes back to the nature of God. The most terrifying and confronting truth in all of Scripture is that God is good. What's terrifying about God being good? The answer is simple. It's terrifying to know that God is good because we are not. If we want to understand the gospel, the good news, we must first understand the bad news and that is, God is good but we are not. God is good because He is holy. Because God is holy, He is just. Because God is just, He cannot do anything other than condemn and purge that which is unholy – and that puts us in the firing line.

Therefore, the problem for God, from almost the beginning of humanity, is that He is good and we are not. God cannot violate His attributes. He cannot do something that contradicts Who He is. Unlike us, God cannot be two-faced. God is a righteous God; that is a good thing because we certainly would not want an evil God to be in charge of the universe, would we? It is a profoundly good thing that God is good, righteous, pure, holy and just. However, herein lies a huge problem for God. If God is just, what does a good God do with sinners like us? We have sinned against God; we have sinned against each other; we have sinned against creation; we are sinners by nature and all of creation calls for our condemnation. If this holy, pure, righteous God is truly just then what does He do with us?

46

If a just God simply pardons the wicked, He is no longer just. What do you call a judge who sweeps crime under a rug? Righteous? No, he is corrupt! In the same way, if a holy God calls the wicked to Himself to have fellowship with Him without dealing with their sin, then He's not a holy God. Therefore, the greatest question running through the whole Bible and all of human history, is this: how can a just God pardon wicked men and women, and still be just? To put it another way: how can a holy God call unholy sinners into fellowship with Himself for eternity, yet remain holy?

The answer is found in the cross of Jesus Christ. In that old rugged cross, we see the unique revelation of the fullness of God's attributes. God is just, so He must condemn sin – but God is also love. Therefore, to satisfy His justice, God's love compels Him to become a man and that Man does what none of us could ever do – He lives a perfect, sinless life as a man. He goes to the cross, where He Who knew no sin became sin for us, as the justice of God – the full wrath of God that we deserve – came down upon one man, Jesus Christ, God's Son and our Saviour.

The exact measure that was required to fully satisfy the justice of God, was brought against Jesus. As He took His final few breaths as a man, Jesus declared, 'It is finished.' That means Jesus has done all that was needed to pay the price for all sin. Let me ask you again : what are you saved from? You are saved from the judgement of God on all sin – past, present and future. Hallelujah, what a Saviour!

Consequently, you are also saved from shame. Shame has to do with not being good enough, being defective, falling short, sinning. You always have and always will fall short against the perfect law of God, so stop looking in that direction. Turn and look to the cross of Christ, the gospel, the good news, the power of God for salvation, and accept that your standing before the law of God and your sinfulness in relation to the law of God is utterly irrelevant in your relationship with God. There are lots of good reasons why you shouldn't sin (I'll get to those later), but you need to know that your personal sins have nothing to do with your relationship to God. If you get this, you are going to be utterly free of shame for the rest of your life!

You are also saved from being self-righteous. That's what the Pharisees were, right? There were puffed up with pride and full of their own 'rightness'. They looked down on 'sinners' and they felt good because they measured up to what they believed was good and right and proper. We still have self-righteous people like that today. But let me ask you something: what do you call people who feel unworthy, who feel that

47

they don't measure up, the ones that the so-called 'righteous' people look down upon? They grovel, they mourn, they cry out, 'I have sinned, I am not right with God. Woe is me, worthless worm that I am.' What do we call these people? We call them self-righteous too!

Don't think for one minute that God will bless the arrogant, proud, self-righteous person because he feels good according to the law, but neither will God bless you for grovelling according to the law. All the blessings of God are already free in the gospel, independent of your boasting or your grovelling. When you compare yourself to a standard of righteousness – whether you compare well or not – it's all self-righteousness and it's all abhorrent. That's what religion is. That's certainly not New Testament Christianity!

Can you just imagine the energy and the power which would be injected into the church if we didn't spend any more time or effort trying to 'get right' with God? Let that sink in – all the energy, time, emotional strength and spiritual might we would have left over if all believers simply accepted that 'rightness with God' is a gift. Instead of working our butts off trying to please God and earn His favour, we would just receive it and respond accordingly: *'God, You love me. Freely You gave to me. How can I freely, with no obligation, manipulation or guilt, give back to You?'*

Even if only a handful of people got that truth in every part of the church across our nation, such a revelation would spread like a fire! That's the power of transformation. That's what births revivals. That's the power of the gospel, a gospel which says, 'I'm okay because God has made me okay. I don't have to spend any religious energy trying to be right with God anymore - I'm given that as a gift. Now I get to respond in gratitude and work my butt off for God because I want to, not because I have to.' When we truly understand the gospel, we will declare every day with the apostle Paul:

> *But by the grace of God I am what I am, and his grace to me was not without effect. No, I worked harder than all of them – yet not I, but the grace of God that was with me. (1 Corinthians 15:10)*

Just imagine what that would do to our relationship with God from our end if we really believed and lived that. Imagine the gratitude, the emotion, the affection, the passion we would have for God as the reality of what happened on the cross for us really hit home. He loved us so much He gave His only Son to die for us so that He could share life with us for eternity. Imagine the change that would come in how we related to other people. Imagine if we thought for one minute that God loved everybody else just as much as He loved us and gave His Son for them just like He gave Him for us, and that they too are right with God because of what God has done for them, not because of their behaviour (which we may not accept). Imagine as that reality hit us, the love and acceptance that would flow from our hearts to everyone.

Are you catching a glimpse of how the real gospel will change people's lives, change Christians' lives, if they will just believe it and live it? Do you see why the enemy has gone to such lengths to camouflage the true, radical, free grace of God behind a lot of legalistic, religious 'do's and don'ts'? The true gospel of Jesus Christ scares Satan to death, and he will do anything he can to deceive, distort and drag you away from the truth, because he knows that the truth shall set you free – forever!

'I'm not ashamed of the gospel, because it is the power of God for the salvation of everyone who believes … and as it is written: "The righteous will live by faith."' Do you want to know what righteous living by faith is? I'll show you.

Just imagine to your left there is a big stone tablet or ancient scroll containing the holy law of God, a long list of requirements. 'Thou shalt love the Lord your God with everything that's in you.' Let me put your score next to that: F, failed. 'Thou shalt love every other person in the world as you love yourself.' Another F. 'Thou shalt never worry about anything again.' Failed again. 'Thou shalt forgive your enemies every time.' F. And so on. You go down the list of requirements to try to fully obey the holy, perfect law of God one hundred per cent of the time. Your true score will be one huge F – utterly and completely hopeless.

Now turn and look in the opposite direction and ask the Holy Spirit to give you a fresh revelation of Jesus dying on the cross for you. 'Holy Spirit, I ask you to come and make real to me now the cross of Christ. Give me a revelation of the Son of God, wounded and bruised, His blood flowing for my sins.' Look at Him, and as you do, understand that you are seeing the One Who kept all those laws on your behalf. He loved God with all His heart, soul, mind and strength. He loved His neighbour to the bitter end, even dying for them. He always forgave His enemies. He met God's standard for you.

Behold the Man. Behold the righteousness of God – beaten, tortured, spat on, pierced for your transgressions, bruised for your iniquities, brutally nailed to a cross because you could not, cannot and will never be able to meet the holy standards of the law of God. This Man gathers up all of your sin and everything you've failed to do and to be and takes it all upon Himself. If you have ever felt guilty about your sins, look at His wounds. There is the punishment for everything which brings you shame

– everything. There is the justice of God. There is the judgement of God. There is the love of God. Look at Him. Ask the Holy Spirit to give you a fresh revelation of what that means.

Do you want to know how to truly live by faith? I just showed you. Every day of your life you look in one direction at the law of God and say, 'Not a chance! I'm dead before I start!' Then you look in the other direction at Jesus, the cross and an empty tomb and say, 'He is the way, the truth and the life!'

If you want to be happy in your life of faith, in which direction are you going to be looking every single day? You will look to Jesus, you will remember Jesus, you will meditate on Jesus, you will read about Jesus, you will pray in Jesus' name, you will embrace the mission of Jesus, you will worship Jesus. You will turn your eyes upon Jesus and look full into His wonderful face, and the things of earth will grow strangely dim, in the light of His glory and His amazing grace. That's what living by faith looks like.

The gospel is the message of God's grace to fallen, sinful mankind. The perfect obedience of Jesus is applied to our account in heaven; the punishment which we deserved was borne by Jesus and His death was credited to us also. In rising to new life, Jesus made the way for us to have life too. This gift of God is totally free to us – we neither earned nor deserved it – yet it sets us free and empowers us to live a life pleasing to God as we believe in His Son for our salvation.

Put simply, the gospel sets you totally free from all the 'got to' demands of religion and replaces them with the 'get to' privileges of life in relationship with God through Jesus Christ. Religion says, 'You've got to read your Bible. You've got to be part of a church fellowship. You've got to serve in ministry. You've got to give 10% of your income. You've got to pray. You've got to worship ...', and the list goes on. The gospel says, 'Now you get to read your Bible. Now you get to be part of a church fellowship. Now you get to serve in ministry. Now you get to give ten per cent of your income. Now you get to pray. Now you get to worship', and the list goes on. What was once a law and an obligation is now a privilege and a blessing. What was once a legalistic duty now becomes the fruit of God's grace in your life.

As we move on in this book we will see how and why the Old Covenant was powerless to deal with sin or to give life but demonstrated our need for a Saviour and foreshadowed the New Covenant in Christ. A clear understanding of the Old Covenant and the New Covenant, and the difference between the two, is absolutely essential. The Scriptures are abused millions of times every day as people pluck verses out of the Old Covenant to justify or explain their actions and God's actions under the New Covenant. When we understand the difference, we will treat both with a new respect and we will be able to counter much of the nonsense that masquerades as the gospel today. Only then can we begin to understand God's grace in all its truth. Only then will we know the depth and breadth and power of the freedom which is ours in Christ. Only then will the captives truly be set free!

'Speak, Lord, Your children are listening. Remove the scales from our eyes and empower us to bring this gospel to all those who so desperately need to embrace the power of Your love and grace. Amen!'

CHAPTER SIX
The Battle Between Grace and Law

The apostle Paul found himself defending the gospel of God's amazing grace many times to Jews and also to Gentile unbelievers. Some of the most powerful teaching in our possession comes from Paul's letters to people in the church who should have known better. He rebukes the Corinthians for their abuse of the freedom which is theirs in Christ. He is scathing in his letter to the Galatians because their acceptance of false teaching had destroyed the very freedom that Jesus died to give them.

The Jewish believers had a problem with Paul's teaching on grace because they and their forefathers had been working their tails off for generations to obey the holy law of God. They had questions like: 'Where does the law fit in? If we are all justified by trusting God alone and not by keeping the law, then why was Israel put under the law in the first place?'

Both Paul and the writer of Hebrews try to answer these questions. In his letter to the Galatians, Paul not only has to hammer home the priority of grace over law, but he also has to explain God's use of the law in the first place. Paul was a Jew, so he knew how controversial his teaching was, but for the sake of the gospel of Christ and the freedom of the believers, he had to totally undo the teaching of the religious leaders of that day. Paul knew that to mix a little law with grace destroys grace and in so doing, we render Christ's death meaningless (Galatians 2:21).

Either Jesus is your everything – your justification, your sanctification, your abundant life irrespective of your performance – or He is nothing. It's law or it's grace, but it can never be a little bit of both. Contrary to the impression he may have given them, Paul had a very high view of the law of God. He poses the question he intends to answer: What then is the purpose of the law (Galatians 3:19a)? Let's look at the setting of this teaching first.

Paul had planted the church in Galatia on a foundation of God's grace which came through the life, death and resurrection of Jesus Christ. The theme of his message was 'in Christ'. He preached that forgiveness of sin is found in Christ; a new relationship with God is found in Christ; life after death, and more importantly, abundant life before death, is found in Christ; Further to that, he emphasised that this was all a free gift from God, experienced by us when we simply believe the gospel. The liberating gospel of grace itself births in us the love and acceptance of God through the Holy Spirit.

After Paul had left that region, some other teachers followed him. They were probably converted Jews from the Jerusalem church who had received Jesus as Lord and Saviour, but who felt that they ought to hang on to the Law as well. Old habits die hard. They saw Christianity as nothing more than an updated version of Judaism. Effectively they were saying:

> *'We are here to follow up and build on what Paul has taught you. He was absolutely right in saying that you need Jesus. That's essential, that's how you get started in the Christian life, salvation is found in no other … but what he failed to tell you is that in addition to accepting Jesus and His atoning work for you, you need to follow certain religious laws and rules.'*

The church in Galatia allowed these well-meaning teachers to destroy the heart of the gospel of Jesus Christ as they opened the door for religion again. As we have already discussed, whenever this happens, the focus shifts from God and His finished work in Christ to our performance which is never finished and never good enough. Relationship is replaced by religion, and the more we work to please God, the more we suppress the life of Jesus Christ in us and through us, thereby suppressing and effectively rejecting the very substance of the Christian faith.

Paul seeks to explain why their acceptance of the law is a repudiation of the grace of God. He turns to their history to establish for them that grace, the promise of God, came first; it was a covenant established and secure forever. The law, which was given later, was for a purpose other than relating us to God. The law came not to replace grace and faith, but to highlight their necessity. This is what the religious leaders that Paul addressed could not understand.

> *… let me take an example from everyday life. Just as no one can set aside or add to a human covenant that has been duly established, so it is in this case. The promises were spoken to Abraham and to his seed. Scripture does not say "and to seeds," meaning many people, but "and to your seed," meaning one person, who is Christ. What I mean is this: The law, introduced 430 years later, does not set aside the covenant previously established by God and thus do away with the promise [that you can be saved by grace, through faith]. For if the inheritance depends on the law, then it no longer depends on a promise; but God in His grace gave it to Abraham through a promise. (Galatians 3:15–18)*

The covenant of grace was made by God with Abraham and his Seed – meaning his descendant in the flesh through Mary - Jesus the Christ, the seed, singular. Abraham is dead and gone. But his offspring, Jesus, is alive and here right now. We can be in Christ, the living Seed, and we can have a living, justified relationship with God in Him. Paul goes on to say:

> *Why, then, was the law given at all? It was added because of transgressions until the Seed to whom the promise referred to had come. (Galatians 3:19)*

The law was given to define sin, to tell us how God feels about it and to set out the consequences of sin. Before the law was given, people would have felt bad about sin, but they didn't know how awful sin really was. For instance, the law told them that it's not just inconvenient to have someone steal your wife; it's a dreadful sin with terrible consequences.

> *Is the law, therefore, opposed to the promises of God? Absolutely not! For if a law had been given that could impart life, then righteousness would certainly have come by the law. But Scripture has locked up everything under the control of sin, so that what was promised, being given through faith in Jesus Christ, might be given to those who believe. Before the coming of this faith, we were held in custody under the law, locked up until faith that was to come would be revealed. (Galatians 3:21–23)*

The law lets us know that we are prisoners of sin. The law is good in that it's true and right, but bad in the sense that it curses us all!

> *For all who rely on the works of the law are under a curse, as it is written: "Cursed is everyone who does not continue to do everything written in the Book of the Law." Clearly no one who relies on the law is justified before God, because "the righteous will live by faith." (Galatians 3:10–11)*

Everybody feels that curse, Christian or not. Modern society wants to get away from the guilt, shame and misery revealed in and inflicted by the law, so we say that everything is relative, and we compose a hierarchy of sins. Taking the law away or softening it will not make us feel better, because it cannot change the reality of sin. It does not give us salvation; it cannot give us life or a right standing with God. The law makes us ready for the day when Someone says to us:

> *Come to me, all you who are weary and burdened and I will give you rest. (Matthew 11:28)*

> *Christ redeemed us from the law by becoming a curse for us, for it is written: "Cursed is everyone who is hung on a pole." He redeemed us in order that the blessing given to Abraham might come to the Gentiles through Christ Jesus, so that by faith we might receive the promise of the Spirit. (Galatians 3:13–14)*

For the wages of sin is death, but the gift of God is eternal life in Christ Jesus our Lord. (Romans 6:23)

As John reminded us in the most quoted verse in the Bible, God so loved His broken, fallen, twisted, rebellious children, that He gave His only begotten Son, that whoever *believes* in Him should not perish because of their sin, but have everlasting life. That's why the law was given before Christ came to die. The law was 'put in charge of us'.

Before the coming of this faith, we were held in custody under the law, locked up until the faith that was to come would be revealed. So the law was our guardian until Christ came that we might be justified by faith. (Galatians 3:23–24)

The RSV translation says the law was made a 'custodian' of us. Other translations say the law was made our 'tutor'. The Greek word translated in these different ways is *paidagogos*, from which we get the English word 'pedagogue'. Wealthy families hired a pedagogue, an educated slave, who was responsible for training the children in every area of life, from the time they got up to the time they went to bed. If he had done a good job, the child was mature and responsible; if he failed, the child was a rebellious, ignorant slight on the family. Either way, his job was finished when the child was considered an adult. Paul says this describes the law. It serves a particular function for a limited time. It teaches the rudiments of knowledge and morality, and it is something which the child is destined to outgrow.

You may be asking, 'How does this grace message fit into all the rules and expectations of child-rearing? How can you believe in grace, yet punish your child?' It makes sense when you understand that the law is for children. To be trained by the law, there must be consequences when they transgress it. We teach them that they live in a cause-and-effect world and that, regardless of how God feels about them, there are consequences to their actions. There are moral absolutes that undergird society, and children need to know that.

However, the time comes when laying down the law has either done its job or it hasn't, and the children move on. The law must go as children mature, and grace, faith, unconditional love and acceptance must take over in a practical sense in the outworking of their lives. God gave the responsibility to parents to raise their children and there are many rules involved in that task. If the parents don't parent well, it's not the church's responsibility to finish their job. The church is not there to pile on legalistic rules and regulations, yet many people have that idea. Paul says it clearly, 'Now that faith has come, we are no longer under the supervision of the law.'

The church of Jesus Christ relates to adults and therefore treats people as though they have been raised properly. Do people still need teaching? Absolutely! There will be those in our midst who didn't learn basic morality, how to be a good citizen or a good husband or wife. So, we continue teaching, not by making rules for people to follow, but rather how God says to teach adult, by walking in the Spirit, because if we walk in the Spirit, we will automatically fulfil the requirements of the law. It happens because the love of Christ in our heart flows out into others' lives as we treat them with respect.

Everyone who is in Christ has the promise of His indwelling Spirit. The Holy Spirit will show you the deep things of God in His Word and your life will be transformed as you walk with Him, trust Him and yield to Him. He is your teacher now, not the law. He is your counsellor and companion.

> But when he, the Spirit of truth, comes, he will guide you into all truth. He will not speak on his own; he will speak only what he hears, and he will tell you what is yet to come. He will glorify to me because it is from me that he will receive what he will make known to you. All that belongs to the Father is mine. That is why I said the Spirit will receive from me what he will make it known to you. (John 16:13–15)

If we agree that the purpose of the law was to lead us to Christ, it follows that any efforts in keeping the law are a backward step. What sets Christianity apart from religion is God's unconditional favour towards us, in saving us and empowering us to live in a way that's pleasing to Him. All of the world's religions are an attempt to get right with God, to establish a relationship with Him through our own efforts and performance.

Every religion has a code of ethics which they claim has, in essence, been handed down by God, or evolved and been refined by the community. In essence, that code says that God likes you more or less, depending on how well you perform in relation to those ethical standards. Therefore, to advance in any religion, you need to learn what's expected and then work hard to meet the criteria. All of those religious systems are what the Bible refers to as Old Covenant – by nature at least. The Old Covenant basically says that God gives us something to do, and if we do it well, He blesses us; if we don't, He punishes us or withholds His blessing. It is conditional. This is described well in Deuteronomy.

If you fully obey the LORD your God and carefully follow all his commands I give you today, the LORD your God will set you high above all the nations on earth. All these blessings will come on you and accompany you if you obey the LORD your God:

You will be blessed in the city and blessed in the country.

The fruit of your womb will be blessed, and the crops of your land and the young of your livestock – the calves of your herds and the lambs of your flocks.

Your basket and your kneading trough will be blessed.

You will be blessed when you come in and blessed when you go out.

The LORD will grant that the enemies who rise up against you will be defeated before you. They will come at you from one direction but flee from you in seven.

The LORD will send a blessing on your barns and on everything you put your hand to. The LORD your God will bless you in the land he is giving you.

The LORD will establish you as his holy people, as he promised you on oath, if you keep the commands of the LORD your God and walk in obedience to him. Then all the peoples on earth will see that you are called by the name of the LORD, and they will fear you. The LORD will grant you abundant prosperity – in the fruit of your womb, the young of your livestock and the crops of your ground – in the land he swore to your ancestors to give you. The LORD will open the heavens … (Deuteronomy 28:1–12a)

The list continues with all the good things that result from doing the right thing. If you fail according to Old Testament law, this is what will happen to you.

However, if you do not obey the LORD your God and do not carefully follow all his commands and decrees I am giving you today, all these curses will come upon you and overtake you:

You will be cursed in the city and cursed in the country.

Your basket and your kneading trough will be cursed.

The fruit of your womb will be cursed, and the crops of your land, and the calves of your herds and the lambs of your flocks.

You will be cursed when you come in and cursed when you go out.

The LORD will send on you curses, confusion and rebuke in everything you put your hand to … (Deuteronomy 28:15–20a)

In the Old Covenant, we are blessed or cursed depending on our performance. This law came from a holy, righteous, perfect God, so what could possibly be wrong with God's law, His Covenant, old or otherwise? Let me stress that there is nothing wrong with the law of God. What's wrong is us! A conditional covenant will not work for sinful people in a fallen world; we simply cannot keep our end of it. The New Covenant in Christ is God's solution to *our* weakness and inadequacy.

The genius and effectiveness of the New Covenant is in the person and work of the Lord Jesus Christ. In the performance of Jesus Christ as a man on earth, the law of God was kept perfectly for the very first time by a human being. Now, as far as every believer is concerned, that old covenant law has been taken away and nailed to the cross (Colossian 2). You don't need to struggle and strain trying to keep the New Covenant. It has already been kept for you by Jesus. No matter how badly you mess up today, you cannot break the New Covenant; it's too late for that. It is kept by Jesus Christ in heaven at the right hand of God the Father, perfectly, completely and eternally. The book of Hebrews is particularly helpful in our understanding of the old and new covenants.

For if there had been nothing wrong with that first covenant, no place would have been sought for another. But God found fault with the people and said:

'The time is coming, declares the Lord, when I will make a new covenant

with the people of Israel and with the people of Judah.

It will not be like the covenant I made with their ancestors

when I took them by the hand to lead them out of Egypt,

because they did not remain faithful to my covenant, and I turned away from them, declares the Lord.

This is the covenant I will establish with the people of Israel after that time, declares the Lord.

I will put my laws in their minds and write them on their hearts.

I will be their God, and they will be my people.

No longer will they teach their neighbor, or say to one another, 'Know the Lord,'

because they will all know me, from the least of them to the greatest.

For I will forgive their wickedness and will remember their sins no more.'

By calling this covenant 'new,' he has made the first one obsolete; and what is obsolete and ageing will soon disappear. (Hebrews 8:7–13)

The writer continues in the next chapter:

> *But when Christ came as high priest of the good things that are now already here, he went through the greater and more perfect tabernacle that is not made with human hands, that is to say, is not a part of this creation. He did not enter by means of the blood of goats and calves; but he entered the Most Holy Place once for all by his own blood, thus obtaining eternal redemption [this covenant is eternal, it's a closed deal, it's fulfilled completely for you]. The blood of goats and bulls and the ashes of a heifer sprinkled on those who are ceremonially unclean sanctify them so that they are outwardly clean. How much more, then, will the blood of Christ, who through the eternal Spirit offered himself unblemished to God, cleanse our consciences from acts that lead to death, so that we may serve the living God!*

> *For this reason, Christ is the mediator of a new covenant, that those who are called may receive the promised eternal inheritance – now that he has died as a ransom to set them free from the sins committed under the first covenant. (Hebrews 9:11–15)*

Jesus died for those sins committed under the first covenant and so, because of what Jesus did for you, your sins are remembered no more, and not just your past sins or your present sins but the sins you're going to commit in the future! There is now no condemnation for those who are in Christ Jesus – none whatsoever. Any condemnation or fear of punishment you may feel is coming from your own tortured conscience, or from the devil; it has no basis in reality if you are in Christ. You have been set free from the penalty of sin and when that truth really sinks in, you will be set free from the power of sin.

You are forgiven – totally, completely and permanently – from all sin. Under the old order, we were all born spiritually dead and under the control of the law. We were judged on the basis of our performance. If we did well, we were rewarded; if we didn't, we were punished and we didn't perform well! We were born into a moral universe governed by moral and spiritual laws, and we were all judged in light of those laws. Laws are good for some things, but not for mediating a relationship with God. Understanding grace in all its truth is only possible when we understand the new covenant and its stark difference to the old covenant.

Paul also discusses the difference between the Old and New Covenants in his letter to the Romans, and to do, this he uses the analogy of marriage. The concepts are a little complicated but absolutely essential to our understanding of the Christian life. Let me take you through the first six verses of Romans chapter 7:

Do you not know, brothers and sisters - for I am speaking to those who know the law ... (Romans 7:1a)

Now that's crucial. Paul is speaking to people who know the law, have a relationship to the law, are bound by the law, are intimidated by the law and have been under the law. Many who grow up in the church today are sadly still in this category.

... that the law has authority over someone only as long as that person lives? For example, by law a married woman is bound to her husband as long as he is alive, but if her husband dies, she is released from the law that binds her to him. So then, if she has sexual relations with another man while her husband is still alive, she is called an adulteress. But if her husband dies, she is released from that law and is not an adulteress if she marries another man. So, my brothers, you also died to the law ... (Romans 7:1b–4a)

One reason why it's complicated is that Paul jumps from his analogy of marriage to our relationship to the law. He was talking about the husband dying; now he's talking about us dying.

... you also died to the law through the body of Christ, that you might belong to another, to him who was raised from the dead, in order that we might bear fruit for God. For when we were in the realm of the flesh, the sinful passions aroused by the law were at work in us, so that we bore fruit for death. But now, by dying to what once bound us, we have been released from the law so that we serve in the new way of the Spirit, and not in the old way of the written code. (Romans 7:4–6)

Now this may be harder for men to equate with than women, but I want to encourage you to enter into this analogy today and let God teach you. You were born 'married' to the law. The law was your 'husband', and you stay married until 'death do you part'. What's so bad about that? Isn't the law a holy husband? Yes, absolutely; this is God's law, pure and right. In its own way, the law is good, and Jesus said the law will never pass away, so what is bad about being married to the law?

Well, first of all, this husband can only relate to you in a negative way. The law only ever tells you what not to do: don't lie, don't steal, don't lose your temper, don't sleep in, don't speed, don't lust, don't gain weight, don't spend too much money, don't in any way be unfaithful to the law. The only word you ever hear from this husband is a rebuke or a correction.

Second, this husband will never comfort or encourage you, never give you understanding and never praise you. There are no extenuating circumstances. If you break the law, you must be punished, and that's all there is to it. For example, a highway patrol officer is an instrument of the law, and when you see those blue lights in your rear-view mirror, you know what's coming! Is the policeman likely to pull you over to compliment you on your superb driving? No! He's there to enforce the law. He's there to tell you what you did wrong and punish you for it. Law only speaks when it is offended. That's your husband from birth. That's the relationship that you were born into, and that describes religion perfectly!

Your conscience is also like the highway patrol. It's a function of law. You may get past the radar or the speed trap, but your conscience never sleeps. Your conscience is there to accuse you of wrong and to dispense the punishment through anxiety, guilt, shame and even depression. Your husband (the law) is impersonal. He's always right, he cannot be appealed to, he always speaks in condemning tones. His strength is fear of punishment, and he never lifts a finger to help you. This is what the Pharisees were all about and why Jesus said:

> ... you experts in the law, woe to you, because you load people down with burdens they can hardly carry, and you yourselves will not lift one finger to help them. (Luke 11:46)

That's how Jesus described the law. The worst thing of all – this husband never dies! He will always outlive you. Jesus said the law will never pass away. As well as that, the law will never change its nature. Now Paul says that we are no longer under law. How can both be true? Let's work through this slowly. Let's read it again:

> For example, by law a married woman is bound to her husband as long as he is alive, but if her husband dies, she is released from the law that binds her to him. So then, if she has sexual relations with another man while her husband is still alive, she is called an adulteress. But if her husband dies, she is released from that law and is not an adulteress if she marries another man. So, my brothers and sisters, you also died to the law through the body of Christ, that you might belong to another. (Romans 7:2–4)

If you're married to the law until death, one of you has to die for you to be freed from the law. We already know the law is never going to die, so it has to be you! One of the realities of the Christian life is that those who have believed into Christ have participated in His experience, and part of His experience is death. Therefore, if you have believed in Christ, you no longer have any obligation whatsoever to the law, because in Christ you have died to the law.

Or don't you know that all of us who were baptized into Christ Jesus were baptized into his death? We were therefore buried with him through baptism into death in order that, just as Christ was raised from the dead through the glory of the Father, we too may live a new life. (Romans 6:3–4)

So, your old life is in the past. The life that you now live, you live in a sense beyond the grave. This is a little hard to grasp because the day after you believed in Christ, you looked in the mirror and saw the same person that you saw the previous day. People still waved to you and knew who you were. But spiritually speaking, you died to your old husband. This is a great mystery but as far as God is concerned, your old life is dead and if you believe that truth and act on it, you will experience the power and reality of that new life. The Spirit of God will make it a reality for you. If you're waiting for it to make sense, like I was for years, but never act on it, you'll never experience it.

Your conscience is a function of law. It will still accuse you because you have broken the law of God. Religion is also a function of law. It doesn't want to go out of business, so it doesn't want you to embrace this truth. Most of all, the devil doesn't want you to embrace this truth, because if you do, you will no longer be subject to him in any way. At the beginning of Galatians 3, Paul says very strongly, 'You foolish Galatians! Who has bewitched you?' The Greek term behind the word 'bewitched' is much stronger in the Greek than it is in English and is the same term used for someone under the influence of an evil spell or a demonic spirit of some kind. It is linked to Satan and his power. It was the only explanation Paul could come up with for why they would exchange the freedom they had experienced in Christ, by the power of the Holy Spirit, for the law and religion.

Satan uses the law of God more than any of us think. He wants us to try and keep the law to prove that we are good, then we can boast and be proud; or he wants us to fail so we can feel guilty. Either one is okay with the devil. He wins both ways; both pride and guilt will destroy our experience of the life in Christ in us. You live in a world in which Satan roams to and fro, a world in which religion and religious spirits run rampant. However, you can live in that world and not be of that world. The devil will still accuse, religion will still nag, but you can get to the point where none of that has any impact on you. This is what God wants for you, and that means He's going to help you get free – if you'll let Him. The first step is to be absolutely convinced from the Bible, and by the Holy Spirit, that what I am saying here is all true.

When you believed in Christ, you were set free from the law and put on the right side of the law. Your relationship to the law is now null and void, due to death. So, all those religious do's and don'ts have no more power over you. Instead of a husband who never lifts a finger to help you, your new Husband is Jesus. You can do all things through this new Husband Who strengthens you. Your new Husband doesn't just help you with the 'spiritual' part of your life; He helps you in everything and with everything.

There are also now no rules; there is only a relationship. Your new husband is always there, He's attentive, He can be reasoned with, He's helpful, He's encouraging, He blesses you, He's always saying He loves you, He's always picking you up when you fall. When you do sin, all you have to do is talk it over with Him. His love and acceptance of you is unaltered by your sin because He was punished for it long ago.

Most importantly, your new Husband, unlike the law, is able to produce life and fruit in you. He impregnates you with the ministry of the kingdom of God. Through the intimacy of prayer, Bible reading, worship, listening and responding to good teaching, obedience, fellowship with other believers etc., this life which He put in you is released. Through your own personal devotion to Him, that intimacy impregnates you with life and in time, the fruit will come.

Now this rescue from the old husband, the law, and your transfer into a relationship with your new husband, Jesus, is an unconditionally free gift. It cost the Giver everything but costs you nothing. It is cataclysmic and radical. Yet this happened to many of us without even a ripple. Part of the problem is that it didn't cost you anything – which is the whole point!

You see, the beauty of grace is also the problem of grace. You cannot and should not try to pay for this gift by your obedience or sacrifice. To attempt to do so by anything you do for God or for others is to cheapen something of inestimable value. The other thing you are doing is attempting the impossible! You are trying to buy something that's free, and you just can't do that. God has nothing to sell and even if He did, you have nothing with which to buy it; you are spiritually bankrupt. Whatever you have has to come from Him in the first place.

The radical truth which lies at the heart of the gospel is that you owe God nothing for your salvation. The riches of His grace and His eternal kingdom have been lavished upon you as a free gift. That makes religious people very nervous and often quite angry.

Look at this powerful illustration of grace in Luke's gospel. Jesus is dying on a cross along with two criminals. What happens is as shocking as it is amazing.

Two other men, both criminals, were also led out with him to be executed. When they came to the place called the Skull, they crucified him there, along with the criminals – one on his right, the other on his left. Jesus said, "Father, forgive them, for they do not know what they are doing." And they divided up his clothes by casting lots.

The people stood watching, and the rulers even sneered at him. They said, "He saved others; let him save himself if he is God's Messiah, the chosen One."

The soldiers also came up and mocked him. They offered him wine vinegar and said, "If you are the king of the Jews, save yourself."

There was a written notice above him, which read: THIS IS THE KING OF THE JEWS.

One of the criminals who hung there hurled insults at him: "Aren't you the Christ? Save yourself and us!"

But the other criminal rebuked him. "Don't you fear God," he said, "since you are under the same sentence? We are punished justly, for we are getting what our deeds deserve. But this man has done nothing wrong."

Then he said, "Jesus, [I want you to know something. This is the first time anybody calls the Lord 'Jesus.' This thief uses the familiar first name of Jesus, but everybody else calls Him Lord, Master or Teacher.] "Jesus, remember me when you come into your kingdom."

Jesus answered him, "Truly I tell you, today you will be with me in paradise." (Luke 23:32–43)

Do you see what just happened? A man asked for a gift and got it, just like that! What had he done to deserve it? Nothing. How much time did he have to love and serve and obey Jesus as payment for that gift? None whatsoever. He had nothing but sin, stupidity, broken opportunities, abuse, neglect and irresponsibility. That was his life, and from that pit of sin, he simply asked Jesus, *'Remember me, won't you?'*

Jesus didn't hesitate: *'Today, you'll be with me in paradise.'* There's Jesus Himself, giving the free gift of God's grace and eternal life. No confession, repentance, baptism or fruitful life from this man, and he certainly wasn't on a church membership roll. But right there on the cross, Jesus gives this man eternal life.

That story makes the little Pharisee inside us want to vomit and people get angry and try to explain away this whole scene as some special, exceptional circumstance. There isn't anything which is exceptional about that scene. That story is the gospel. That is the good news. That is *grace*!

Why are we humans suspicious of something that is free? Perhaps if we had to work for years to buy our eternal freedom, it might be more real to us. Ask Jesus dying on the cross if it's rea. Ask Jesus dying on the cross if it cost anything to get you out of the old husband's house and into the new husband's house. Ask Jesus if it's cataclysmic. Ask Jesus if it's radical! That realisation is only possible by the supernatural illumination of the Holy Spirit that it will change your attitude and actions from then on. To ask you to keep the law of God then would be stupid. Your heart will be so full and overwhelmed by the reality of what God has done for you and in you that you'll be doing much more than the law requires anyway, and you'll be doing it because you want to, not because you have to. None of that will happen until you believe this is the truth; nothing will change until you believe the heart and soul of the gospel. Look at these powerful words from Paul to you as first recorded in Romans 5:

> *Therefore, just as sin entered the world through one man, and death through sin, and in this way death came to all people, because all sinned –*

> *To be sure, sin was in the world before the law was given, but sin is not charged against anyone's account where there is no law. Nevertheless, death reigned from the time of Adam to the time of Moses, even over those who did not sin by breaking a command, as did Adam, who is a pattern of the one to come.*

> *But the gift is not like the trespass. For if the many died by the trespass of the one man, how much more did God's grace and the gift that came by the grace of the one man, Jesus Christ, overflow to the many! Nor can the gift of God be compared with the result of one man's sin: The judgment followed one sin and brought condemnation, but the gift followed many trespasses and brought justification. For if, by the trespass of the one man, death reigned through that one man, how much more will those who receive God's abundant provision of grace and of the gift of righteousness reign in life through the one man, Jesus Christ!*

> *Consequently, just as one trespass resulted in condemnation for all people, so also one righteous act resulted in justification and life for all people. For just as through the disobedience of the one man the many were made sinners, so also through the obedience of the one man the many will be made righteous. (Romans 5:12–19)*

Paul reminds us that Adam was the head of the human race. In fact, in the beginning, Adam *was* the human race. Therefore, when Adam sinned, he took the whole human race with him, and we all came under the judgement of God. We were born as a child of that first Adam and came under the law. We were born married to the law. After we believed and became a Christian, our experience was that of the second Adam, Jesus Christ. The gift that came was Jesus, who gathered us up into Himself. We were born again into a new life, subject to the new Husband, the Lord Jesus Christ. Paul sums it up in one sentence:

> For the wages of sin is death, but the gift of God is eternal life in Christ Jesus our Lord. (Romans 6:23)

This is where faith comes in. When you believe the gospel of God's amazing grace and act on it, it will become your experience. Legalism can creep into our lives whenever we start to trust in anything we do, say or think, to improve our performance or standing with God apart from Jesus and His ongoing love, acceptance and work in us.

God is a God of grace. His nature is to give and invite and include. The holy standards expressed in the law show us God's purity, holiness and righteousness, and point us to His plan and purpose in Christ for bringing His lost children home to Him. In that sense, the law is a promise to us. The law gives us a picture of who we are becoming in Christ, and not in our own strength. A proper understanding of God's law and its purpose only shows us our dependency on Christ and draws us closer to Him. It is a tutor which leads us into maturity in Christ.

We were given a new relationship and new life in Christ Jesus when we believed in His life, death and resurrection. He has become our new Husband and He births fruit in us which leads to life. In Him alone, we have a right standing with God, so we can throw the rule book out of the window. The message of grace is as simple as it is powerful – we have peace with God just as we are, and it all came to us free in Christ, through Christ, for Christ. Believe it, receive it and then watch everything change in you and around you.

CHAPTER SEVEN
Free from Accusation

As we have seen in the previous two chapters, the apostle Paul speaks of the law of God in a positive and in a negative way. In the positive sense, the law is a tutor – it brings us to Christ, it reveals God's will to us, it reveals the majesty and holiness of God. Paul has lots of good things to say about the law. The law becomes negative when it's used as a way of judging us or assessing our behaviour in order to improve our relationship with God or derive a blessing from Him. Here Paul is talking about the law being used in a religious sense and about the man-made rules and codes that are added to the law of God by which we are supposedly judged by God and by which we judge one another.

That's exactly what the Pharisees had been doing when Jesus showed up in town. They had hundreds of laws, all supposedly derived from the law of God which included the Ten Commandments. One of the terrible things about the law (used in this negative sense) is that it completely corrupts our relationship with God because we start trying to relate to God through our performance. For example, under the law, prayer, Bible study, worship, service and obedience become requirements. Under grace in Christ, the same things are the fruit of something within us, or more precisely, someone within us and that someone is Jesus.

Without faith in Jesus Christ, it is impossible to fully experience God. The only way you can have a relationship with God is to believe that God has already done everything for you to secure and protect that relationship. All you have to do is believe it, receive it, participate in it, enjoy it and let that reality produce fruit in your life. Those good works everyone exhorts you to 'do' will actually be the fruit of what God has already done in you. He gives His grace, love, mercy, power and intimacy as a free gift and from that gift, fruit will grow spontaneously.

Not only does trying to live under the law wreck our love relationship – our new covenant with God – it also wrecks our relationship with each other. Once we have the law which judges exterior behaviour, we can say, 'I'm doing pretty good and you're not' or 'You're doing pretty good and I'm not!' Instead, we should be saying, 'You're okay with God because Jesus has made you okay. That means you're okay with me too! Now let's see how we can spur one another on to love and good works.'

Good works are still important. How do we know what kind of tree it is if we can't see the fruit? How do we know what life is in us if it doesn't show? How do we reveal the character, love and beauty of Jesus Christ if it's not by what we do, which is radically different to most of the world around us? Good works are the fruit of the power of God within us.

If you're not producing the fruit of the gospel – if you're not a fruit-bearing disciple of Jesus – the only conclusion I can draw from Scripture is that you have never tasted the grace of God in the first place, or you tasted it once but, like the Galatians, you have allowed the enemy to drag you back under the law so that now you're now striving to produce fruit which will never come. You cannot be a fruitful Christian by trying to obey the law of God. If that were possible, Jesus wouldn't have needed to die in your place.

When you understand grace in all its truth, you will just do what you do out of love; you'll enjoy it and you'll go out and do it some more! You will encourage others as you do it, and you will give people a place to rest up when they fail. Not *if* they fail, but *when* they fail – it's inevitable. When you fail, you need someone to accept you and love you anyway, because those who succeed are no different from those who fail. We are what we are by the grace of God. That acceptance is what the body of Christ is all about.

The law was a heavy burden in Jesus' day. Jesus came into a society that was riddled with sin. There was organised crime, sexual immorality, political oppression, military occupation, slavery and the violation of human rights. However, Jesus never ran a campaign against any of those things, as much as I'm sure He detested them. Jesus' strongest criticism and condemnation was reserved for religion! Jesus ran a campaign against the law. Allow me to paraphrase Luke:

> *You Pharisees, you teachers of the law, you bind up heavy burdens, you make people feel guilty because they're not living up to an impossible standard, and then you do nothing to lift that burden or make it possible for them to carry it.* (Luke 11:46)

But this same Jesus says:

> *Come unto me all you who are weary and burdened [come unto me all you who are under the yoke of the law] and I will give you rest.* (Matthew 11:28)

In the Greek, the word translated here as 'rest' is a very strong word. Jesus is effectively saying, 'Come to me and I will give you a permanent vacation from the law.'

When most people think about the great conflict or war that's going on in the New Testament, they think in terms of good versus evil, as personified in Jesus versus Satan. I want to suggest that this is not the case at all. While the battle of good against evil is certainly present, I would suggest that the greatest conflict in the New Testament is between Jesus and the law (in the negative sense).

> Out of his fullness we have all received grace in place of grace already given. For the law was given through Moses; grace and truth came through Jesus Christ. (John 1:16–17)

The great conflict in the New Testament is not between Jesus and Satan but between Jesus and the law. We see the same thing in Paul's letter to the Galatians:

> We who are Jews by birth and not sinful Gentiles know that a person is not justified by the works of the law, but by faith in Jesus Christ. So we, too, have put our faith in Christ Jesus that we may be justified by faith in Christ and not by the works of the law, because by the works of the law no one will be justified. (Galatians 2:15–16)

Throughout the New Testament you have this contrast: you can try (in vain) to have a relationship with God through the law, or you can have a relationship with God through faith in Jesus Christ. That is not to say that Satan is unimportant as a player in that battle. However, more often than not, Satan uses the law (i.e. our wrong understanding of the law) to achieve his purpose. But as we will see soon, the power of Satan just melts away when we understand and walk in God's amazing grace and come out from under the yoke of the law.

There are many Christians who go to great lengths and engage in all kinds of spiritual warfare to get Satan out of their way. I believe that the devil will be automatically repelled and defeated as we begin to understand grace in all its truth. For as we'll see later in this study, the grace of God embodies the power of God, and when we understand that, the power of God is released in us to live a victorious Christian life, without ranting, raving or yelling at Satan.

In the New Testament, the greatest threat to the relationship that God desires for each of us is the law in the restrictive, legalistic sense. It is a greater and more powerful enemy than Satan. Paul makes this point clearly in the following words to the Colossians:

> When you were dead in your sins and in the uncircumcision of your flesh, God made you alive with Christ. He forgave us all our sins, having cancelled the charge of our legal indebtedness, which stood against us and condemned

us; he has taken it away, nailing it to the cross. And having disarmed the powers and authorities, he made a public spectacle of them, triumphing over them by the cross. (Colossians 2:13–15)

Jesus triumphed at the cross, by keeping the law perfectly to the bitter end and by taking the punishment once and for all for our inability to keep the law. The law was intended to say, 'You're okay, and you're not.' That's its power. The cross took that power away. Through the blood sacrifice of Christ, we are accepted by God, independently of the law. The law is useless as a tool against you once you understand that you are completely forgiven, for all time!

In Revelation 12:10, Satan is referred to as the 'accuser'; that's actually what his name means. That's why the law is such a powerful weapon in his hands. Take away any reference to the law and the accuser is out of business. If you forget everything else, remember this: when you were dead in sin, God made you alive! He took away the code that defined your sins, and by doing that, He disarmed the principalities and powers, and He disarmed Satan. Jesus made a public spectacle of Satan, dragging him through the streets, so to speak – defenceless, weaponless and an object of mockery.

A major reason why some people are depressed and burnt out in the church, and not living a victorious, joyful, fruitful, abundant Christian life, is because they still live under the condemnation of the accuser. They may well be born-again Christians, but they still listen to the lying voice of their old master. We need to understand the tactics of the enemy who accuses us night and day before God. When you know the truth, the truth will set you free from all accusation.

Imagine for a moment that you are taken to court and are standing before the Judge. The prosecuting Attorney (the accuser) says: 'I accuse this person of this crime.' The Judge asks, 'What law has this person broken?' Because of the finished work of Jesus, the accuser is forced to say, 'Well, actually, your Honour, now that you mention it, there isn't any law. It was nailed to the cross.' The Judge's response is quick and decisive: 'Then I rule that in the absence of a law to convict them, they shall go free!'

You need to accept that you still sin, yet (and here's the point) there isn't a law that your sin relates to anymore. The law has been taken away and nailed to the cross. The legal means of convicting you and sentencing you and the power of accusation has been taken away. It exists only in your fallen imagination and tortured conscience. So, invite Jesus into that conscience and ask Him to heal you.

(Jesus said), But do not think I will accuse you before the Father. Your accuser is Moses, on whom your hopes are set. (John 5:45)

In this verse, Moses represents the law, the good and glorious law that reveals God's perfection, His standard, His holiness, His heart. As wonderful and as glorious as it is, Jesus describes it as the accuser and He says, 'Do not think I will accuse you before the Father.'

Let the lights go on here. This is pure gold for the poverty-stricken, religious church – Jesus says, 'Don't even think that I will accuse you!' He couldn't make it any clearer if He tried. Your accuser is the law, and those religious and demonic powers that still use the law against you. That is why the preaching of grace disarms religion, because it disarms the devil. When you understand that the law has already been fulfilled, once and for all, and is effectively taken away, then the power to accuse you, the power to squash your spiritual life and expression, or to depress you and burn you out as a believer is completely removed.

When the things that suppress the gospel in you are disarmed and taken away, the fruit of the Spirit (which you have been sweating and struggling to manufacture yourself) just rises up from the depths of your being by the power of God's amazing grace. When that happens, overwhelming joy, a positive attitude and good works will just ooze out of you because they're no longer suppressed by the accuser. Jesus says, 'Think instead that, because I am in you, rivers of living water and life and fruit will spontaneously flow out of you. I have come to give you life, and life more abundantly. It's the enemy that comes to rob and to steal and to destroy, to bring guilt and shame and fear and depression.'

Tragically, however, all over the world, the devil is being re-armed every day, especially on Sundays! So many preachers are unconsciously re-arming the devil by preaching sermons full of 'shoulds' and 'oughts' and 'do-more-try-harder' guilt trips. You've got to hand it to Satan – he's a lot of despicable things, but he's not stupid. He has been doing this for over two thousand years, and because it works so well, he's not going to give it up.

The blessings, gifts, power and fruit of God are already in you! The Bible says, 'Christ is in you, the hope of glory' (Colossians 1:27). Everything that is in Christ is in you. You simply need to believe that and act on it. It's so simple that many of us miss it! When this revelation comes from the Holy Spirit, your whole life and relationship with God and others will be transformed. We need to pray that God will give us this liberating, empowering revelation. Colossians 1:6 tells us that the gospel of Jesus Christ will spread across our community, our nation and all over the world – it will grow and bear fruit – when we understand God's grace in all its truth. The apostle Paul warned us about this battle between Jesus and the law a long time ago:

Are we beginning to commend ourselves again? Or do we need, like some people, letters of recommendation to you or from you? You yourselves are our letter, written on our hearts, known and read by everyone. You show that you are a letter from Christ, the result of our ministry, written not with ink but with the Spirit of the living God, not on tablets of stone [in light of the law] but on tablets of human hearts [in your very personality].

Such confidence we have through Christ before God. Not that we are competent in ourselves to claim anything for ourselves, but our competence comes from God. He has made us competent as ministers of a new covenant - not of the letter but of the Spirit; for the letter kills, but the Spirit gives life. (2 Corinthians 3:1–7)

He's talking to Christians here – and so am I. It's amazing that with the life of Christ inside, so many believers still feel dead. They're not just tired; they are spiritually burned out. That is what the law does to Christians. It continues to rob us spiritually, emotionally and relationally. Death of every kind is the ministry of the law.

By stark contrast, the grace of God, when understood in all its truth, releases the life of Christ in you. When you are born again, that life is put into you. I have every confidence in the gospel. I have confidence in the life of Christ in you. When the religious load is taken off you, the life that is in you can manifest and bubble up spontaneously. I have confidence in the Holy Spirit's gifts in you. I know that they are in there and all we have to do is encourage them to be released into your church and into your community and across your whole nation. Then the sleeping giant will finally be awakened, and the world will see the church as she was always meant to be!

Let me wrap up this important chapter by including some selections from Romans 3, 4 and 5 from *The Message*. May the Lord bring understanding as you read these very powerful words of truth.

But in our time, something new has been added. What Moses and the prophets witnessed to all those years has happened. The God-setting-things-right that we read about has become Jesus-setting-things-right for us. And not only for us, but for everyone who believes in him ... Since we've compiled this long and sorry record as sinners ... and proved that we are utterly incapable of living the glorious lives God wills for us, God did it for us. Out of sheer generosity he put us in right standing with himself. A pure gift. He got us out of the mess we're in and restored us to where he always wanted us to be. And he did it by means of Jesus Christ.

God sacrificed Jesus on the altar of the world to clear that world of sin. Having faith in him sets us in the clear. God decided on this course of action in full view of the public - to set the world in the clear with himself through the sacrifice of Jesus, finally taking care of the sins he had so patiently endured. This is not only clear, but it's now - this is current history! God sets things right. He also makes it possible for us to live in his rightness.

God does not respond to what we do; we respond to what God does ... We've finally figured it out. Our lives get in step with God and all others by letting him set the pace, not by proudly or anxiously trying to run the parade ...

God sets right all who welcome his action and enter into it ...

But by shifting our focus from what we do to what God does, don't we cancel out our careful keeping of the rules and ways God commanded? Not at all. What happens, in fact, is that by putting that entire way of life in its proper place, we confirm it. (Romans 3: 21–31)

So how do we fit what we know of Abraham, our first father in the faith, into this new way of looking at things? If Abraham, by what he did for God, got God to approve him, he could certainly have taken credit for it. But the story we're given is a God-story, not an Abraham-story. What we read in Scripture is, "Abraham entered into what God was doing for him, and that was the turning point. He trusted God to set him right instead of trying to be right on his own."

If you're a hard worker and do a good job, you deserve your pay; we don't call your wages a gift. But if you see that the job is too big for you, that it's something only God can do, and you trust him to do it - you could never do it for yourself no matter how hard and long you worked - well, that trusting-him-to-do-it is what gets you set right with God, by God. Sheer gift ...

That famous promise God gave Abraham - that he and his children would possess the earth - was not given because of something Abraham did or would do. It was based on God's decision to put everything together for him, which Abraham then entered when he believed. If those who get what God gives them only get it by doing everything they are told to do and filling out all the right forms properly signed, that eliminates personal trust completely and turns the promise into an ironclad contract! That's not a holy promise; that's a business deal. A contract drawn up by a hard-nosed lawyer and with plenty of fine print only makes sure that you will never be able to collect. But if there is no contract in the first place, simply a promise - and God's promise at that – you can't break it.

73

This is why the fulfilment of God's promise depends entirely on trusting God and his way, and then simply embracing him and what he does. God's promise arrives as a pure gift. That's the only way everyone can be sure to get in on it, those who keep the religious traditions and those who have never heard of them. (Romans 4:1–5, 13–16)

By entering through faith into what God has always wanted to do for us - set us right with him, make us fit for him - we have it all together with God because of our Master Jesus. And that's not all: We throw open our doors to God and discover at the same moment that he has already thrown open his door to us. We find ourselves standing where we always hoped we might stand - out in the wide, open spaces of God's grace and glory, standing, tall and shouting our praise. (Romans 5:1–2)

CHAPTER EIGHT
The Performance Treadmill

Many of us struggle to accept God's free gift of grace and are not prepared to admit as believers or as a church that we are not where God desires us to be. We will do the most outrageous things with the Bible to justify what we currently do or don't believe and how live and act inside and outside the church.

If we have not experienced the grace of God in any significant way, then to admit that we cannot meet our own standards or improve our performance can be incredibly threatening. The moment we accept that, we are admitting that we need to move from where we are; we need to change or be open to God changing us. If we resist change, then the power of the gospel of God's amazing grace will always elude us.

As we continue to explore the relationship between grace and law, it helps our understanding to consider how the law works in us from a practical, experiential point of view. I want us to begin by looking at two statements from the apostle Paul that radically illustrate what happened to Paul when he allowed a full understanding of the grace of God to change his life.

> *We know that the law is spiritual; but I am unspiritual, sold as a slave to sin. I do not understand what I do. For what I want to do I do not do, but what I hate I do ... So I find this law at work: Although I want to do good, evil is right there with me. For in my inner being I delight in God's law; but I see another law at work in me, waging war against the law of my mind and making me a prisoner of the law of sin at work within me. What a wretched man I am! Who will rescue me from this body that is subject to death? Thanks be to God, who delivers me through Jesus Christ our Lord!*

> *So then, I myself in my mind am a slave to God's law, but in my sinful nature a slave to sin. (Romans 7:14–15; 21–25)*

Paul's raw confession of his struggle with sin removed him from any pedestal his followers may have put him on and firmly planted him on level ground before the cross of Christ with the rest of us. Paul struggled with sin just like everyone else. But then, in stark contrast, the same man said this in his letter to the Philippians:

> *I can do all things through Christ who strengthens me. (Philippians 4:13, NKJV)*

Note that Paul doesn't say he can do *some* things – the easy things, or the things that he's good at or has been trained to do, or the things he has worked hard at. He says he could do *all* things through Christ who strengthened him. So how did this great apostle go from Romans 7 to Philippians 4? How did he move from 'The good I want to do I don't do,' to 'I can do all the good I want to do, through Christ who strengthens me.' More to the point, how do we make that transition? How do we turn from 'I can't quite make it' to 'I can make it, with power to burn?'

The Bible clearly teaches that it's the right and heritage of every Christian to live above sin. So how does that happen? How do we break that deadly cycle of trying harder, succeeding for a while, failing and feeling guilty again? How do we get off the merry-go-round of failure to the place of affirming that we can do all things through Christ who strengthens us?

The world, and even some churches, teaches us that the way to be okay in order to gain acceptance and love is by doing what is 'right'. That varies according to which group of people you want to impress or belong to. The guys at the bar or the footy game have one set of rules; the corporate jungle of deals and profit and market share have another set. Some churches have a different set of rules: the rules say (or imply) that if you do these things well, you're loved and accepted; and if you don't there will be consequences, and you'll feel rejected pretty quickly. Whether people intend to reject you or not is secondary; that is always the effect when external standards are given prominence or importance. These church 'rules' state that you're okay and you gain acceptance and love by meeting certain religious standards.

This is the law at work. It may include reading the Bible, praying, witnessing, attending services, giving money, being baptised, becoming a church member and plenty more. All these things may be very good, and some of them are things that we are exhorted to do in the Bible. However, if just doing them made us okay as Christians, then Jesus didn't need to die. We would just need a really good self-help program and we'd be right. If trying to do the right thing is all we need, those good little Christians who are working their tails off in the church doing more and trying harder should be the happiest, most accepted, most victorious people in the world! But they're not. Human performance as a means of acceptance doesn't work, and it's certainly not the gospel.

As Christians, we know that doing more and trying harder never makes us happy and never brings us closer to God. We know from experience, but it's as though we don't know any alternative. We can't find anyone that it's worked for, but we keep doing it anyway. There is a very real, dark spiritual force behind performance-based religion which masquerades as true Christianity. Flesh can never change or overcome flesh.

Let's look at an everyday illustration. Suppose you overeat, and you think you weigh too much. That may be a true assessment. You feel bad about it, not just because you're vain, but because it's bad for your health and you are potentially shortening your life. Your actions are denying the richness and fullness of the life that God gave you to live. Now the performance answer is simple: go on a diet, get control of your eating and commence an exercise program. This is what our weight-conscious, 'slim is beautiful' society has been preaching to us for many years. But if the 'do-more-try-harder' approach ever worked, we would be the skinniest people in the world. Yet, all indications are that we're fatter now as a nation than ever before. That is our reality in spite of a preoccupation with losing weight – doing more and trying harder. It doesn't work in the world, and it doesn't work in the church. It actually makes things worse.

The church in the Western world has never been as riddled with gross sins like infidelity, immorality, sexual abuse and fraud as it is at present. Why is that the case when we have heard so much preaching about sin and know very well what is acceptable and what is not? A lot of people say that the preaching is too weak these days – I would agree; but it's not weak on laying down the law and loading expectations on us. All that guilt about not doing enough has made us Christians even more inactive and guilt-ridden. Why is that so? Well, let's analyse this.

There's no argument about the great worth of Bible study and prayer. Christians who neglect either will be poorer in their lives. But what happens when you realise you are not reading the Bible or praying as often as you feel you should? You feel bad about it, and when you finally feel guilty enough to address this bad behaviour, you resolve to set a schedule for Bible study and prayer. It starts well and God meets you in those quiet times of reflection. But eventually you miss a few days and get down on yourself. The further you punish yourself the further you seem to slip away from the discipline, until finally you crash in a heap and give up. This cycle of good intentions – trying harder, succeeding, failing, feeling guilty and trying again – is something that many of us know all about, and it is doomed from the start. Let me explain why.

This cycle begins with your feelings of guilt or shame because you are doing something you shouldn't do, or not doing something you feel you should do. These feelings build up to where they are strong enough (listen to this language) to motivate you to spur into action. You want to eliminate the shame and the guilt. You're ready to do something about it. So, you make a resolution. You re-dedicate your life, you commit yourself to the Lord's work again, you make promises, you come forward for prayer. You do whatever you need to change your behaviour.

At this stage, you're full of energy. You can spot this 'do-more-try-harder' cycle by the levels of energy you have at the various stages. At the beginning stage, after a long time of feeling guilty, you've got hope, energy and discipline. It can even be a little intoxicating. 'Maybe God's going to do it this time; maybe He's going to be pleased with me *this* time; maybe it will work *this* time and I'll never have to go through that horrible cycle again. Maybe I'll know the power of the Holy Spirit *this* time; maybe *this* time if I *just try harder*, God will be there for me!'

As a result, your prayer life becomes regular, or you watch what you eat or you hit the gym again. You get in tow whatever the bad behaviour is. Everything you felt guilty about you now feel master of. One week, two weeks pass; you feel great. But why do you feel great? Because of your good behaviour. Hello? Reality check! What do we call it when we feel okay because of our performance? The victorious Christian life? No, we call that *self-righteousness*! So, when you feel okay before God because you're finally doing things right, you turn into a Pharisee!

That's why God hates religion more than you'll ever know. Religion is this lying, horrible, deceitful, cruel hoax which tells you that you're not okay because you don't perform properly. When you do, it turns you into one of the people for whom Jesus reserved His most savage criticism! Anything that you put faith in to make you okay, or to restore self-esteem, or to quieten the guilt – anything you do, or any power you appeal to – is your idol. Religion is an idol. It can properly be seen as an addiction. Some people take alcohol to ease the pain of life. Some take drugs, or run marathons, or get lost in pornography or sexual sin. There are lots of ways that people deal with inner pain, guilt, shame and inadequacy. Christians just have a more respectable, but far more dangerous idol – religion.

The inescapable lesson that we must learn sooner or later is that self-help goodness is not the Christian life, and it doesn't work. The world's terms of living – obsession with money, looking out for number one, putting confidence in possessions etc. – is called 'living according to the flesh'. Am I right? Being good, going to church, reading the Bible, praying, serving on committees, being baptised, singing Christian songs etc. may be just as much living according to the flesh, depending on your motivation.

The only difference is the audience you are trying to impress; one is outside the church and the other is the church or, in reality, God Himself. That's right, we are deceived enough to think God is impressed by our performance! It doesn't matter whether you do good things or bad things from God's perspective; if you're trying to earn His favour and be accepted by Him in any way, it's useless. It's also an insult to God and an offence to the cross of Christ.

This is why Jesus told the Pharisees that the prostitutes and criminals He hung around with were actually closer to the kingdom of heaven than any of them. Ouch! What a low blow to a godly, passionate, committed Pharisee. Jesus said that because we are either all the way in or all the way out of the kingdom of God, and the only way to be in is through the finished work of Jesus Christ. The Pharisees thought that if they lived better lives than the sinners around them, they were closer to the kingdom of God. But Jesus said that only takes us further away, because our self-righteous, 'good' behaviour was harder to confront than the sin of those we look down on. They're more likely to repent than we are. Did you get that? *It's easier to get the world to repent of its worldly behaviour than it is to get the church to repent of its religious behaviour.*

Now let's see exactly why this cycle of self-effort is so deadly and doomed to fail. You may go for one, two, even five weeks cranking out the good behaviour and feeling really good about your performance. Now, if you were initially motivated to perform by guilt and shame, what motivates you six weeks later? Answer: nothing!

The law can produce guilt, anxiety and shame in you, or it can produce pride, but it cannot produce spiritual life or genuine, godly fruit. So, if guilt and shame was the basic motivation to get you off your backside to do more and try harder, you are setting yourself up for certain failure, because the moment you start performing better, the guilt and shame will start to disappear and sooner or later you lose the motivation behind your performance.

You slack off and before you know it, you're at the bottom of the roller-coaster and the deadly cycle starts all over again. The distance between your highs and your lows can be breathtaking.

Some Christians spend their whole lives in this cycle. So, when preachers talk about the victorious Christian life, they may as well talk to the wall. Most of the people listening have no idea how to get off this religious roller-coaster and back into reality where God loves them unconditionally and is ready, willing and able to fulfil all those disciplines and more in their lives in His strength, not theirs.

Others catch on a lot sooner and realise that this is a dead-end street and it's never going to get any better, so, they stop doing more and trying harder and just leave the church. There are hundreds of thousands of people in this nation who were once involved in the church but aren't anymore. Why? Because all they encountered was religion – they never embraced the transformational, New Covenant gospel of Jesus Christ. These people need to hear the true gospel at least once before they die. They have not rejected Jesus; they just never got to meet Him in their experience of church.

Let me demonstrate the grace of God in action by telling you a story. You will have heard it before, but maybe not this way. A father had two sons. Both of them were good boys; they were performing well. But one day the younger son said: 'I'm tired of all this do-gooder stuff. I want to go off and be bad.' So, he demanded his inheritance, got permission from Daddy (who knew that if his son didn't want to be there, then he wasn't really there anyway) and the boy left the family farm and travelled a very long way from home and from his father.

As planned, he lived like hell. He was as bad as he wanted to be. He got to do all the stuff that was in his heart. Eventually he hit a wall going really fast in the sin lane and woke up one day on his face in a pig pen. He then realised that this father's servants were treated better than him, so he decided he would go home and strike a deal with dear old Dad to hire him as a servant. At least he would have a roof over his head again and some real food.

He thought, 'I really blew it. I have disqualified myself from being a son. I'm no longer acceptable because of my bad behaviour, so maybe I can live as a servant and repay my father with my good behaviour.' So, he headed home. His father saw him a long way off. Why? Because he was looking for him and had been looking and longing for his son since the moment he left his side.

The father ran to the boy, his heart beating in his throat with excitement as he welcomed him home. Just as the boy started out with what some people call repentance (but it really has nothing to do with what biblical repentance is), the father crushed him in an avalanche of love and grace and unbridled affection. In effect, he cut off the boy's sob story and confession, stopped his pathetic plea to buy the favour of his father again and said, '*You don't understand, son. Your behaviour has nothing to do with whether you are my son or not. You are my son because you are my son! Bring the robe, bring the ring, bring the sandals; here is full and free restoration of your sonship. All the symbols, all the power, all the reality of total, unconditional reinstatement, acceptance and love are yours, in spite of your behaviour, in spite of your bad choices, in spite of your sin. My acceptance of you has nothing to do with your performance; it has everything to do with me and my character.'*

You have just seen how to be okay with God and how to feel okay with God when you're feeling shame or guilt, or you don't measure up in some way. How do you break the deadly cycle of self-effort? First, you come home and receive God's free grace, love and acceptance as you are, where you are with no exceptions. Come home in your sin, rebellion and stupidity and just be loved by your heavenly Father. You need to feel okay on His terms. Don't make any promises. Don't do anything. Just bask in His grace and love until that has its effect in you.

The father in the story wouldn't listen to any promises or resolutions about the future. He simply restored his son again – totally, completely and unconditionally. That is exactly what your heavenly Father will do for you every time you come to Him. As that wave of love and grace saturates you, the gift of true repentance is birthed deep within you and your life is never the same again.

I came to God fifty years ago, full of sin and desperate for mercy and grace. He gave it to me, and I will never outgrow that humble dependence on a saving God. Our dependence on His saving and empowering grace never ends. As believers, sin doesn't break our fellowship with God; it just fills us with shame, and we turn away from God. But He never turns away from us. So, the solution is always to turn back and head for home. That's the only place to go when you feel bad – when you need to be loved, forgiven and accepted. The writer of Hebrews says it best:

> *Therefore, since we have a great high priest who has ascended into heaven, Jesus the Son of God, let us hold firmly to the faith we profess. For we do not have a high priest who is unable to empathize with our weaknesses, but we have one who has been tempted in every way, just as we are – yet he did not sin. Let us then approach God's throne of grace with confidence [The KJV translation says, 'Let us boldly approach'] so that we may receive mercy and find grace to help us in our time of need. (Hebrews 4:14–16)*

You can approach the throne of God's empowering with confidence and receive mercy every time. You don't deserve it, but you get it anyway. And not just mercy, but also grace, God's empowering presence. Do you want power to do better next time? Here's the power; go for it! You want mercy? Just ask for it and it's yours!

Do you see why the true gospel rips the heart out of works-based religion? You have to take it for free or you don't get it at all. God's mercy, love, forgiveness and acceptance are not bought at any price – except the blood of Jesus. God's grace – the empowering presence of God Himself - is also not bought at any price. It is freely given to those with the sincere belief that it is theirs for the taking. Can you see how religion doesn't fit here at all?

Look again at the cross of Christ, at the blood streaming from His murdered body. Keep looking until you've got it, until you know that there is nothing you can do that will ever make it okay. Stay there, totally forgiven in the loving embrace of your compassionate Father. When that hits home, when you come face to face with His amazing grace, you will say, 'I don't want to live like this anymore. Give me the grace to live a real life. Get me off this religious roller-coaster and give me the power to become like Jesus. I want to do what I do because I love you. I want to live before I die, not just play out a role that has no reality in it. I want to live by Your grace and for Your glory, Lord.'

How will you respond to this truth today? Perhaps you've identified with this deadly cycle of self-effort recently and you need God's empowering presence to lift you off that roller-coaster. Maybe you're tired – you've been serving the Lord a long time – but the glow has left you. It's become more of a habit or lifestyle than a living relationship, and so little things become big things and crush you.

You need to be brought out of the rut and given new purpose, a new direction and power to travel a new road. Perhaps you are one who knows all the right answers about God. You've grown up in the church and heard hundreds of times about the real, authentic Christian life, the Spirit-filled, powerful life that makes an impact in the church and in the world. You've been exhorted to press on and know God better, but you wonder if you really know Him at all. Maybe you lack the power to deal with a particular problem, whether it be relational, financial, spiritual, emotional, physical. If you want the power of God for healing in any area of your life, prepare to enter the throne room of God now.

I want you to imagine you're standing before a huge, thick, heavy door. It's the door to the throne room of grace, the place of God's empowering. You're nervous and you wonder if you even have the right to go in. 'How could a holy God even look upon my sinful face, let alone give me what I need?' Just when you're about to turn away gripped by shame and inadequacy, you feel someone's hand on your shoulder. You turn to see who it is. It's Jesus, standing right there next to you. His eyes are filled with indescribable compassion, love and understanding.

He leads you gently towards the door and says, 'It's okay. Don't be afraid; I'm with you. Our Father knows you're coming. He's expecting you. I've already been in and cleared the way for you. You have nothing to fear.' With that, He just walks towards the door which opens in His presence, like it knew He was coming. As you enter, you see the Father seated on the throne of grace. His look of love and acceptance melts your heart and all your fear vanishes. You feel like you could ask Him for the whole world, and He would give it to you. You pour your heart out to him.

'Father, I love You and I stand in awe before You. I cannot understand why You would go to the lengths You did to bring me into this throne room today. I am overwhelmed by Your love for me. You have promised me so much, things I am too fearful or ignorant to claim. Among those promises is the one You've given me again today, that I may boldly approach your throne and ask for mercy and grace, for unconditional forgiveness and the power to change and become the person You always knew I could become.'

Now, in the quietness of this moment, tell God what you need. Tell Him what burdens you have right now and ask Him to strengthen you to face that challenge, or if possible, remove the challenge altogether. Lay all those burdens at His feet now and watch as Jesus picks them all up one by one and takes them upon Himself. That's what living in Christ, through Christ and for Christ really means. You give Him all your burdens, all your guilt, all your shame, all your shortcomings, and He gives you His strength, His life and His resurrection power. Amazing grace, how sweet the sound!

Until we are set free from the religious expectations of the law by a proper understanding of God's free acceptance of us, we will engage in an endless cycle of futile human effort. We simply need to return to our loving heavenly Father and accept His love. When we turn to Him, we find all that our heart has ever desired is there, given to us freely and without condemnation. When that happens, and only when that happens, we will experience true repentance and radical transformation. All those expectations we used to beat ourselves up trying to fulfil to please God will begin to emerge in us as the fruit of the gospel, as the life of Christ, is released deep within us. All that we ever hoped to be and struggled to achieve will become a reality in Christ, through Christ and for Christ.

CHAPTER NINE
You are Radically Free!

As you have been engaging with the teaching in this book, has the thought ever crossed your mind, 'When is he going to get around to talking about sin and repentance? Can we just go on sinning if we're forgiven?' If you haven't thought that or something similar, then I probably haven't made the gospel free enough yet! In Romans 6, we see one of the times Paul was asked this. He was accused of making the gospel too free and so he responds to his critics a couple of times:

> *What shall we say, then? Shall we go on sinning so that grace may increase? What then? Shall we sin because we are not under law but under grace? By no means! (Romans 6:1, 15)*

When grace is preached in all its fullness, that question will rise to the surface – it has to. Have you ever thought that you could sin without condemnation? Or have you always known what the rules were, what God and others would condemn you for, in spite of all the evidence which says that rules are useless at making people holy and the fear of judgement can never, ever produce righteousness?

Look at the nation of Israel in the Bible, God's called out people. Judgement came through the Philistines, snakes, scorpions, death, destruction and curses galore. Did that keep the people from sin? Did that make them holy? No, it didn't do them any good at all. In fact, one could argue that it just made them more sinful. By contrast, however, let me say this: in all my years of Christian ministry, I have never once observed a situation where a genuine understanding of God's unconditional love, grace and goodness has actually had a sinful effect on anyone.

In one of the least quoted but most important verses in the New Testament (Romans 2:4), Paul reminds us that 'it's God's kindness that leads us to repentance'. It's our experience of God's love that cleans up our life. I have yet to meet a person who was made more evil by reflecting on God's love for them. Conversely, I have never met a person who was made holy or good by reflecting on their sin or God's judgement. So those people in Paul's day (and today) who fear that making God's grace and power too free will cause people to sin without concern first of all do not understand God's grace to even think that, and secondly, they are worrying about something that has not happened.

The true gospel is designed to set you completely and radically free, as Paul said so clearly, 'It is for freedom that Christ has set you free' (Galatians 5:1). Yet that is not what a lot of modern preaching is designed to tell you. It is more likely to give you standards to 'make' you good. Now if some people want to make up rules and others are silly enough to subject themselves to those rules, that's okay, I guess. There are all sorts of organisations where, if you want to belong, you have to agree to their rules. There is nothing wrong with that. Just don't ever call such an organisation the church of Jesus Christ! We can have our rules and regulations if we want to, but let's never dish out those rules with a Bible in our hand, suggesting that Jesus is building that kind of church – because He isn't.

When people are set free to be who they really are in Christ, and not who someone else wants them or expects them to be, all the fruit of the gospel will spontaneously break out in them, in the church, in their community and across the whole nation. That's the power of the gospel! You are free; you are radically and dangerously free. This issue of freedom is not an insignificant one in the Bible. It's a major and central issue. Jesus said himself:

> *The Spirit of the Lord is on me, because he has anointed me to proclaim good news to the poor. He has sent me to proclaim freedom for the prisoners and recovery of sight for the blind, to set the oppressed free … (Luke 4:18)*

He wasn't talking about people in jail; He was talking to and about people who were imprisoned by religion. As I've said before, Jesus' strongest criticism was reserved for the law and the custodians of the law: the religious leaders. The Pharisees were the good, conservative, religious people of His day, yet Jesus deliberately picked a fight with them many times to expose their restrictive, law-burdened teaching. This same Jesus said:

> *Then you will know the truth and the truth will set you free. (John 8:32)*

That truth is not abstract theological truth. That truth is Jesus Christ, the One Who said,

> *I am the way, the truth and the life … (John 14:6)*

If you know Jesus Christ personally, you know the Truth and you will be free. Freedom does not come from the knowledge of certain theological truths; it comes from a relationship with Jesus. He goes on to say:

> *So if the Son sets you free, you will be free indeed. (John 8:36)*

Paul picks up on this in hundreds of places. Let me just mention some:

... through Christ Jesus the law of the Spirit who gives life has set you free from the law of sin and death. (Romans 8:2)

It is for freedom that Christ has set us free ... (Galatians 5:1)

You, my brothers and sisters, were called to be free ... (Galatians 5:13)

Freedom is your calling in life. It is your commissioning. You are meant to be totally unable to be manipulated by religion, religious leaders or the devil himself.

But now he has reconciled you by Christ's physical body through death to present you holy in his sight, without blemish and free from accusation ... (Colossians 1:22)

Now the Lord is the Spirit and where the Spirit of the Lord is, there is freedom. (2 Corinthians 3:17)

In him [Christ] and through faith in him we may approach God with freedom and confidence. (Ephesians 3:12)

The Spirit and the bride say, "Come!" And let the one who hears say, "Come!" Let the one who is thirsty come; and let the one who wishes take the free gift of the water of life. (Revelation 22:17)

Freedom is not a minor issue with God. It's a big deal. In all the congregations I have pastored over the years, I always prayed that a sense of His real presence would be present when we met together. If God was there, then I didn't have to worry about much. He would take care of things; for where the Spirit of Lord is, there is freedom. Human institutions seem to want to control people. God wants to set us free in our hearts from all that control, be it governmental, religious, relational or emotional control. I would suggest there are two basic reasons why God wants this.

First of all, it's only when you are free that you can be who God created you to be. That sounds simple, but it's vitally important. God wants you to be free from anybody's manipulation so that you can do what you want, act out what you feel, make choices and follow through on them. He treats you with dignity and respect. He values you. The second thing God wants (and longs for) is for you to use that freedom to choose to return to Him in love.

When the gospel of God's amazing grace is preached, someone invariably comes forward with the warning: 'If you keep preaching this stuff and make people completely free, then you're not going to get them to do anything in the church. If they take this stuff to its logical end, they may even stop coming to church! They may stop tithing! In fact, they'll do anything they like and think that's okay with God.'

Well, that's the risk you take when you preach the full gospel of God's amazing grace, and that's precisely the point of grace! God wants to see everyone in the church doing anything they want to do and doing nothing out of obligation, manipulation or expectation from their pastor, from their church, or even from God Himself. Either we will return to Him freely or we won't. If we go back to Him after being set free, then it's the real thing; if we don't, it was never real to begin with. He wants us to be free, not slaves; choosers, not robots.

By contrast, religion holds the carrot out in front and then swings a stick behind. The carrot out in front is: 'We will like you and accept you if you become like us, do the things we do and believe the things we believe.' The stick behind is: 'If you don't, then we'll reject you, we won't like you, we won't give you the same position of freedom in Christ's church that we have given ourselves.' Now everybody knows that the thing in between the carrot and the stick is a donkey! That's not the way God wants His children to be treated. That's not His plan for those precious ones who are created in His image and for whom Christ died.

I need to caution you that you may not want this freedom. This is an observation of fact among all Christians when radical freedom of this biblical nature is taught – many people simply can't handle it. The main reason there is so much religious, legalistic, do-more-try-harder pseudo-Christianity is because there's such a big market for it. I used to think that we were all victims of some kind. Yet as hard as it may be to swallow, I don't think we've been victims of anything. Many people submit to this legalistic garbage because deep down they want to. People are scared of freedom. They are afraid to make choices that they're responsible for.

So many of us are like those in the vision of the prison without doors I shared back in chapter 2. All the people in that prison are there by their own choice. They are not prepared to sacrifice the familiarity and predictability of life in captivity for the wide open spaces of freedom which await them. They seem to prefer submitting to the church telling them what's right and wrong, rather than embracing a personal, one-to-one relationship with Jesus Christ where He guides their steps each day. That seems too scary. Whenever I have called on people to take their own God-given freedom seriously, many of them have struggled. They just can't let go of the need to relate to God through a set of rules. In effect they are saying that they want something other than the unconditional acceptance of God in Christ.

As a church, this radical freedom in Christ will challenge us in all what we do and why. If I am to preach and teach His Word as it is, then I have to be prepared to let the chips fall where they may and let Him pick up the pieces. If that threatens the way we do things or challenges any sacred cows in regard to what we believe or how we act, then so be it. If a rule, regulation, belief or practice is not from God, then why would we want it? If it's not birthed in the gospel, why should we tolerate it?

Let there be no misunderstanding: Christ accepts you; therefore I accept you. I trust you because I trust the Holy Spirit in you. I want you to do whatever He leads you to do in the church and in the community. It is that unconditional acceptance of each other as fellow pilgrims that God wants in every church congregation that names the name of Jesus. Yes, there are guidelines and biblical principles of leadership and a general understanding of what is helpful and edifying and what is not, but these are not put forward as rules to restrict and harness people in a way that hampers them fulfilling their potential.

Jesus came to lift that yoke of religion completely off our shoulders and give us His yoke which is light and easy. Yet for some reason, many in the church still cling to the heavy yoke of religion and wonder why God is not real and why the presence and power of God is not evident in the way it seemed to be in the early church. I've said it many times – God hates religion! Until we accept and embrace our total, radical freedom in Christ, we will not see God move in our nation the way so many of us desperately desire. God wants you to be radically free so you can be yourself.

The second reason that God wants you free is so that you can freely return His love to Him, or not. He's prepared to take that risk. He wants a free love relationship with you more than anything else. He's willing to sacrifice control and to risk His good name. He gave the life of His own Son to express His free, un-manipulated sovereign love to you in the hope that His love will ignite love in your heart. True love demands freedom. God established our freedom from the law through the blood of His Son so that not even He could manipulate us. When you truly see and feel that love in your heart, you will love Him back freely, without obligation.

We have already seen this in the story of the prodigal son. The Father was under absolutely no obligation, legally or culturally, to give in to the demands of his son. In fact, there would have been much advice to the contrary from friends and family. The father chooses to give the boy what he asks for. He puts him in charge of his own life. He gives him control over his own destiny. He gives him freedom in the hope his son would make the right choices in that freedom – but they were his choices regardless. That is exactly what God has done for us.

Let me put it another way: you cannot give yourself to God if you're not free, if you're not in possession of yourself. If you are acting out of some compulsion or manipulation from your conscience, religion or the expectations of the people around you, then you can't truly give yourself to anyone. I object to the view that says, 'God owns me. I have no choice in the matter. I just do everything He says because He bought me with a price.' If people really believe that, they haven't read the Bible. We choose every single day, and that's the way God wants it to be.

We can see this when we look at some of the teaching concerning tithing and giving money to the Lord's work. Some say: 'God owns all of your money. Everything belongs to Him really, and He expects you to give Him ten per cent back. We owe God a tithe.' Let's think about that view for a moment. If your money isn't your money, then you can't give it as a gift. God gave you that money; he equipped you to earn it. You can give it to Him as a gift, an act of love, but not as a result of manipulation.

In the same way, a god who gives his subjects eternal life, but then demands sacrifice and obedience to pay him back for that gift, has not given them a gift at all. He's bought them but expects them to pay the price. That is the essence of Pharisaism, legalism and religion, and unfortunately much of what passes for Christianity today. The acid test of a true gift is that when you give it, you let it go. It costs the giver, but it's totally, unconditionally free to the receiver – and that's why it's so difficult to receive it.

There are so many well-meaning Christians who want to *do* something – anything – to get even with their conscience before God. They just can't believe that it has all been given to them for free. If you get this, not only will your spiritual health improve, but also your relational health and maybe even your physical health. The gospel is a gift. Salvation is a gift. There are no strings attached. Paul says,

> *Therefore, there is now no condemnation to those who are in Christ Jesus. (Romans 8:1)*

That is unconditional. It is a gift, now and forever. If we say or think or imply by our actions, 'Much obliged …', or 'I owe you one, Lord', we are slapping the Giver in the face! So, if you want to give service in the context of the church, that's great. If you want to give money to support the ministry of the church, go for it. Just make sure you never do it out of obligation. We should want to be an obedient servant of the Lord Jesus

Christ out of love for Him, and we'll do it side by side, together. I believe in the covenant of grace, not the contract of works. Sadly, the latter is what so many of us have been dished out for years and we don't even know it! We've let the enemy distort the truth and mix grace with works so beautifully that it even sounds believable.

Let me say it so that you can't possibly misunderstand: the life, death and resurrection of Christ – and everything that flows to us because of that – is a free gift and we owe God nothing for it. That is the gospel truth; that's how radical and free it is. If you don't get that, or can't accept that as biblical truth, then you can't get anywhere in your Christian walk.

This is the foundation to all that is written in this book and everything I ever teach in the name of Jesus. I know that God has called the church of Jesus Christ to do great things, and that will cost a lot of money. I also know that I have just made it impossible for me or anyone else to manipulate that money out of you, and that's the way it should be. If the money doesn't come back to God and to His purposes as an act of love on your part, then go ahead and keep it.

Once the gospel of grace takes hold of your imagination, once it sinks into your heart and begins to grow and bear fruit by the power of the Holy Spirit, once you accept that the punishment for your sins has already been dished out and received, once you realise that Jesus traded your sins for His righteousness, when the lights are finally turned on and you see that you are already right with God, then you will be overwhelmed with joy and gratitude. You will see many ways to return that love.

Once, on a honeymoon, the groom carried his new bride over the threshold and welcomed her back to her home as his wife, not his maid. As soon as he put her down, she went to the kitchen, tore the list off the wall and rather dramatically ripped it into a hundred pieces as her worried husband looked on.

'Why did you do that?' he exclaimed. 'Are you not, as my wife, still going to cook for me and maintain the house?' She smiled at him and said, 'Of course I am, darling, but now I will do it because I want to, not because I have to. Now I will do it out of love, not obligation.' I know of no better way to portray the radical difference between a contract and a covenant. I believe this man's wife would have done ten times what was on the previous list once her heart had been set free by the power of love.

The Bible is not an index of answers to your questions, nor is it a book of rules or a list of your daily obligations before God. The Bible, particularly the New Testament, is your new Husband's heart on paper, and as you experience His love, you are going to want to approach the Bible in a brand new way. You will be searching the Scriptures to find ways to return His love freely. You'll find lots and lots of things to do, but you won't do them to fulfil a contract, or to ease your conscience, or to be accepted by Him or by the church. You'll do them because the grace and love of God has so filled your heart that you cannot help responding to Him in love.

You are totally, radically and dangerously free in Jesus Christ. Do you really know that today? You are free to do anything you want to do. God invites you to return to Him and know that He will always run to you with open arms with nothing but love, acceptance, grace and the power to be whoever you want to be. We're all prodigals in some way. We all need to return to our Father – but never on a contract. He wants us to come to Him knowing that we are accepted, loved and set free from any obligation to the law whatsoever. You are free – radically, totally and unconditionally free!

A true understanding of God's grace, that we have been set free from death itself, empowers us to really live. It destroys the fear that was the basis of law. It is stupid, then, to go back to small living and narrow-minded pursuits. Those things are certainly out of place in the church. God set us free because He loves us. He set us free to be ourselves the way He made us to be. He stands against anything that binds up His children. He desires that we return His love and be in relationship with Him, but He gives us that choice.

Many people choose to stay under rules because they feel safer, rather than trusting their lives to their loving Father who has given everything to secure their freedom and has committed Himself to them totally and unconditionally. When we truly understand God's amazing grace and love for us, our hearts will be moved to give freely to Him.

CHAPTER TEN
Grace Meets our Deepest Needs

The first part of the good news of the New Covenant says that your position in Christ is secure and it's freely given to you at His expense. The second part of the good news is that when you're born again into this New Covenant, you receive a power to live the life that you ought to live and want to live. Grace is not just a passive theological or abstract concept; it is the personal, empowering presence of God in our lives, enabling us to be all that we can be and to do all that we can do.

We can look at our lives and see what God has done for us. The grace of God has reassured us eternally of His love and acceptance of us. He has committed Himself to us, to conform us to the likeness of Christ. We can see the promises that He has given us through His Word and know that they will be formed in us as the Holy Spirit imparts the life of Christ to us.

> *His divine power has given us everything that we need for a godly life through our knowledge of him who called us by his own glory and goodness.*
> *(2 Peter 1:3)*

Through eyes of grace, we find answers to all our questions as we continue to allow God to reveal Himself to us. The effects of this grace in our lives are life-changing and life-defining. We are given the power to grow, the power to change, the power to live humble, peaceful, non-threatened lives, free from anyone's manipulation.

Here is an objective truth: no matter how badly you mess up today, you are right with God through Jesus Christ, and you are accepted in Him. You might feel bad about yourself. You might feel guilty or unloved, defeated or oppressed, even accused and judged by God. You may even feel condemned. Such feelings are subjective, yet they are real, and you can't ignore them, nor do you need to deny them. You can be honest about your emotions. I am not saying you will never feel any of those things when you understand grace in all its truth. The devil will continue to fuel all kinds of lying emotions in us while he is allowed to reign in this world in any way. *Having* those feelings is not wrong – it's inevitable – but *believing* those feelings is most definitely wrong. They are not from God; they have no basis in reality, and therefore you must reject them.

You might be thinking that's easier said than done, but it all depends on what you want. If you want to be free from accusation and condemnation, then you will make a choice to reject those feelings and move on. Just keep telling yourself the truth:

'This does not reflect reality. It's a direct attack from the father of lies, the accuser of the brethren, the one who comes to kill, steal and destroy. In Jesus' name, I reject these lying emotions and ask God to release peace and joy to flood my soul and wash away all of Satan's lies.'

There are two things that human beings need in life: acceptance and change. We want to be accepted as we are, warts and all, sin and all. We don't want to have to jump through any hoops to earn that acceptance. However, there is another desire at work in us, the desire to change. While we want acceptance as we are, we don't want to stay as we are. Every normal human being I have met wants to change. They want to grow; they do not want to mark time and let life just pass them by. Sadly, our need for acceptance can often lead us to seek it through human affirmation and that can so quickly see us taken captive again by performance-based religion which always leads us away from the gospel and its power.

So many people in this nation have grown up without the experience of a father's love. Fathers in particular have an incredible influence depending on whether (or not) they affirm and accept their children as they are, encouraging and assuring them in spite of failure. Many people never had that experience. We are trained by an education system which affirms us on the basis of our performance. We find the same thing in our employment. It is no wonder that we see it in the church. Coming into the kingdom of God doesn't change the fundamental pain of rejection and insecurity in us, so we may seek acceptance from the pastor, leaders or those around us. Even when we gain affirmation on the basis of our performance, we cannot relax. Tomorrow, we might get it wrong with the people who are important to us. Sadly, in such a situation, it is only our performance which is accepted, not us.

There is only one place we can go to find affirmation which is independent of our performance, and that is to God. He will give you the same affirmation He gave His only Son that day when He was baptised. At the commencement of Jesus' ministry, before any preaching or miracles, God said: 'This is my beloved Son in whom I am (already) well pleased.' That kind of affirmation from God is not only a possibility for you, but your birthright. Your right standing with God through Jesus, your freedom from condemnation and your total acceptance by Him, is an objective truth, no matter how you feel subjectively. That acceptance comes in the glorious package of the gospel.

Paradoxically, the second thing we really need in life is the power to change. The New Covenant, the gospel of Jesus Christ, gives us acceptance and the power to change; that is what God wants the church to be about! We are meant to be channels of acceptance and change. He wants us to accept people the way they are, but not let them stay that way. When the impact of God's free grace really hits home and we understand that His grace is the only thing we really need, then we will be able to give the same acceptance to others that God gives to us. When that happens, there won't be a building large enough to hold all the people! But it won't happen until we deal with our attitude towards other people. We desperately want people to accept us the way we are, but we can often have a problem accepting people the way they are.

Through this wonderful New Covenant relationship, we now have with God in Jesus Christ, we are empowered by the Spirit of God to live up to the performance that Jesus credited to us freely. The power of God, which is part and parcel of His grace and love, transforms us to be more and more like the One who kept the Covenant for us in the first place.

Therefore, as you read things like 'love your enemies', 'don't worry about anything ever', 'don't lust', go into all the world and preach the gospel', 'heal the sick', 'cast out demons' – those things that seem so impossible to you, exhortations that you just can't live up to – they are in fact wonderful promises to you! God's bidding is His enabling. What He calls us to do, He also empowers us to do, and He is in the process right now of training us to do just that. Let's look at what Paul wrote to the Corinthian believers:

> You show that you are a letter from Christ, the result of our ministry, written not with ink but with the Spirit of the living God, not on tablets of stone but on tablets of human hearts. Such confidence we have through Christ before God. Not that we are competent in ourselves to claim anything for ourselves, but our competence comes from God. He has made us competent as ministers of a new covenant – not of the letter but of the Spirit; for the letter kills, but the Spirit gives life. (2 Corinthians 3:3–6)

This New Covenant is not just something we understand in our head. This New Covenant carries with it the very power of God who makes us competent ministers of the New Covenant. We are altered in such a way as to make us different people. When you become a Christian, when you are born-again into the New Covenant by believing in Christ, you find yourself having new desires. The things of God are now important to you. You want to meet with the body of Christ, whereas before it was either a threat or just boring. You receive a longing for prayer, for the Word of God and for intimacy with God. Your attitude has radically changed.

When you enter into the New Covenant, you are empowered to do something about the new desires which the Spirit of God has birthed in you. You long for peace, to help people, to be one with God in prayer and worship, to forgive your enemies and love those who are unlovely. You also find the power is there to do so. You are accepted in Jesus Christ. Therefore,

- you don't know how to worship? No problem – He did, and He does.
- you don't know how to pray? No problem – He did, and He does.
- you don't know how to heal? No problem – He did, and He does.
- you don't know how to obey? No problem – He did, and He does.
- you don't know how to truly love? No problem – He did, and He does.

Jesus has done all that for you, and that is all credited to you! The New Covenant (and what should be New Testament Christianity today) gives people exactly what they really need. You will recall that the Old Covenant was unable to bring that about. In the book of Jeremiah, we read this:

"The days are coming," declares the LORD, "when I will make a new covenant

with the people of Israel and with the people of Judah.

It will not be like the covenant I made with their ancestors

when I took them by the hand to lead them out of Egypt,

because they broke my covenant, though I was a husband to them," declares the LORD.

'This is the covenant I will make with the people of Israel after that time," declares the LORD.

"I will put my law in their minds and write it on their hearts.

I will be their God, and they will be my people.

No longer will they teach their neighbour, or say to one another, 'Know the LORD,' because they will all know me, from the least of them to the greatest" declares the LORD.

"For I will forgive their wickedness and will remember their sins no more." (Jeremiah 31:31–34)

A long time ago, God said through Ezekiel that the Old Covenant wasn't working. It was right, it was perfect, but it was not working for sinful people. God was so eager to have an intimate relationship with His children that He foreshadowed the day when He would usher in a New Covenant whereby that could happen. He said He will forgive the people's sins, He will accept them, and He will change them from the inside out. We read this in Ezekiel 36.

> For I will take you out of the nations; I will gather you from all the countries and bring you back into your own land. I will sprinkle clean water on you, and you will be clean; I will cleanse you from all your impurities and from all your idols. I will give you a new heart and put a new spirit in you; I will remove from you your heart of stone and give you a heart of flesh. And I will put my Spirit in you and move you to follow my decrees and be careful to keep my laws. You will live in the land I gave your forefathers; you will be my people, and I will be your God. (Ezekiel 36:24–28)

There it is again: acceptance and change – 'I will forgive you and accept you, I will remember your sins no more, because I'm going to look at the performance of Jesus and accept you in Him, and I'm going to send the Spirit which empowered Jesus into your hearts to empower you.' If you cooperate with that empowering Spirit, you will start to change.

The Old Covenant can only ever produce guilt, shame and more sin, and it leads to spiritual death, not liberating life and joy and peace. But if we know that we can try and fail and that God is not going to punish us, then we'll try and try again, and keep on trying and believing and trusting until that life-giving power bursts out like an underground stream of water and floods every part of our life and the lives of those around us.

One of the reasons people don't experience the power of the Holy Spirit in their lives is that they're trying too hard to pay for it, and that's impossible with God. We will never experience God in His fullness on our terms. When we stop trying to buy the power of God by trying to do the right thing and live the right way in order to get it, He'll give it to us along with the power to repent and grow to be more like Jesus. Let me point you to a powerful passage in John's gospel:

> On the evening of that first day of the week, when the disciples were together, with the doors locked for fear of the Jewish leaders, Jesus came and stood among them and said, "Peace be with you!" After he said this, he showed them his hands and side. The disciples were overjoyed when they saw the Lord.

Again, Jesus said, "Peace be with you! As the Father has sent me [full of love, joy, peace, full of power to heal, the power to forgive sins, the power to forgive], I am sending you." And with that he breathed on them and said, "Receive the Holy Spirit." (John 20:19–22)

He gave them power. He gave them authority. He gave them something real. An Old Covenant minister looks at the Bible and studies it and tells you what's in it. A New Covenant minister imparts power to you. Christianity is frustrating to many people because they hear sermons and read books which nag them to live up to a standard that they haven't been empowered to live up to. If you can imagine a job where you've been given responsibility for things that you've not been given authority or power to deal with, then you will know how this feels. What a frustrating situation to be in! So many Christians have that inflicted on them every week.

By contrast, Jesus empowered His disciples to live the life that He commanded them to live. He doesn't go through the Bible and expound on abstract theological notions. Jesus' Bible study on the Holy Spirit was over in one gentle blow – literally! He breathed on them and gave them substance. He imparted something to them.

The New Covenant imparts something to you more and more. When you read all the high ethical demands of the New Testament, don't shrink back and say, 'It's a good thing I'm saved by grace. I'm glad I'm not held responsible for any of that hard stuff.' Instead, look at that hard stuff and say, 'That's what God has empowered me for and that's where I am headed. I'm going to live up to that one day and I can see that I'm making progress.' You'll not be proud of it because you know it's all Him! He did it for you and He's enabled you to do it. So, you stay humble even while your performance improves, because it's grace from beginning to end.

- The Old Covenant was conditional.
  The New Covenant is unconditional.
- The Old Covenant required one hundred per cent obedience.
  The New Covenant requires belief in the obedience of Jesus.
- The Old Covenant was based on fear.
  The New Covenant is based on love and forgiveness.
- The Old Covenant was based on human effort.
  The New Covenant is based on the grace of God.
- Under the Old Covenant, forgiveness was earned.
  Under the New Covenant, forgiveness is given as a free gift.

The list goes on and the contrasts are many. It's bondage or freedom – that's the basic choice. Which will it be for you? Our mind needs to be grounded in truth so as to inform our emotions and spirit. The truth is that God loves us and accepts us as we are in Christ Jesus. Whatever was owing on our accounts, Jesus has paid in full. There is now no cause for guilt, shame or feelings of inadequacy before God. We are set free to boldly approach His throne of grace to find mercy and help in times of need.

The grace of God also imparts the power to change, to be able to live the way we are inspired to live by the experience of freedom from accusation. We receive the life of Christ, and we are empowered to live a fruitful, abundant life by the Holy Spirit. Receiving God's grace enables us to relate to others in a new way too. We can accept them as Christ accepted us. We can give them room to try, to grow, to fail, and to be changed into the likeness of Christ. Our lives only work as God intended them to work when we understand and embrace God's amazing grace.

The church which bears the name of our Lord and Saviour only works and fulfils its purpose on earth when collectively, as a community of faith, we understand grace in all its truth and let that grace have its effect in us just as it did in the apostle Paul, as he affirmed in his letter to the believers in Corinth:

> But by the grace of God I am what I am, and his grace to me was not without effect. No, I worked harder than all of them – yet not I, but the grace of God that was with me. (1 Corinthians 15:10)

When that is the personal affirmation of all believers, then, and only then, will the church Jesus promised to build awaken from its slumber and impact the world the way it once did.

CHAPTER ELEVEN
Justification by Grace, Through Faith

I believe much of the pain in the Christian church throughout our history has been caused by sloppy thinking. If we walk in the light by embracing the truth conceptually and relating to it spiritually, we are largely protected from being manipulated or seduced by all kinds of different doctrines or beliefs. We need to exercise our thinking ability to fully appreciate the life that we have in Christ. When we get theological truths straight in our minds and meditate on them, we are released in true worship. Clear thinking about our forgiveness and the depth of our acceptance and justification inspires our gratitude to God and makes our life more dynamic and our worship more intense. So let us reason together now.

Justification by grace through faith is the heart of the gospel of Jesus Christ. If you understand the essence of your justification before God, you will be able to understand everything that flows from it. Justification is a legal term taken from Roman law courts, and when applied to us, it means we are now justified, made right with God. The opposite of justification is condemnation. Justification is what undoes condemnation, as the apostle Paul reminds us here:

> Nor can the gift of God be compared with the result of one man's sin [that one man being Adam, who sinned for us all]: The judgment followed one sin and brought condemnation [that's the problem you and I were born into and then participated in; and therefore, along with the world, we are condemned], but the gift followed many trespasses and brought justification [it erased condemnation and made us just; that is, justified, perfect before God]. For if, by the trespass of the one man, death reigned through that one man, how much more will those who receive God's abundant provision of grace and of the gift of righteousness reign in life through the one man, Jesus Christ! Consequently, just as one trespass resulted in condemnation for all people, so also one righteous act resulted in justification and life for all people. (Romans 5:16–18)

Through Christ, we reign because we are justified and are no longer under condemnation. We have seen that Paul would allow nothing to be added to the gospel of justification by grace alone, and he got very agitated with anyone who would try! He explains this in his letter to the Galatians when he said:

We who are Jews by birth and not sinful Gentiles know that a man is not justified by observing the law, but by faith in Jesus Christ. So we, too, have put our faith in Christ Jesus that we may be justified by faith in Christ and not by observing the law, because by observing the law no one will be justified. (Galatians 2:15–16)

In other words, your behaviour will never justify you. Your actions, your works or your obedience to the law of God have no bearing on your standing in God's sight.

But if, in seeking to be justified in Christ, we Jews find ourselves also among the sinners, doesn't that mean that Christ promotes sin? Absolutely not! If I rebuild what I destroyed, then I really would be a lawbreaker. For through the law, I died to the law so that I might live for God. I have been crucified with Christ and I no longer live, but Christ lives in me. The life I now live in the body, I live by faith in the Son of God, who loved me and gave himself for me. I do not set aside the grace of God, for if righteousness could be gained through the law, Christ died for nothing! (Galatians 2:17–21)

Justification describes someone who actually committed a sin, who violated the legal system, but nevertheless who somehow gets to walk out free, innocent and pardoned. It does not refer to one who has been falsely accused. The only person who can be justified is someone who was once guilty. Let's look again at those three verses in Romans 5 and see how justification works for us, remembering that the opposite of justification is condemnation.

Nor can the gift of God be compared with the result of one man's sin: The judgment followed one sin and brought condemnation, but the gift followed many trespasses and brought justification. (Romans 5:16)

The gift of God (Jesus Christ) brings justification for all of us who were rightly condemned. Our sins, our crimes against God, demanded punishment. The wages of sin is death, so someone has to die. That someone was Jesus, Who took the complete punishment for our sins when He died on the cross.

For if, by the trespass of the one man, death reigned through that one man, how much more will those who receive God's abundant provision of grace and of the gift of righteousness reign in life through the one man, Jesus Christ! (Romans 5:17)

That is to say, you are now right with God. God didn't overlook your sin; He legally and completely punished all your sins in Christ. That is true whether you know it or not, or feel it or not. The death of Jesus Christ facilitated God's forgiveness of everybody's sin, for all time.

When you believe in Christ, you receive the justification that is available for everybody. Paul continues:

Consequently, just as one trespass resulted in condemnation for all people, so also one righteous act resulted in justification and life for all people. (Romans 5:18)

To return to our courtroom scene, when you believe in Christ and this becomes your reality, you don't have to sneak out of the court hoping nobody stops you. The judge is not going to change his mind. His job is to see that the law is fulfilled and that breaches of the law are punished. That's exactly what happened. Jesus achieved both: the law and the Judge are satisfied. You are free before the law.

A young boy growing up on a large wheat farm was out in the paddock with his grandfather one summer just before harvest. They were talking about the threat of fire which was always present that time of the year. The boy's grandfather told him to always carry a box of matches with him when he was out in the fields. He said that if a fire came and he couldn't escape, he should start another fire around him, let it burn a little and then stand right in the centre of the burnt patch. The grandfather explained to the boy, 'You will be safe there, because fire cannot pass where fire has already been.'

When we believe in Jesus Christ – completely emerging our whole lives into Jesus by faith – we come into the only place in the universe where the fire of God's judgement has already passed. Let's make no mistake about it, the Bible tells us that there is a terrible judgement coming upon the earth. The holiness and purity of God will one day burn against all unholiness and impurity. Our God is an all-consuming fire. In Jesus Christ, you have already been burnt; the fire of God has consumed all that is not holy.

And by that will, we have been made holy through the sacrifice of the body of Jesus Christ once for all. (Hebrews 10:10)

How holy do you want to be? Being holy isn't watching everything you think, say and do, trying your hardest to be like Jesus. This verse says that you have been made holy; it is something that has been given you by God. Holiness is a gift from God.

Day after day every priest stands and performs his religious duties; again and again he offers the same sacrifices, which can never take away sins. But when this priest [Jesus Christ] had offered for all time one sacrifice for sins, he sat down at the right hand of God … (Hebrews 10:11–12)

Why did Jesus sit down? Because the job was finished! The priests who operated within the Jewish sacrificial system never sat down because their job was never done; there was always more sin to be atoned for. But Jesus, after this one sacrifice, sat down,

> ... and since that time, he waits for his enemies to be made his footstool. For by one sacrifice he has made perfect forever those who are being made holy. (Hebrews 10:13–14)

Jesus has, once and for all time, made perfect, made holy, pronounced right, true and just, those who believe. Those who walk in this reality are now being purified and made holy in their own experience. Holiness is a gift; it has been pronounced and it has been given to you. In the New Testament, there isn't a choice between holiness and sin in that sense. Are you a sinner? Yes. Are you holy? Yes. In God's sight, you are completely holy because of what Jesus did for you. So out of good common sense, you step into that life, and you experience more and more of the life that is yours in Christ and act out more and more of the reality that is already there in God's eyes. You step by faith into the holiness that has been declared – once and for all time.

When you understand that in God's sight you have been made perfect, you are far less inclined to sin. When the love of God, as seen in the death of Jesus, really gets a hold of your heart and you realise that He died to make you holy, repentance and holiness will ooze out of you! Sin will no longer attract you. God has said you are holy. It's a divine decree.

When that truth sinks in, then your need to justify or defend yourself, or get angry with those who cross you, disappears. It is a waste of emotional and physical energy. God has declared you holy and blameless in Christ.

> God made him who had no sin to be sin for us, so that in him we might become the righteousness of God. (2 Corinthians 5:21)

What a wonderful exchange – Jesus Christ became sin for us! God has to punish sin. His holiness burns against it. That is the whole meaning of the cross. Jesus bore the consequences of all sin on the cross so that in Him we might become the righteousness of God. How holy do you want to be before you feel okay? You are the righteousness of God. Does that do something for your self-esteem? For many, the answer is 'no' because they don't really believe it! Our prayer must be: 'Lord God, please, through preaching, prayer, by personal revelation, through ministry – somehow, Lord, burn this truth into me that I am the righteousness of God. Bury it deep in my consciousness, and then help me to live it.'

That will do two things: firstly, it will lift all anxiety off you, making you happy and joyful, and life will be worth living. Second, it will make you a better person. Any kind of holiness preaching – do this, don't do that – only makes us more focused on sin and failure. The Bible says that law exacerbates our lusts and desires. If you want to become a better person, just believe the truth, just embrace the gospel!

You are the righteousness of God. Believe it and then you will look at things in your life and see that they are inconsistent with the righteousness of God, and you will choose not to do those things anymore.

That's how sin is dealt with – not by wrestling with it and concentrating on it and praying against it or rebuking the devil over it. No! Concentrate on who you are in Christ, and all that other junk in your life will just fade away, because it's not compatible with who you really are in Christ. This is what makes our legalistic attempts to be justified by our religious behaviour so pointless. Paul cried out to the Galatians (and I paraphrase):

> *Why are you doing this – deserting the truth? It's bad enough that you think you can achieve something better than the righteousness of God by what you do – circumcision, eating the right food, giving alms, fasting – that is so stupid. But when you do that, you raise yourself above others who don't. It's wrong! Don't do it!*

> *We who are Jews by birth should already know that we are never justified by observing the law, but only by faith in Jesus Christ. So we, too, have put our faith in Christ Jesus so that we may be justified by faith in Christ and not by observing the law, because by observing the law no one will be justified.*

As we have already seen, the law is holy and perfect. Just don't try to be justified by it. Paul is not antinomian; he is not anti-law. The law reflects God's character. It is the only absolute standard by which behaviour can be judged. God's holy law lets everybody in the whole world know that they need a Saviour, but nobody is going to be justified by the law because they can't keep it!

So, logic dictates that we have to look somewhere else for our justification. We look to the only One who ever fully obeyed the law – Jesus Christ. We are justified in and through His obedience to the law. That is why, in Colossians 2, Paul tells us that Jesus nailed the law to the cross. As we believe into His life, death and resurrection, the law is no longer over us. Jesus said the law will never pass away. It is a reflection of the character of God and God will never change.

So, the law didn't pass away but it was totally fulfilled in Jesus on behalf of the whole human race and so as we believe in that fulfilment of the law by Jesus, it becomes our reality. In a practical sense, we are now no longer under the law; we live under the grace of God as shown in the giving of His Son. Paul sums it up well here:

> *For through the law I died to the law so that I might live for God. I have been crucified with Christ and I no longer live, but Christ lives in me. The life I live in the body, I live by faith in the Son of God, who loved me and gave himself for me. (Galatians 2:19–20)*

Paul's testimony is clear: He was crucified with Christ. His sins were judged in Christ. Fire has actually passed through him already on the cross – smell the smoke! Paul had already died for his sins in Christ. He had already been judged in Christ and cannot be judged again. Now he is justified, and he can stand before the Judge of all judges dressed in the righteous robes of Jesus Christ.

Now the questions about sin, confession and repentance can be answered. What if you sin tomorrow? The death of Jesus dealt with those sins also, before any of them were committed. Some people struggle with the concept that their sins are already forgiven and blotted out before God before they even confess them or ask for forgiveness. There are a few Bible texts that have been translated and interpreted to infer that God's forgiveness is conditional upon our confession and repentance, or upon our forgiveness of others. That is how they are translated into English, but that can't be what they mean when we understand the whole gospel.

Think about it, not theologically, just logically. Jesus Christ has justified you and now when you sin, you don't look to some external behaviour to make you justified; you look to Him who is your justification. Let's hear from Paul again:

> *Brothers and sisters, my heart's desire and prayer to God for the Israelites is that they may be saved. For I can testify about them that they are zealous for God, but their zeal is not based on knowledge. Since they did not know the righteousness that comes from God and sought to establish their own, they did not submit to God's righteousness. Christ is the culmination of the law so that there may be righteousness for everyone who believes. (Romans 10:1–4)*

Do you understand that? Jesus Christ is the end of the law, and you are in Christ. You don't have to come up against the law and feel condemned by it because it has ended for you. Paul elaborates in his letter to the Colossians:

When you were dead in your sins and in the uncircumcision of your flesh, God made you alive with Christ. He forgave us all our sins, having cancelled the charge of our legal indebtedness, which stood against us and condemned us; he has taken it away, nailing it to the cross. And having disarmed the powers and authorities, he made a public spectacle of them, triumphing over them by the cross. (Colossians 2:13–15)

Now, when you come against the law, you can say, 'Jesus has put an end to this standard for me. The law by which I was judged has been nailed to the cross.' The law now functions for us by showing us the appropriateness of our behaviour. It shows the character of God. It shows the kind of performance which is possible the more we allow the life of Christ in us to flood every part of our being. With overwhelming gratitude, we can thank God for having done that. When we look at the law, we can now say, 'Yes, Lord, that's where I want to be. The things I have done wrong were stupid, inappropriate, immature. I need to deal with the consequences of them. I embrace Your forgiveness where I've hurt someone.'

We don't ask for forgiveness so we can become right with God, but rather so our relationships with one another can remain strong; so that we don't open the door to the enemy to use that sin to mess up more relationships. Sin is evil whether you're in Christ or not. So don't do it! It will hurt you and those around you. The grace, love and acceptance of God does not remove the very real cause-and-effect nature of our sins. Sin needs to be rooted out of the lives of each and every one of us and out of the church, but it does not affect your relationship with God if you are in Christ. The word 'confess' means literally 'to say the same thing about'. It's not a religious ritual with which you buy God's forgiveness. You have that forgiveness whether you confess or not! True confession for a believer in Christ involves sitting down with God and saying:

'Father, I blew it. You know I blew it. I agree with You and affirm that this was a stupid and sinful thing to do but, Father, I've lived with myself long enough to know that if You don't change me by the power of your Holy Spirit, this is where I'm stuck. I'll just go right out there and do it again. Father, I thank you again for accepting me in Christ in spite of my sin, but I want you to change me. I want the life of Jesus that is in me to dominate – more of Him and less of me.'

You are never out of relationship with God because of your sin. You're either in or out of fellowship with the Father depending on whether you are in Christ or not. It's that simple. You are not judged by the law anymore, nor justified by it, and you should not condemn yourself or anyone else by it. Confession also completely delivers us from   all defensiveness. We can honestly admit our faults. We can acknowledge those things that are still not right in our lives, and God will say to us:

'Yes, that is all true, but you're okay with me, because you are in Christ. Now let's work on those things so that you can experience more of the abundant life I have given you freely.'

That gives us true freedom in Christ like we've never known before, and we find that once we open ourselves up to God and others, allowing ourselves to be vulnerable, the power of God is working in us and for us and through us.

The only way for God to release us from the accusation and condemnation of the law and our sin was to justify us. In His holiness, He could not leave sin unpunished. The righteous requirements of the law had to be met, and they were met in Jesus. The fire of God's judgement has passed through Jesus, and we now stand in Him. Fire cannot pass where fire has already been. By placing us in Christ, through faith in Him, we are credited with His performance, His holiness, His righteousness, His perfect life, His sacrificial death and His glorious resurrection. That's where we are now, in Christ.

Justification sets us free from the burden of failing to please God, and our own expectations, and the ways in which we punish ourselves. It sets us free to be ourselves. The power of sin is broken. Although we continue to sin, we are no longer enslaved to it. We deal with it in the power of the Holy Spirit by the grace of God. We take hold of His gift of repentance and respond to His work in us to restore relationships with other people as we allow the life of Christ to bear fruit in us. This is the wonder, the beauty, the power and the reality of the gospel of God's amazing grace. This is the truth, the whole truth and nothing but the truth, and Jesus said, if you know the truth, it shall set you free.

I really want to encourage you to revisit this chapter a number of times. Chapter by chapter in this book I have been unwrapping God's amazing grace and trying to explain each layer and the many different levels of grace. In this chapter, I have exposed the very heart of grace. Justification by grace through faith is the heart of the gospel of God's amazing grace.

You are now into the second half of this book, but this chapter is by far the most important and the pinnacle of the whole message of grace. If you truly understand and embrace the truths I have outlined here, the wonder, the glory and the power of the gospel will explode within you in ways you never imagined.

CHAPTER TWELVE
A New Definition of Grace

In the New Testament, there is an unmistakable connection between grace and power. If overlooked, this has great consequences in our understanding and experience as believers. Standard conservative evangelical theology has defined grace as God's good intentions towards us - His desire to be patient, merciful and forgiving. Many Bible dictionaries define grace as 'God's unmerited favour' meaning that God accepts us on the basis of Christ's life for us and not our effort. While that is certainly true, grace is so much more.

In the New Testament (especially the gospel of Luke and in Paul's writings), the word 'grace' is used in the context of the power of God to change, to heal, to deliver, to connect and to integrate. Grace is not just God's attitude towards us; it is God's power for us and God's empowering presence working in us and through us.

The word grace occurs one hundred and thirty-one times in the New International Version of the Bible. Now if you substitute the popular definition of grace in all of these texts, it makes sense for some, but for many (including some of the most quoted and important texts) it just doesn't fit – it never has. To equate grace simply with God's unmerited favour is actually very misleading and causes us to miss the true essence of God's grace. One of the earliest references to the word grace is in Proverbs.

> Surely He scorns the scornful, But gives grace to the humble. (Proverbs 3:34, NKJV)

No one can be 'rewarded' with unmerited favour; that just doesn't make sense. The word grace is also applied to Jesus:

> When Joseph and Mary had done everything required by the Law of the Lord, they returned to Galilee to their own town of Nazareth. And the child [Jesus] grew and became strong; he was filled with wisdom, and the grace of God was upon him. (Luke 2:39–40)

We also read in John's gospel that Jesus was, 'full of grace and truth' (John 1:14). To say that the unmerited favour of God was upon Jesus is nonsense. Jesus was the only human that ever lived who actually merited God's favour! Grace in these verses must mean something else. Let's look at a few more passages to see if the traditional definition of grace fits.

And now, brothers, we want you to know about the grace [unmerited favour] that God has given the Macedonian churches. (2 Corinthians 8:1)

That's okay so far, but read on and we encounter problems again with that definition of grace:

In the midst of a very severe trial, their overflowing joy and their extreme poverty welled up in rich generosity. For I testify that they gave as much as they were able, and even beyond their ability. Entirely on their own, they urgently pleaded with us for the privilege of sharing in this service to the Lord's people. And they exceeded our expectations: They gave themselves first of all to the Lord and then by the will of God also to us. So, we urged Titus, just he had earlier made a beginning, to bring also to completion this act of grace [unmerited favour] on your part. But since you excel in everything – in faith, in speech, in knowledge, in complete earnestness and in the love we have kindled in you – see that you also excel in this grace [unmerited favour] of giving. (2 Corinthians 8:2–7)

Mark my words! I, Paul, tell you that if you let yourselves be circumcised, Christ will be of no value to you at all. Again, I declare to every man who lets himself be circumcised that he is obligated to obey the whole law. You who are trying to be justified by law have been alienated from Christ; you have fallen away from grace [God's unmerited favour]. (Galatians 5:2–4)

You can't fall away from something you did nothing to merit in the first place, so grace must mean something else here as well.

You then, my son, be strong in the grace [unmerited favour] that is in Christ Jesus. (2 Timothy 2:1)

Each of you should use whatever gift you have received to serve others, as faithful stewards of God's grace [unmerited favour] in its various forms. (1 Peter 4:10)

How can we be strong in, or administer, God's unmerited favour? We can't. The concept of power – specifically God's power – has to be a part of any New Testament definition of grace. A lack of understanding of this will disempower your life and the life of the church. If you go back through those references and insert a more complete and accurate definition of grace – that is, the empowering presence of God – they will make much so more sense. Let's have a look:

When Joseph and Mary had done everything required by the Law of the Lord, they returned to Galilee to their own town of Nazareth. And the child [Jesus] grew and became strong; he was filled with wisdom, and [the empowering presence of God] was upon him. (Luke 2:39–40)

The Word became flesh and made his dwelling among us. We have seen his glory, the glory of the One and Only, who came from the Father, full of [the empowering presence of God] and truth … Out of his fullness we have all received [the empowering presence of God] in place of [the empowering presence of God] already given. For the law was given through Moses; [the empowering presence of God] and truth came through Jesus Christ. (John 1:14, 16–17)

That makes the hair on the back of my neck stand up. This will change your life if you let it sink in.

And now, brothers, we want you to know about [the empowering presence of God] that God has given to the Macedonian churches. In the midst of a very severe trial, their overflowing joy and their extreme poverty welled up in rich generosity. For I testify that they gave as much as they were able, and even beyond their ability. Entirely on their own, they urgently pleaded with us for the privilege of sharing in this service to the Lord's people. And they exceeded our expectations: They gave themselves first to the Lord, and then by the will of God also to us. So, we urged Titus, just as he had earlier made a beginning, to bring also to completion this act of [the empowering presence of God] on your part. But just as you excel in everything - in faith, in speech, in knowledge, in complete earnestness and in the love we have kindled in you – see that you also excel in this [empowering presence of God]. (2 Corinthians 8:1–7)

With this definition, one of Paul's most debated statements will finally make sense to you:

Mark my words! I, Paul, tell you that if you let yourselves be circumcised, Christ will be of no value to you at all. Again, I declare to every man who lets himself be circumcised that he is obligated to obey the whole law. You who are trying to be justified by law have been alienated from Christ; you have fallen away from [the empowering presence of God]. (Galatians 5:2–4)

You then, my son, be strong in [the empowering presence of God] that is in Christ Jesus. (2 Timothy 2:1)

Each of you should use whatever gift you have received to serve others, as faithful stewards of [the empowering presence of God] in its various forms. (1 Peter 4:10)

These, and many other Bible verses, come alive when the definition of grace includes the dimension of God's presence and power. So now we need to understand what we mean by power. When talking about power, I am not referring to the flashy, miraculous, out of the ordinary, signs-and-wonders type of power, but I'm not excluding that either. The word 'power', particularly in the New Testament, has a very simple, yet profound definition; it simply means 'the ability to do'.

… you shall receive power when the Holy Spirit comes upon you. (Acts 1:8)

Christianity is founded on the powerful *works*, not just the words of its Founder, Jesus. If you compiled a book of Jesus' teaching alone, it would be tiny in comparison to the volumes of the world's religions. Yet history is witness to the fact that Jesus has had a more profound effect on humanity than any other teacher. That's because of what He did, not just what He said.

Most Christians know more of the Bible than they ever experience personally. There is only one way to experience that reality – that is with power from God, 'the ability to do'. How are you going to forgive your enemies? How can you look at life and all that it brings and not worry about anything as Jesus commanded? How are you going to heal the sick or cast out demons? How do you maintain the passion to love the unlovely until you drop, and do it with a smile on your face? How are you going to go to the ends of the earth making disciples of all people? None of that is achievable in your own power.

The power of the only One who ever achieved such things, the Lord Jesus Christ, will convert sermons and teaching into real, life-changing experience as He equips His people to fulfil the ministry to which He has called them. Then we will experience the real presence and power of God in worship, in preaching and teaching and in ministry. That real church will grow as the Lord adds to our number daily those who are being saved by His grace.

Luke's gospel is described in Acts 1:1 as 'the things that Jesus began to do and teach'. In 1 Corinthians 2:4, Paul says that the gospel is not a matter of mere words but is a demonstration of the Spirit's power. Jesus said, 'If you don't believe my words, then believe my works' (John 10:38). The Bible is an explanation of powerful events and dynamic experiences, not just a collection of theological ideas and concepts. The power of the Holy Spirit came upon the people at Pentecost, and some said, 'Wow, this is great! I'm hearing the gospel in my own language.' Others said, 'These people are drunk.'

Peter then explained the power that was being displayed, and those words became Scripture. What might have happened if he had preached that sermon before the Holy Spirit had come upon the believers? Probably not three thousand conversions!

The authentic, effective church is one that has power as well as sound Bible teaching. Sadly, however, the church today is more accustomed to words than works. If we can't do any of the things we read about in the Bible, then we just talk about them. This is the cause of much of the anxiety and criticism in the church today. It feels guilty. The fascinating thing is that often it's the ones who are really concerned about the words who get mad at the ones who come along and start doing the works, because that points out what's lacking.

Of course, I need to balance this immediately and say there are those who get carried away with the works and neglect the words too. We need to know the truth and live in the power of the truth. The balance of spirit and truth is essential.

I believe the element of power has been removed from the popular definition of grace by a specific work of the enemy which is intended to rob the church of Jesus Christ of the very power it needs to fulfil the mission of Christ. The Bible warns us in the last days there will be doctrines taught by demons. We really should heed that warning.

The unmerited favour of God alone will not fulfil the mission of Christ. It will not heal the sick, raise the dead, cast out demons and set the captives free. To look around most of the church, one might assume that the ministry that occurs in Jesus' name has changed dramatically since the days of the early church. Some even teach that this is supposed to be the case, but if all we have is a vague, innocuous feeling of God's unmerited favour, then how could it be otherwise?

In Colossians 1:6, Paul said that the gospel was growing and bearing fruit all over the world when the believers understood God's grace in all its truth. They obviously understood something about God's grace that the church today has largely missed. Paul's passionate prayer in Ephesians 1 that we would experience the riches of God's grace and His incomparably great power which is available to us who believe, is answered in the church when we believe that this is what God wants for us all as His loyal partners in fulfilling the mission of Christ.

Satan has nothing to fear from a church that just believes that it is forgiven and saved by grace, but a church that also operates in the power of God's grace does serious damage to the enemy's cause. Captives who have been set free have a passion to come back and rip that prison apart and set others free. The enemy knows the power of God's grace more than the church does, and he fears it! Let me show you an example of how the church has been deceived by this teaching.

The law was brought in so that the trespass might increase. But where sin increased, grace increased all the more, so that, just as sin reigned in death, so also grace might reign through righteousness to bring eternal life through Jesus Christ our Lord. (Romans 5:20–21)

This verse is usually explained by saying that God's forgiveness, unmerited favour and mercy is boosted in some way when sin increases to cover or accommodate that increase of sin. Such teaching is dangerously wrong on two counts. Firstly, it pacifies us before the power of sin. It gives us an excuse to look upon our sin lightly and not deal with it ruthlessly through repentance. Your standing in Christ is not affected by your sin, but to say that sin does not destroy, debilitate and mess up your whole life is to deny the whole experience of human beings and the witness of Scripture.

Secondly, and worse, such teaching misleads us as to the nature of God's true forgiveness and mercy. God's forgiveness cannot increase. It is absolute. It says in 1 John 2:1 that Jesus is the atoning sacrifice for our sins and the sins of the whole world, past, present and future, forever.

The proper term for 'God's unmerited favour' is not grace; it's mercy. Reading this verse with the new definition of grace makes a lot more sense: The law was added so that the trespass might increase. But where sin increased, (the empowering presence of God) increased all the more.

Paul says you don't have to sit passively in the power of sin: you have the empowering presence of God Himself within you that can extinguish the power of sin as simply as blowing out a candle. We just need to believe that and trust God for it to happen. This power of God increases and decreases to meet personal and specific needs. God's grace enables us to see the kingdom of God become a reality. We see the rule and reign of Christ in our midst. Jesus came proclaiming the kingdom of God. He came in power to overcome our enemies, to set us free from Satan's grasp, to drive back evil and remove its effects. In a word, He came to heal.

Jesus brought healing to our relationship with God and with each other. The healing power of Jesus touched us in every way –spiritually, emotionally, relationally and even physically. Being born again is to be born into God's immediate blood family, which includes all the resources of God. You can participate in those riches and that power, assuming you know it's there.

It's like living all your life on a farm that is relatively worthless, until that day when a gold mining company discovers the largest single deposit of gold in the world right underneath your very old broken-down house.

Are you wealthy? Absolutely! However, you've been sitting on that wealth all your life and you never knew it until someone showed you.

I think this is where millions of Christians are at present – living totally unaware of the infinite riches and power of God in Christ. The power of God is grace to us through the life of Jesus Christ, which is credited to us, gifted to us and enables us to participate in His ministry.

> *But to each one of us ([the empowering presence of God] has been given as Christ apportioned it. (Ephesians 4:7)*

Christ did not apportion God's unmerited favour or mercy. He did not give some people one variety of mercy and others a different variety. He apportioned the power of God. You are given the measure of God's empowering to do what God has called you to do. When you understand this, there are some logical conclusions that you can make when you face frustration and setbacks in your life and ministry.

First of all, it might not be your job! God personally tailors or apportions His power to each of us according to our own custom-made gifts, abilities, personality and calling. It is important to hear from God for yourself, to get to know God and get to know yourself. Be honest, stop your religious thinking and listen to God; otherwise, you'll be torn in different directions.

Secondly, we need to receive all that God has apportioned to us. The problem is not just that we don't hear from God, but that we have not participated fully in the grace that He has given us already. A child will, more often than not, ask for another biscuit before they've eaten the first one. We too often want more grace and power from God, yet He's still waiting for us to use what we have! Paul said of himself:

> *But by [the empowering presence of God] I am what I am, and his [empowering presence] in me was not without effect. No, I worked harder than all of them - yet not I, but [the empowering presence of God] that was with me. (1 Corinthians 15:10)*

Paul participated in the power that was given to him but admits that even the desire to do that came through the power of God. We must open up to the empowering presence of God to experience and walk in the measure of grace that Christ has apportioned us.

Everybody in the church has been given gifts. They have been given grace and power from God, but because of spiritual abuse, bad teaching, laziness or other reasons, many are not operating in those gifts and contributing to the kingdom of God when they could be having the adventure of their lives.

Paul says, 'I am what I am because of the grace apportioned to me by God, and because I responded to that grace with my own hard work.' There are great reasons for working hard: gratitude to God, a desire to have an authentic life, to help people, to be a fully alive human being experiencing all that God desires for you, to glorify God in all that you do – to mention just a few. Religious efforts are those done in our own strength. We see this more when we understand that God's grace is God's enabling.

> *You who are trying to be justified by law have been alienated from Christ; you have fallen away from God's grace - you have fallen away from [God's empowering presence]. (Galatians 2:4)*

Some use this verse to say that we can lose our salvation. That's impossible. A gift is not a gift if it can be taken back or given back. However, you certainly can fall away from the *experience* of your salvation. You can fall away from the empowering presence of God and effective, victorious living – and many in the Church have done just that. We will never see the fruit of the gospel until we admit to God that we have fallen away from His grace, His empowering. We need to be honest with Him and say:

> *'Lord, I guess I really have never known Your empowering presence in the way You planned. I've been trying to minister as a Christian on my own and in my own strength. I ask You to show me a different way, the authentic way. Enable me to walk in Your grace, in Your empowering presence.'*

There is a tragic tendency among Christians, who were accepted and empowered by God simply by believing, to trade that experience for law, religion and human effort. God works miracles, not because you're a good Christian, but because you believe the gospel. Miracles are just God on the job! Empowering is not just an event, but a process. Some things will happen quickly, but usually this is an ongoing process. Expect great things from God, long for His presence and power, but make sure the enemy doesn't take away your patience and faith as you trust in God's timing.

James says, 'You have not, because you ask not' (James 4:2). God is waiting on us to ask Him, sincerely and persistently for things that He already wants to give us. He wants a close, intimate relationship with His children. He will not treat us like plants that get fertiliser whether they ask for it or not. He's rich and He's very generous, and it glorifies Him to have us ask for something, so you never have to worry about imposing on God. If He didn't withhold His own Son, then He won't hold back in giving to you.

If you then, though you are evil, know how to give good gifts to your children, how much more will your Father in heaven give the Holy Spirit to those who ask him!" [In the original Greek, it means 'keep on asking'.] (Luke 11:13)

Keep on asking, keep on seeking, keep on knocking. Persistence in our asking is a real act of faith, and very often it is persistence and determination in prayer that brings fruit. Just like Paul did:

I keep asking that the God of our Lord Jesus Christ, the glorious Father, may give you the Spirit of wisdom and revelation, so that you may know him better. I pray also that the eyes of your heart may be enlightened in order that you may know the hope to which he has called you, the riches of his glorious inheritance in the saints, and his incomparably great power for us who believe. (Ephesians 1:17–19)

That's what life is; that's what grace gives us. The conventional definition of grace as being 'God's unmerited favour' falls far short of our reality and all the experiences described in the Bible. A more complete, accurate and helpful definition of the word 'grace' is 'the empowering presence of God.'

Grace describes God's power in our lives, both in what He has done for us and what He does in and through us. Without the power of God, Christianity becomes another religion based on a collection of moral teachings. You could memorise the whole Bible and still miss the heart of the Christian faith, because it is a personal relationship with Jesus, and the indwelling power mediated to us by His Spirit, that makes us real Christians.

God's grace is not raw, impersonal, spiritual power, but rather the presence and personality of God Himself, which enables us to be effective in His kingdom. We experience God's empowering presence when we believe, receive and walk in His amazing grace.

CHAPTER THIRTEEN
Opening the Door to Grace

In Romans 1:16, the apostle Paul affirms that the gospel is the power of God for the salvation of everyone who believes, and it's not limited to the initial act of conversion. It is ongoing and includes healing, deliverance, fullness of life and abundant grace – the empowering presence of God, enabling you to be all that you can be and to do all that you can do. Paul is not ashamed of the gospel because it is the power of God, bearing fruit and expanding throughout the world whenever God's people understand grace.

> *[the gospel] has come to you. In the same way, the gospel is bearing fruit and growing throughout the whole world – just as it has been doing among you since the day you heard it and truly understood God's grace. (Colossians 1:6)*

As sincere Christians, we want the gospel to bear fruit and to grow in us, among us and through us into our community. We want to minister in the empowering presence of God. Therefore, we seek to understand grace in all its truth and that's why we need to hear about grace over and over again, because a fuller understanding of grace will empower us to be all that God created us to be.

We should note that both the Old and New Testaments make a connection between our attitude and God's grace. Proverbs 3:34 tells us, 'God resists the proud but gives grace to the humble.' So, if we want to participate more in the grace of God, then we need to seek an understanding of the relationship between grace and humility. Let's look at some more texts.

> *You save the humble, but your eyes are on the haughty to bring them low. (2 Samuel 22:28)*

> *If my people, who are called by my name, will humble themselves and pray and seek my face and turn from their wicked ways, then will I hear from heaven and will forgive their sin and will heal their land. (2 Chronicles 7:14)*

> *Then he [the messenger from the Lord] continued, 'Do not be afraid, Daniel. Since the first day that you set your mind to gain understanding and to humble yourself before your God, your words were heard, and I have come in response to them.' (Daniel 10:12)*

Likewise, you that are younger be subject to the elders. Clothe yourselves, all of you, with humility toward one another, for "God opposes the proud, but gives grace to the humble." Humble yourselves therefore under the mighty hand of God, that in due time he may exalt you. Cast all your anxieties on him, for he cares about you. (1 Peter 5:5–7, RSV)

It appears that humility in us is the open door to God's grace – to God's empowering presence in our lives and in the life of the church. The word 'humility' has a number of definitions, concepts and feelings attached to it that are mostly negative, so we're not too sure if we want humility or not. We'll give lip service to it, but deep down we don't think it is that inviting. Not many people want to pray, 'God, grant me humility'. The reason is because the images that come to mind about humility in our culture are not that attractive. However, those are not biblical images; they have evolved in our Western language and culture.

When you have an accurate understanding of humility, you will be crying out to God from the depth of your being for humility, for there's nothing negative about it. It's all profoundly positive. Let's start off with some standard dictionary definitions of humility:

(1) poor, wretched and pitiful. (We speak of humble circumstances. We wouldn't ever pray for poverty or wish it on anybody.)

(2) servile, cringing and shameful, the attitude of a slave. (That is certainly not attractive. God's grace has set us free from such humiliation.)

There are lots of prayers and worship songs that talk about the humility of Jesus. I can't imagine anyone praying, 'Jesus, I love your wretched and pitiful heart'. We wouldn't sing, 'Jesus, you are so cringing and servile.' That hardly inspires worship, does it? These definitions, which are common in our usage, do not reflect the biblical concept of humility. Just as we had to re-define grace in the previous chapter in order to unlock its real meaning and power and to be able to actually participate in it, so too, we must take a fresh look at humility. This third definition comes a lot closer to the biblical concept:

(3) unpretentious, not demanding attention.

Does that sound better? Don't you want to be around people like that? Of course you do. In the first place, we need to understand that God Himself is supremely humble. Humility has absolutely nothing to do with status or class or rank. It only has to do with character. God is God and He is Supreme and transcendent – yet God is humble. God deserves and welcomes our worship and praise, and He does so without any embarrassment at all, yet He is not proud.

You can actually see this beautiful quality of humility within the three persons of the Trinity as they relate to each other. God the Father points to the Son. The Father stays in heaven out of sight and sends His Son to earth and gives Him the leading role on centre stage, saying, *'Look, here is My beloved Son.'* God the Son immediately points back to the Father and says, *'Without Him, I can do nothing. I only do what I see the Father doing. I am here to do his bidding. All honour and glory goes to Him.'* The Holy Spirit hides altogether and takes the things that are Christ's and makes them known to us, bringing to our remembrance everything that Christ spoke. There is a beautiful mutual deference and profound humility within the relationships between the Father, Son and Spirit.

Many people wonder why, when God came to seek and to save the lost, He didn't make a spectacular entrance for all the world to see His glory. He chose not to impress us with how great He is and how small and insignificant we are by comparison. He didn't force us to pay attention. He very quietly, almost secretly, came into our world through the womb of a young village girl. He did that because it is essential to His nature. He came in a barn because He is supremely humble; He doesn't push himself into inns which have no room.

The most amazing thing in this universe – God becoming man – happened in a barn full of smelly animals, because our God is humble. He came to invite us to respond voluntarily to Him, and then He died for us. He didn't just issue a divine decree and make it all happen, because that is not how God operates.

There is no play-acting with God, no performance, no spectacle. He operates according to who He is all the time, whether that makes sense to others or not. If you want to see who God is, just look at Jesus in the New Testament. Simply put: *God does Who Jesus is - all the time.* The fullness of the deity was in Jesus, which is why He said:

Anyone who has seen me has seen the Father … (John 14:9)

This could be the most winsome, wonderful and attractive aspect of God's character – His profound humility. It's a shame we don't talk about it more in church because this is a powerful evangelistic tool. It's a powerful discipleship insight. Who wouldn't want to hang around with somebody like that? We love being with humble people. In many ways, true humility is reward enough in itself.

If humility was the end goal, it would be a great thing to strive for, but you can add to this the fact that God grants grace to the humble. He actually gives His personal presence and power to the humble.

Now the opposite of humility is pride, and conversely, it is the most repulsive of all personal traits. We hate to be around people who are constantly drawing attention to themselves, dominating every conversation, demanding their rights, pushing their programs and ideas, insisting on their views, forcing people to hear about their problems all the time. You may end up having to buy something from somebody like that, but you definitely don't want to be around them!

You're in good company because God detests pride too. Over and over again, the Bible tells us that God resists, mocks, curses, and thwarts the proud, but He gives grace to the humble. So, if pride was not by itself curse enough on our lives, we have this added active resistance from God. We all want to be delivered from pride and embrace humility, but how do we do that? True humility is rooted in security. A truly secure person is free to be humble. Let's hear from Paul again:

> Have this attitude in yourselves which was also in Christ Jesus, who, as He already existed in the form of God, did not consider equality with God something to be grasped, but emptied Himself by taking the form of a bondservant and being born in the likeness of men. And being found in appearance as a man, He humbled Himself by becoming obedient to the point of death: death on a cross. For this reason also God highly exalted Him, and bestowed on Him the name which is above every name, so that at the name of Jesus every knee will bow, of those who are in heaven and on earth and under the earth, and that every tongue will confess that Jesus Christ is Lord, to the glory of God the Father. (Philippians 2:5–11, NASB)

Jesus was able to humble Himself because He was totally, utterly secure. He knew who He was, and He knew His Father's love. He had nothing to prove, nothing to hide, nothing to defend, nothing to lose and nothing to gain. He had everything of God, so He could humble Himself all the way to the point of death. We see Jesus acting out this profound humility just before His death when He washes the feet of His followers:

> The evening meal was in progress, and the devil had already prompted Judas, the son of Simon Iscariot, to betray Jesus. Jesus knew that the Father had put all things under his power, and that he had come from God and was returning to God … (John 13:2–3)

Jesus knew that He had all power, He knew where He came from, He knew where He was going. He had total freedom and complete control over everything – and He chose to be a servant.

> ... *so he got up from the meal, took off his outer clothing, and wrapped a towel around his waist. After that, he poured water into a basin and began to wash his disciples' feet, drying them with the towel that was wrapped around him. (John 13:4–5)*

The Bible tells us that Jesus was full of grace because He was profoundly humble. Jesus had the full measure of God's empowering presence which enabled Him to be all that He was and to do all that He did. His ability to suffer in the garden and die on the cross was not just His strength of character. The beautiful humility of Jesus opened Him up to receive the all-sufficient, empowering grace that God the Father poured into Him. It is the love and acceptance of God that produces that kind of security.

Before Jesus even began His earthly ministry, the Father spoke at His Son's baptism and told the whole world that 'This is my beloved Son in whom I am well pleased'. Jesus' constant fellowship with the Father through prayer enabled Him to maintain that unbroken sense of security because He experienced moment by moment the acceptance and love of His Father. The essential place to start in building mature Christian character is not by doing something but by receiving God's love. Here is true love – not that we loved and went out and were good Christians, but that God first loved us and enabled us to love by His empowering presence working in and through us.

So, the very first thing you need to do is sit down and bask in the Father's love. Open yourself up to His love, directly through worship and prayer and reading the Bible and indirectly through the ministry of the body of Christ, the church. Find some regular way of experiencing God's love, because you simply won't have the foundation to move on to anything else if you don't.

If security produces humility, it follows that pride is related to insecurity. Those people who are insecure often compensate by calling attention to themselves. They are trying to earn the love and favour of people. At the base of such dominating and dogmatic behaviour is often a genuine insecurity. Some express pride in terms of standing out above the crowd and doing things that make people notice them, while others express pride by exhibiting a false humility: 'Oh, it's nothing, don't mention it; it's just the Lord.'

Therefore, just as humility is produced by security, which is rooted in acceptance, pride is produced by insecurity which is rooted in rejection. After a time of being rejected and betrayed, people think they are forced to take care of themselves, and they do this by asserting themselves through various manifestations of pride. A truly fascinating thing about pride is that it is self-perpetuating; it feeds itself. What do you feel like doing to proud, arrogant people? Rejecting them, right? You don't like being around such people; you feel like pushing them away from you. The response to that inevitable rejection is to feel even more insecure and so their behaviour becomes worse.

It is a common pattern that bad things tend to breed bad things and good things tend to breed good things. For example, if a husband is critical of his wife, she will back away because of the criticism. He becomes more critical of her because she's backing away from him, which pushes her further away, which pushes him further away. If that cycle is not identified and cut short, the marriage is doomed. In reverse, we can see that a man's unconditional acceptance and love of his wife produces a security in her and a response from her which draws her closer to him. This makes him even more secure to, in turn, love, respect and honour her, which gives her even greater confidence to love and honour him and there you have it: 'one flesh', the closest thing to heaven on earth.

So instead of rejecting the prideful and arrogant, we should do what God does – He resists them. That is, we confront them and say: 'This is not good behaviour. This will drive you away from people. Don't do this.' Secondly, we affirm them and say, 'You're accepted despite your behaviour. You're loved whether you measure up or not.' Too many of us don't know how to confront destructive behaviour without rejecting the person, but it is something we can learn. Also, most of us don't know how to be confronted about our own behaviour and still feel accepted – but we can learn that too!

In identifying rejection as a root cause of pride, I am not suggesting that the person has no responsibility because they were rejected by others. We are each responsible for the choices we make, regardless of our life's story. Rejection becomes insecurity when we do not believe God when He has told us that we are valuable in His sight. We choose to turn away from His display of love in Jesus on the cross, and therefore we reject His grace. Obviously, God does not reject the proud, He accepts us all. So, what does it mean that God *resists* the proud?

Pride, by definition, is living life on your own and in your own strength. Pride is really our attempt to be independent from God and God won't have anything to do with that. God resists that way of living because He does not want to be shut out of our lives. You can thank God that He is determined to resist anything that gets in the way of a close personal, dependent relationship with Him, because your life is never going to work the way you want it to apart from that relationship.

God wants to get into your life, and He can't do that when you're functioning in self-sufficient pride. God's deepest motive in resisting pride is His desire to give Himself to us and be involved intimately in our lives. He wants us to be the best version of ourselves, and that only happens when we voluntarily humble ourselves before Him and open ourselves up to Him. Humbling yourself is not grovelling on the ground; it is simply admitting that you can't make it work on your own and that you are totally dependent upon God and His grace, His empowering presence, to achieve anything worthwhile. The Bible doesn't say to pray that God will humble you; it says humble yourself, then God will give you His grace, His empowering presence. The apostle Peter said it clearly:

> Likewise you that are younger be subject to the elders. Clothe yourselves, all of you, with humility toward one another, for 'God opposes the proud, but gives grace to the humble.' Humble yourselves therefore under the mighty hand of God, that in due time he may exalt you. (1 Peter 5:5–6, RSV)

If you humble yourselves now – maybe not instantaneously, but in God's time – He will lift you up. Peter then tells us how we can do this:

> Cast all your anxiety on him, because he cares about you. (1 Peter 5:7, RSV)

God tells us how to grab pride by the throat and choke it to death. You take those things that make you feel insecure and bring anxiety and you cast them on the Lord. You give them to God. Cast your anxiety on Him because He cares for you. Meditate on this fact. God the Father cares about you and thinks about you constantly. God wants to give you His grace, His empowering presence, but He needs you to open the door to His grace through your humility. God wants you to cast all your insecurities and anxiety upon Him so He can take them away.

If the experience of God's grace has had any effect in us, we will want to participate in it more and more. Western civilisation mostly has a negative view of humility, but we find that God Himself is supremely humble. He is not boastful or prideful in His attitude. Humility comes from security. Too often we define ourselves by other peoples' opinions and attitudes towards us, but God gives us a picture of ourselves in Christ. He loves and accepts us, and we are valuable in His sight. Therefore, we are completely secure in Him. Out of that security, we can humble ourselves over and over again, and through that humility we open the door to God's grace, to God's empowering presence in our lives. You can't jump a step; one leads to the other. There are no short cuts.

God gives grace to the humble and grief to the proud. Our pride deceives us, and we try to live our lives in our own strength. We shut God out by our own choices and turn away from Him. When we humble ourselves, when we admit that we need and desire Him, then we are open to receiving and responding to God's empowering presence.

CHAPTER FOURTEEN
The Unmistakable Proof of Grace

In one of the most confronting verses in the Bible, we see the unambiguous link between the presence of God and joy.

In Your presence there is fullness of joy. (Psalm 16:11, NKJV)

Therefore, every human on the planet must concede that, if at any point in time they are not experiencing fullness of joy, they are not experiencing the presence of God in their life. Consequently, now that we have more accurately defined grace as the empowering presence of God, we can confidently say that joy is the proof of that grace in our life. Just ponder that for a moment before we move on.

One of the key signifiers of the empowering presence of God in a believer is the presence of real joy. You can't manufacture real joy; it's the fruit of the life of God within us. It is the one infallible proof of God's amazing grace in a person's life. God is love, and where His empowering, loving presence is, there is joy. If our lives are not marked by this deep, peaceful joy, bubbling up like a stream from the depth of our soul, then we have a lot to look forward to because we have yet to experience the fullness of joy that has been given to us freely in God's grace. God is in you, so joy is in you and if you don't experience that joy, it's because the stream is blocked. When we identify those blockages, God can deal with them and release the spirit of joy that lies within each of us. That's what grace does. The presence of God is characterised by joy. If Christ is in you, joy is in you. If Christ is in you, power is in you. And if you're a Christian, Christ is in you. It's that simple. It's that clear.

Many of us remember the joy we felt when we came from the kingdom of darkness into the kingdom of light and embraced God's gift of salvation. CS Lewis described his whole conversion experience as being 'surprised by joy', in the book by that name. The Bible itself describes our conversion experience as coming to joy. When the Ethiopian eunuch heard and believed the good news preached to him by Phillip, he went on his way rejoicing (Acts 8:39). When the Philippian jailer received salvation through the preaching of Paul and Silas, he was filled with joy (Acts 16:34). Joy is the mark of the conversion experience. The apostle Peter said it best:

Though you have not seen Him, you love Him; and even though you do not see Him now, you believe in Him and are filled with an inexpressible and glorious joy, for you are receiving the goal of your faith, the salvation of your soul. (1 Peter 1:8–9)

You are embracing salvation, so you are filled with an inexpressible and glorious joy. I've had people say, 'Well, yes, that is the conversion experience, but you get over it. The emotion dies down and you mature into a deeper understanding of your faith.' What a load of codswallop! What they're effectively saying is that when they first met Jesus, they were thrilled and excited and full of life and spontaneity and joy, but the longer they knew Him, the duller He became!

I believe religion has dealt a fatal blow to joy and openness to God in so many of us. It replaces the free, unbridled life of grace with works, guilt and shame. The enemy of God has robbed so many believers of that inexpressible and glorious joy through false teaching and bad role models. Satan has done all he can to remove any emotion or spontaneity from us, particularly with the men in our culture. Some people stand before the living God Himself in worship looking like they're sucking on a lemon or like they'd rather be somewhere else, and when they see someone responding to God enthusiastically or showing some emotion during worship, they might think, 'Well, if they want to do that, that's fine. It's just not my cup of tea.' However, we wish deep down that they wouldn't do it, because it makes it look like they've got something we haven't. We might even consider these people as immature, highly emotional or unstable in their faith, when in fact they are actually encountering the power and reality of God in worship, and they cannot contain the joy within them.

When the enemy of God took away our true understanding of God's grace and replaced it with an abstract theological concept, he took us away from the real presence and power of God, and consequently the joy, excitement and spontaneity that goes with the presence of God also disappeared. I put a question in a home group study book many years ago which read, 'What excites you most about your relationship with God?' Believe it or not, one group in that church spent an entire night debating the word 'excitement' and whether that is an appropriate emotion in our relationship with God. Some suggested that excitement was shallow and inappropriate and perhaps not even from God. They were fearful and equated excitement with the Pentecostal wing of the church, the people who were 'out there' in their emotional response to God. How sad – but how incredibly common. These people had been robbed of the joy of the Lord and the reality of God's presence and the enemy was using them to keep it that way and keep their congregation that way. The joy of the Lord was simply not there.

Why do we do this to ourselves and to each other? The more we look at our sins and how bad we are, the more depressed we get. Why should that surprise us? When you stop looking at Jesus and start looking at your sins or the sins of others, how do you expect to feel? Next time there's a beautiful sunrise, just sit there and gaze at it and see how you feel. Then hop in your car and drive out to the local rubbish dump and sit there in the hot sun and watch a million blowflies on the rotting food and rubbish, then see how you feel. You don't need a university degree to work out why you would feel a little depressed gazing at garbage but feel a deep sense of peace in your soul as you focus on a beautiful sunrise.

So where is your focus? That's why worship is so important. It shifts our focus back to God – His love, His grace, His power, His mercy, His ability and desire to fulfil His plan and purpose in us and through us. Intimate and personal prayers and songs lead us to relate to God one-to-one. When your focus is upon Him and Him alone, joy will just rise up within you and take over. Corporate worship is one of the few opportunities we have each week when we can come together and support each other in forgetting about ourselves. We take our eyes off what's wrong with us and the world and focus our attention on what's right with God. If nothing else happens, that alone should cheer you up!

The New Testament makes it clear that the ongoing experience of a Christian is to be marked by joy. We have been born again into the kingdom of God. The whole Christian life is a participation in the words and the works of the King, Jesus. So, see if you notice something in these passages that talk about the kingdom of God.

> *The kingdom of God is like treasure hidden in a field. When a man found it, he hid it again, and then in his joy went and sold all he had and bought that field. (Matthew 13:44)*

When a man or woman sees the kingdom of God, their first reaction is not 'Well, this is the way to overcome the evil one. This is the way to truth and life …' All of that is absolutely true, but their first reaction is 'Yippee! Hallelujah! Praise the Lord!' Their first response is joy!

> *The seventy-two returned with joy and said, "Lord, even the demons submit to us in your name."*
>
> *He replied, "I saw Satan fall like lightning from heaven. I have given you authority to trample on snakes and scorpions and to overcome all the power*

of the enemy; nothing will harm you. However, do not rejoice that the spirits submit to you, but rejoice that your names are written in heaven."

At that time Jesus, full of joy through the Holy Spirit, said, "I praise you, Father, Lord of heaven and earth, because you have hidden these things from the wise and learned, and revealed them to little children. Yes, Father, for this is what you were pleased to do." (Luke 10:17–21)

They come back after doing the works of Jesus and they're full of joy, and so is Jesus. Participating in the life of the kingdom of God is not only joyous for you and me, it also brings joy to God. There's joy in heaven and there's joy on earth when we're connected with God as human beings, fully alive in Christ.

For the kingdom of God is not a matter of eating and drinking [not a matter a religious dos and don'ts], *but of righteousness, peace and joy in the Holy Spirit.* (Romans 14:17)

The kingdom of God is righteousness, peace and joy in the Holy Spirit. It is a kingdom characterised by joy! Is that the witness and testimony of the majority of people in the church today? It was really obvious in the first-century church when the kingdom of God came in Christ. When you're converted to Christ, you're converted to a life of joy from beginning to end, unless it is blocked or stifled in some way. It is joy even when things don't go our way.

Blessed are you when people hate you, when they exclude you and insult you and reject your name as evil, because of the Son of Man.

Rejoice, be full of joy in that day and leap for joy because great is your reward in heaven. (Luke 6:22–23)

And now, brothers, we want you to know about the grace that God has given the Macedonian churches. In the midst of a very severe trial, their overflowing joy and their extreme poverty welled up in rich generosity. (2 Corinthians 8:1–2)

The joy that bubbled up inside them overcame adversity and enabled them to rejoice and be full of gladness and to give sacrificially of their money even in severe poverty. The power of persistent joy lies at the heart of the power of God in our lives to overcome all our enemies and to undo all the bad stuff in our life. That's why we can do all things through Christ who strengthens us.

The joy of the Lord is our strength, and that joy will not quit or be thwarted; it will not be stopped by adversity or even Satan himself. What stops our joy is wrong thinking or a wrong focus. Taking our minds and our focus off Jesus and putting them on ourselves will stifle joy quicker than anything I know. Your sins can't stop joy – we've all proven that. Time doesn't stop joy and neither does suffering – the early church proved that! The only thing that will stop joy is taking your focus off Who Jesus is and what He has done and what He is doing, and looking instead at your own flawed, sinful life.

This is true inside and outside the church. Thousands of people are trying desperately to be happy and joyful, and none of them are finding it outside of Christ. If you go after joy as an end in itself, you will never find it. If you go after Jesus, you get Him, and joy comes as a bonus! Joy is a by-product of knowing Jesus. Joy is the fruit which comes from worshipping and connecting with Jesus. There is nothing that's wrong with you that a connection with Jesus won't fix.

That is why so much of what masquerades as counselling today is utterly useless. The focus is always on the person, identifying their problems and finding ways to change their behaviour and fix it without having the power to do any of it – because the power comes from Jesus! I can't imagine a more frustrating and pointless way to spend a life than to be a secular psychologist. They do not know Jesus nor the empowering presence of God. They cannot connect people to the only true source of joy and peace. When are we ever going to learn that we can't fix us or anyone else, that only Jesus can? We need to stop thinking about ourselves. Sooner or later, we've got to move on and get a life, a life characterised by joy in spite of the circumstances around us.

Consider it pure joy, my brothers and sister, whenever you face trials of many kinds … (James 1:2)

There's no way you can have that kind of joy in the midst of trials, insults and opposition if you shift your focus away from Jesus. He is the source of that joy; you cannot manufacture it. When somebody's down and depressed and very aware of how bad they are, you can't just say, 'Snap out of it, be joyful, praise God!' That just adds another do-more- try-harder burden that they are already failing in. Joy is something God does in you; all you need to do is create a possibility for that to happen. If you're a Christian, joy is in you. If you're not experiencing it, there's a blockage. Paul knew that there was something seriously wrong with the Galatian church, because he asked, 'What happened to all of your joy? (Galatians 4:15)' He didn't say, 'What happened to your quiet time or your scripture reading or your prayer or your tithing or your witnessing?' He asked about the absence of joy in their life. He then spends the rest of the letter telling them what happened to their joy, as they started replacing Jesus with something else, mainly their performance.

Joy is something you get for free, and as long as you keep the channels open, you go on experiencing that joy all your life. It won't diminish from your conversion experience; it will actually intensify! If a marriage can get better between two sinful people, don't you think that an intimate relationship between you and the King of Kings and the Lord of Lords can get better too?

The most noticeable trait of churches that are struggling under the weight of abusive, legalistic teaching or are starved of good teaching all together is the absence of joy. But the joy that is talked about in the Bible is a force that bubbles up from within us like an artesian spring. When Paul comes to describe his motivation for ministry, he describes it in terms of promoting joy in his people.

> *If I am to go on living in the body, this will mean fruitful labour for me. Yet what shall I choose? I do not know! I am torn between the two: I desire to depart and be with Christ, which is better by far; but it is more necessary for you that I remain in the body. Convinced of this, I know that I will remain, and I will continue with all of you for your progress and joy in the faith, so that through my being with you again, your boasting in Christ Jesus will abound on account of me. (Philippians 1:22–26)*

This is absolutely amazing! Paul says, 'I'd like to be with Jesus, to be with the Lord and away from this old, tormented body, but you need more joy so I'm going to stick around!' He doesn't say, 'My mission is not completed yet, I have more churches to plant, I haven't finished writing the New Testament, there's still a lot of sin in you I've got to root out and fix.' No! He says, 'I'd like to check out of here, but you need some more joy, so I'm going hang around until you get it!'

Friends, that is exactly why I'm here. Through teaching, equipping and ministering among God's people, my primary purpose is to release the joy of the Lord in people. I want people to be *happy* they are part of the church. My own philosophy of ministry is summed up in 2 Corinthians 1:24. Paul is writing to the church at Corinth; remember what yahoos these Corinthian Christians were? He says, 'Not that we lord it over your faith, but we work with you for your joy, because it is by faith you stand firm.'

We work with you for your joy. If ever there was a stupid and sinful church, if ever there was a church that needed to be slapped around and straightened out, if ever there was a church that needed some discipline, it was the Corinthian church. Yet Paul says, 'My first obligation is not to fix you; my first obligation is to increase your joy.' He did that by preaching grace over and over and over again until they understood it in all its truth, because he knew that the joy of the Lord would just well up inside them and flow spontaneously when they understood and experienced the empowering presence of God.

Whenever I teach about grace, somebody will invariably ask, 'Why the emphasis on God's grace? Now that we've had grace, when are we going to move on? How do we get people to stop sinning and read the Bible? Too much of this grace and our kids are going to rebel and do whatever they like.' If you're thinking anything like that, then you haven't heard the message of grace yet.

I preach and teach about grace and will continue to do so because that is the gospel. That is what changes people's lives and produces in them an inexpressible joy that floods their whole being and overflows to those around them. The cleverest perversion of all is when we start to understand grace and the enemy says, 'Wow, you understand this stuff better than those legalistic Christians!' Once you focus on your understanding of grace and take your eyes off Jesus, just watch the joy dissipate. Grace is not to be your focus. Humility is not to be your focus. Joy is not to be your focus. *Jesus* is to be your focus! It's worshipping Him, hearing about Him, looking at Him, talking to Him, reflecting upon Him, being filled with joy by Him – that is to be your focus.

You might be thinking, 'There's more to me than I'm experiencing, there's more to me than people have seen yet, there's more worship in me than has been expressed, there's more prayer in me, there's more joy in me than I've experienced, but for some reason it's just not getting out.'

Childbirth is the best analogy I can think of. Many women have had to have emergency caesarean operations because the placenta had moved into the wrong position and was blocking the path of the fully developed unborn child. If they were to go into labour, both mother and child would be at risk. Years ago, there were many mothers and babies who died in the process. It is tragic. They have a fully developed life within them, but it can't get out. That's what it's like for some of us.

The life of Jesus within us is blocked because of an obstruction. Constant exposure to God's grace and the joy of others will gradually erode that obstruction, so stick around and it will happen eventually. But there is also a very real, anointing of joy from God. We see this in the book of Hebrews:

And again, when God brings his firstborn into the world, he says,

"Let all God's angels worship him."

In speaking of the angels, he says,

"He makes his angels winds, his servants flames of fire."

But about the Son he says,

"Your throne, O God, will last for ever and ever; and a scepter of justice will be the scepter of your kingdom.

You have loved righteousness and hated wickedness; therefore God, your God, has set you above your

companions by anointing you with the oil of joy." (Hebrews 1:6–9)

There is an anointing of joy that Jesus has in Him, and people who have experienced it have been radically changed. Jesus is joy, Jesus is full of joy, and Jesus is in you. So, in the name of Jesus, I bless you with joy right now. I bless you with the full inheritance of your salvation – joy that will defeat depression, joy that will defeat evil, joy that will defeat anxiety. Be anxious for nothing because God is in you and God is joy. Be fearful for nothing for Christ is in you and He is anointed with joy. Be optimistic about the future because the Spirit is in you leading you into the future, and He is the Spirit of joy. I pray that God would release that spring within your spirit and cause that joy to bubble up to the surface now and flood every part of your life, removing the barriers of self-pity, bitterness, shame, anger, unforgiveness, self-hatred, judgements spoken against you and repression of emotion.

So, choose today to enter into the presence and working of God in your life and the joy of the Lord will be your strength. It is simply the product of the life of Christ in you. When you are lacking in joy, it is a sign that the life of Christ is somehow being blocked. Loss of joy is the first thing you will notice when you fall away from grace and come under the burden of the law, when even joy becomes an effort. You can remove the blockage and recapture your joy when you take time to connect with God in worship, and in the presence of His people. You participate in the joy of the kingdom through partnering with God in ministry.

Even trials and persecution for the sake of the gospel cannot quench your joy; that only happens when you take our eyes off Jesus and look at yourself again. As in all things, you can make the choice to allow grace to have its effect in your life. When you do, your joy will be restored, and you can freely serve others so that their joy too may increase.

CHAPTER FIFTEEN
Freedom! Freedom! Freedom!

Our life in Christ is characterised by dignity, freedom, flexibility and self-government, or to be more precise, Spirit-government. However, as we've seen in many different ways throughout this teaching as well as in our own experience, people seem to give up their freedom too all easily. Why is it that some people, set free by God's grace, make free choices to return to bondage? The apostle Paul questions the believers in the Galatian church:

> Formerly, when you did not know God, you were slaves to those who by nature are not gods. But now that you know God – or rather, are known by God – how is it that you are returning to those weak and miserable forces? Do you wish to be enslaved by them all over again? You are observing special days and months and seasons and years! I fear for you, that somehow I have wasted my efforts on you. (Galatians 4:8–11)

He wants to know why they would give up the freedom of intimacy with God for rules and religion, trying to manipulate Him when He has already given them all things in Christ. Paul is scratching his head over these believers who are now trying once again to impress one another (and even God?) with their performances. Let's look at more of Paul's confronting teaching in Galatians 5.

> It is for freedom that Christ has set us free. [Perhaps the most terrifying verse in the whole Bible!] Stand firm, then, and do not let yourselves be burdened again by a yoke of slavery [religious dead works]. (Galatians 5:1)

If you turn to religion, you've turned your back on Jesus Christ. How much clearer can he be?

> Mark my words! I, Paul, tell you that if you let yourselves be circumcised [do any of these dead religious works], Christ will be of no value to you at all. Again, I declare to every man who lets himself be circumcised that he is obligated to obey the whole law [and we know that no one can obey the whole law]. You who are trying to be justified by law have been alienated from Christ; you have fallen away from grace. (Galatians 5:2–4)

There are only two choices – you can attempt to relate to God by trying to be good; or you can be related to God through Jesus.

For through the Spirit we eagerly await by faith the righteousness for which we hope. For in Christ Jesus neither circumcision nor uncircumcision has any value. The only thing that counts is faith expressing itself through love. (Galatians 5:5–6)

Verse 1 encapsulates this whole passage and possibly the whole message of the New Testament: *'It is for freedom that Christ has set us free.'* It is difficult to imagine a more radical or extreme definition of authentic humanity. God's purpose in setting us free in Christ is not, first of all, to go into all the world and preach the gospel or become a missionary or serve the local church or find our destiny.

He set us free, first and foremost, for freedom itself. God made us free to be authentically who we were created to be. Many people have difficulty with this concept because it is not what is taught by religious teachers. They effectively preach (but would never express it this way!) that you come out of the bondage of sin and rebellion straight into the bondage of religion.

The devil wins both ways; the effect is the same – we are robbed of our God-given freedom. The devil's plan is to keep us away from Christ and he doesn't mind how that happens; in church or out of church, either way is okay with him. In fact, I believe it's easier for Satan to keep people away from Christ in church! Religion is much more subtle than full-on rebellion because the modern-day Pharisees do not recognise how far from Christ they have strayed. The Westminster confession of 1646 states:

The chief end of man is to worship God and enjoy Him forever.

That sounds great but think if you had asked Paul what the chief end of man was when he was writing to the Galatians. I think he'd say, *'to get free and stay free, through Christ, by the power of the Holy Spirit.'* Paul doesn't want to see Jesus die in vain for anyone. Rather than set these two statements against each other, perhaps we could combine them: *So we can worship God and enjoy Him forever, we need to get free and stay free, through Christ, by the power of the Holy Spirit!*

Why did Christ die to set us free if we were not meant to be free? If He wanted us to be enslaved to religion, He could have stopped with the Sermon on the Mount. In the beginning, we were made in the image of God, and one major aspect of that is our freedom. God is free, and we are meant to be free also. Freedom is our true native environment. That is where we function best. That is where we are fully alive and fully human in all its God-given glory!

The Christian church will realise her full potential when believers live abundant lives totally free in the presence of God – free from manipulation, expectation and control by others, even God Himself! God never wanted to control us, and He still doesn't. Why can't we see that? Why do we still run to Him like little kids and long for Him to call all the shots in our life in a way that He never intended? (More about that later.)

Paul's letter to the Galatians has two parts. In the first part, he tells us who we are in Christ and about all the blessings bestowed upon us. He says we are much loved sons and daughters of God, set free for freedom's sake. Then he goes on to say, 'in the light of that fact, this is how you ought to respond.'

Now in saying that 'you are free, it's all by grace, and you can't do anything to earn it or pay it back', please don't think that it doesn't matter how you act. That is not what Paul is saying at all. After emphasising our freedom in Christ, he immediately goes on to say, 'Stand firm, then, and do not let yourselves be burdened again by a yoke of slavery'. He puts the responsibility fairly upon our shoulders to protect the freedom that Christ has given us. The fact that Christ set you free on the cross doesn't mean that you just settle back and watch it all happen in your life. We live in a world where all sorts of pressures are brought to bear to rob us of that freedom and enslave us again.

In our Christian lives, there are demonic forces, religious forces, social forces and forces from within our own personalities which will undermine that freedom, and we are going to have to fight every day to protect it. This is true at every level of society and in every culture. These are the forces which have shaped every world system. They are spiritual as much as environmental or cultural, and they are strong and persistent – but they are no match for the life of Christ within us. He that is in us in greater than he that is in the world, so we have nothing to fear.

So why do we give up our freedom so easily and fall for religious externals? This is speculation, but I believe the answer may lie within our own personalities. There is something strangely comforting about someone else taking responsibility for our decisions. When you look around in the world, you will see most people are ready to give up their freedom if someone will take responsibility for the terrifying freedom we've been given as human beings. Freedom represents a lot of hard work, so it's often easier to let someone else take the risk and wear the consequences. Then we have someone to blame when things don't go as planned.

People get into a habit in church where they don't think about what they hear preached, and don't read the Bible for themselves nor wrestle with God about deeper issues. They trust someone else to tell them what to think or believe. That is so much easier than operating in the freedom that is ours in Christ and being led by the Holy Spirit. It does away with having to study the Bible personally and pray or fast to discern God's heart on issues.

Freedom is frightening for people who are used to having decisions made for them. We can see this in those people who have been institutionalised for long periods of time. Criminals released from jail will often re-offend, just to get back into prison. They become so dependent on having someone else take care of their needs and direct their time and activity that the freedom for which they longed night and day actually frightens them straight back into bondage.

The same is true in our spiritual lives, and that is why religion in all its subtle shapes and forms can be so enticing. Deep down, we are happy to let someone else take responsibility for us. People invent theologies of restriction and legalistic regulation which deny people's freedom and take away their responsibility for thinking for themselves. There must be a market for it because hundreds of thousands of people submit themselves to those churches.

When this is full-blown, as in some cults, even the most mundane decisions are directed by the 'church' – the style and colour of clothes, who they are allowed to have as friends, who they must marry, and of course, what translation of the Bible they must use. Sometimes the manipulation and intimidation inflicted by the leaders is horrific and it becomes very difficult to ever find freedom again. People have been separated from their families or have had to move away because they chose to leave the group.

Deep down many of us fear relating to God, naked spirit to naked spirit, as totally accepted sons and daughters in an intimate, uninhibited, no-rules relationship of love. When you combine that fear with the very powerful spiritual forces behind religion, guilt and shame, you start to understand why so many people over so many years have allowed themselves to be beaten up in church every week. There is no other explanation.

There is another manifestation of insecurity in our relationship with God, one that looks respectable but is just another display of religion. There are people who desperately seek the Lord for every little decision they make. They genuinely want to do His will, so they want confirmation before they take every step. Often, they don't get the guidance they want because the Lord is effectively saying, 'I've set you free to make your own decisions. Whether you are right or wrong won't affect how I feel about you. Learn to operate in that freedom.'

I am not suggesting we shouldn't pray about anything and everything – go right ahead as God is always happy to talk to you about anything. But if He does not give any clear insight or reason for not proceeding, you are free to do what you think is appropriate. Your moment-by-moment dependency on Him is not intended to hold you back like an immature child.

There are many things we do not need to seek His mind on because He has already told us clearly in Bible. There are other things which are given to us as choices and God wants us to exercise our freedom creatively and use the growing wisdom which He is releasing in as we draw near to Him. If it doesn't work, we don't blame God. He smiles lovingly at us, picks us up, dusts us off, encourages us and sets us back on the bicycle and pushes us down the hill again. That's what freedom is all about. It's scary – it's a wild ride sometimes – but it's what God ordained for us all.

It is for freedom and dignity that Christ has set us free. We can fight it or hide from it, we can deny it or run away from it, but we cannot change the fact that we are, objectively speaking, totally, radically and completely free because of Christ. However, down through history, the gospel of God's free grace has been repeatedly replaced by the bondage of religion because men and women in key places have faltered because of fear.

Too many Christian leaders are weak and dependent people. Some choose helping professions like social work and psychology to meet their own needs by being needed by others. In my opinion, too many counsellors, social workers and psychologists that I have met and known should never have entered those fields. They did so because of needs in them. That sounds pretty harsh, but I believe it is true. If you're not secure in yourself and need others to make you feel okay, prop you up or need you, you are absolutely vulnerable to those people. If they ever remove that acceptance, you're in big trouble. This has happened to many Christian leaders, and it's tragic. They become controlled by other people.

It's important to reflect on the sources of your own fears. A lot are tied up with the threat of rejection or abandonment. Many people have had painful experiences of rejection which makes them quite vulnerable. I have had to face these fears personally over many years. Since the age of fifteen, I have found myself in leadership positions and positions of influence over others and, therefore, I have been open to this danger for most of my life. I know what this is like, and if I had not let God bring me through this issue into freedom in Him, the rejection I have experienced from people around me over the years would have bound me in such a way that I would have been utterly useless to anyone. Worse than useless – I would have been dangerous if I had remained in leadership.

It is no picnic fighting the forces which try to bind and rob us of this freedom. At times every emotion in us cries out and pushes us in the opposite direction, but we have to respond in spirit and in truth, not from our emotions, if freedom is where we desire to live.

Another inner enemy of freedom is the past, or at least our attitude to the past. Your past has absolutely no power whatsoever; it is only your attitude to the past which can impact the present and the future. Don't let the enemy blind you to the truth. Someone may say, 'My father abused me; therefore, my life is a mess.' In Christ you have been made free, so you can't blame your father forever. You can make new choices. You can respond any way you want, so if you stay messed up, it's your choice. What was your father's fault back then is not your father's fault now; you are free to choose.

Another person may say, 'My wife isn't interested in me anymore; therefore, I started looking for other women to meet my needs.' Your wife didn't make you do anything; you made a choice to walk away from your marriage. You are free, and with your freedom comes the full responsibility for your decisions. Someone else may say, 'My last pastor was spiritually abusive, so that's why I'm dysfunctional in this church.' Well, stay as long as you need to get healed, but if you stay dysfunctional, that is a choice you have made, because Jesus is the One Who has set you free to choose. We have been doing this for a very long time now:

Adam said, 'I disobeyed you, God, because the woman made me do it.'

Eve said, 'I disobeyed you, God, because the serpent made me do it.'

God said, 'No, you were free. You made choices, and real consequences follow real freedom.'

That little dialogue has been going on between us and God ever since, yet so many people still don't get it and still try as hard as they can to shift the responsibility for their lives to someone else. At that point, they are not operating in freedom. That's why real freedom is scary, because real freedom brings real choices, and at the end of the day, your life is not going to be labelled Social Forces or Life's Chances – your life will be labelled My Choices.

You may ask, 'Does that mean I no longer have an excuse for the way I am, for being broke or depressed or lonely or anything else?' Yes, it does! We can't alter many of the circumstances into which we are born or which come our way, but we are in complete control of our reactions to those circumstances. When failure comes, we can let our lives stop at that point, or we can choose to embrace a new opportunity and press on. We are free to not be held captive by anything that happens to us. In Christ you are not condemned for the way your life looks, because all your good choices and all your bad choices are covered by the blood of Jesus. You are forgiven and cleansed for all time.

What a tragic shame it is if you allow fear or failure to rule the way you live. Failure is not the worst thing that can happen to you. The worst thing is to let yourself be imprisoned by fear of any kind and not do anything, to not take any chances, to never make any radical choices. That is to miss out on life itself!

When you are acting under the compulsion of public opinion or external pressure to conform to man-made standards, rules or expectations, you are not free. You have alienated yourself from Christ and fallen away from the experience of the empowering presence of God. When this happens, you shouldn't fall on the floor in despair; you just need to change your mind, repent of religion and go back and allow God to bathe you in His freedom again.

Let the Spirit of God set you free from the bondage of the fear of freedom – the fear of making wrong choices, the fear of forgiving somebody who's hurt you and may hurt you again. These fears, and many more, keep us from walking and ministering in the freedom that Jesus bought for each of us with His life's blood.

Paul goes on to explain what true freedom is. He was accused of being soft on sin, of encouraging lawlessness by emphasising the grace of God, so he wrote this:

> You, my brothers and sisters, were called to be free. But do not use your freedom to indulge the flesh; rather, serve one another humbly in love. For the entire law is fulfilled in keeping this one command: "Love your neighbour as yourself." If you bite and devour each other, watch out or you will be destroyed by each other. (Galatians 5:13–15)

Paul defines freedom. He says you know when you're finally free in Christ when you are free to serve others. Freedom isn't lying in bed all day doing nothing and filling your life with self-indulgence. You can love and serve one another because you have first been loved by God. God's amazing grace has so overwhelmed you that it flows out into those around you. You no longer have to trade or barter to get acceptance from anyone else ever again. You can just give them your love and acceptance the way God does, whether you receive any back or not. That is the ultimate test of freedom. That is setting others free as you have been.

True freedom is not freedom *to* sin; it is freedom *from* sin. It is finally defined in serving one another in love. When nothing and no one can keep you from loving others, then you are walking in the freedom that is yours in Christ. You are walking in the Spirit because *'where the Spirit of the Lord is, there is freedom'* (2 Corinthians 3:17).

It is often observed that people set free from some bondage over their lives will return to it. Many people have a concept of freedom and consider it to be one of the basic human rights, but don't really know how to live in that freedom every day.

God has set a very high value on human freedom – Jesus gave His life to secure it for us. The apostle Paul took it very seriously when the church gave its freedom away. There are many reasons why we return to the confines of religious life, but they are all rooted in one thing – we don't trust God to keep us and work in us and through us. We keep returning to our own efforts to find security.

Our security, our significance, our purpose and our destiny are all found in Christ, and in Christ alone. That is the truth which will set us gloriously and permanently free, the freedom for which Christ has set us free.

CHAPTER SIXTEEN
Our Struggle with Unbelief

Throughout this book, I've been stressing that our relationship with God is absolutely secure through the work of Jesus Christ, because He paid the price for us. I have also emphasised that all the benefits of that are completely free to us. It is a sovereign gift of God's grace which we could never earn. We can never manufacture the power, peace, joy, gifts and fruit which come with that gift, and we can never pay it back. We can only accept it as a free gift, or we can refuse it. However, we must understand that if we are to experience the reality of this life which is ours free, in Christ, we must choose to participate in it. Let me put it this way. Our life in Christ is free; we can't work *for* it, but we can work *in* it. We can walk in it.

Some of this we have discussed at length from different perspectives, so let's look at some stories of the lives of people like you and me who understood this principle. The Bible is a record of the experiences of men and women with God as their Creator, Saviour and Redeemer. That is why it is such a relevant and rich document, because you and I are effectively on every page!

The story of Abraham begins in Genesis 11. We are told that Abraham received, by grace through faith, a whole new life through a child born to him in his old age. In Romans 4, it says he inherited the earth by believing God. Along with his believing, Abraham acted on his belief. He didn't work to obtain, earn or create God's promise of a child, but he worked with God in receiving it. He would never have received the promise otherwise.

Abraham acted in faith in accordance with the promise God had given him, being fully persuaded that God had power to do exactly what he promised (Romans 4:19–20). Abraham acted as if the Word of God were true. He believed God and acted accordingly! The next story is about Naaman.

Now Naaman was the commander of the army of the king of Aram. He was a great man in the sight of his master and highly regarded, because through him the LORD had given victory to Aram. He was a valiant soldier, but he had leprosy.

Now bands or raiders from Aram had gone out and had taken captive a young girl from Israel, and she served Naaman's wife. She said to her mistress, "If only my master would see the prophet who is in Samaria! He would cure him of his leprosy."

Naaman went to his master and told him what the girl from Israel had said. "By all means, go," the king of Aram replied. "I will send a letter to the king of Israel." So Naaman left, taking with him ten talents of silver, six thousand shekels of gold and ten sets of clothing. The letter he took to the king of Israel read: "With this letter I am sending my servant Naaman to you so that you may cure him of his leprosy."

As soon as the king of Israel read the letter, he tore his robes and said, "Am I God? Can I kill and bring back to life? Why does this fellow send someone to me to be cured of his leprosy? See how he is trying to pick a quarrel with me!"

When Elisha the man of God heard that the king of Israel had torn his robes, he sent him this message: "Why have you torn your robes? Have the man come to me and he will know that there is a prophet in Israel." So Naaman went with his horses and chariots and stopped at the door of Elisha's house. (2 Kings 5:1–9)

When Naaman arrives at Elisha's house, with his robes, chariots and in great pomp, the prophet of God doesn't even come out of the house! He's out the back, fixing the washing machine!

Elisha sent a messenger to say to him, "Go, wash yourself seven times in the Jordan, and your flesh will be restored and you will be cleansed."

But Naaman went away angry and said, "I thought that he would surely come out to me and stand and call on the name of the LORD his God, wave his hand over the spot and cure me of my leprosy." [He was expecting something religious or magical.] Are not Abana and Pharpar, the rivers of Damascus, better than any of the waters of Israel? Couldn't I wash in them and be cleansed?" So, he turned and went off in a rage.

Naaman's servants went to him and said, "My father, if the prophet had told you to do some great thing, would you not have done it? How much more, then, when he tells you, 'Wash and be cleansed!'" So, he went down and dipped himself in the Jordan seven times, as the man of God had told him, and his flesh was restored and became clean like that of a young boy. (2 Kings 5:10–14)

The Word of God to Naaman was clear, through Elisha. He was effectively given healing by the grace of God through Elisha's command to wash in the Jordan seven times. Naaman could act on that and receive the healing from God – or he could ignore it and die from leprosy. The Word of God was true, but he would never have experienced it unless he had acted as though it were true. The irritating thing for Naaman (and every religious person that followed him!) is that it just sounded too simple!

We face the same problem today. We can fall into the trap of waiting for some flashy, miraculous, sudden intervention from God to solve our problems and make us believe Him, that one thing that is going to make life work – the conference, book, preacher or experience that will fix us and unlock the blessings and reality of God.

What God gives us is so simple that we often miss it. That's why Jesus said we must come as little children, with the same child-like faith. We receive the free gifts and blessings of God by believing that they are free and then acting on that belief in faith.

> *Then Naaman and all his attendants went back to the man of God. He stood before him and said, "Now I know that there is no God in all the world except in Israel. Please now accept a gift from your servant."*

> *The prophet answered, "As surely as the LORD lives, whom I serve, I will not accept a thing." And even though Naaman urged him, he refused. (2 Kings 5:15–16)*

Naaman tried to pay for something that was free. As understandable as that is for fallen humans like us, it's an insult to God who gives freely in love. How would a parent feel if a young child started giving their pocket money back in payment for each meal? It must wound God's heart when His children try to pay Him back for His love and empowering grace. The apostle Paul tells his own story:

> *For I am the least of the apostles and do not even deserve to be called an apostle [I don't deserve anything I have], because I persecuted the church of God. But by the grace of God I am what I am [and I say what I say, and do what I do, and write what I write], and his grace to me was not without effect. No, I worked harder than all of them – yet not I, but the grace of God that was with me. (1 Corinthians 15:9–10)*

Paul clearly says he didn't deserve it; it came to him freely. He got what everyone else in the kingdom got. But it didn't come to him without effect because he worked harder than everybody else. He worked in response to the resources of God's grace. He could have received God's grace and not worked, and the gift would have been without effect. Abraham could have waited forever if he hadn't acted upon God's word.

Naaman would have died in his pride and disease had he not acted. You may believe in God's free, radical grace, you may affirm that you can never deserve or earn it or pay it back, but if you don't act as though that is true, you will never experience the liberating power of that free gift. It will have no effect.

Jesus explained this to His disciples in Luke 8, with the parable of the seed and the four types of soil. The seed is the Word of God. It comes to you by reading the Bible, listening to sermons, discussion in a small group and sometimes directly to your spirit. The seed remains the same, but the different soils determine whether the seed will germinate and grow. The good seed sometimes falls on the path. The soil is hard, the seed cannot take root there, so it blows away or is snatched by a bird. Other seed falls on shallow soil and it can't grow there either. It may fall in good soil, but weeds grow up faster and choke the seed to death. But the same seed which fails to grow in those places produces a bountiful crop in fertile soil which is rich, receptive and prepared. The power isn't in the soil, the power is in the seed; but the life and fruit within the seed will never produce its crop without the resources of the soil.

We should spend as much time as we can in the Bible, not for any religious reason to please God, or because it's a discipline we've developed, but because it contains the seed – the life-changing, mind-blowing Word of God Almighty that will produce life in us. If we read it and allow it to penetrate our heart and take root, we will find everything God has promised to begin to manifest in our life and that great old hymn, 'Joy unspeakable and full of glory', written over a hundred years ago by Barney Warren will be our testimony. You should look it up and read the words!

Does that sound like your life? That's the promise of God which will become a reality in your life as you provide the best environment (soil) for His Word of truth. First believe it; then start acting as though it's true and you will receive all the fruit God desires. Seeds don't come up overnight and babies don't arrive the next week. Sometimes there is a time delay as the fruit forms in a hidden place, but the promise will be delivered.

All those great promises of God will in time become your experience: 'I will keep you in perfect peace', 'You will be able to do all things through Christ who strengthens you', 'Ask anything in my name and I will do it for you' etc. The Word of God will produce fruit because it has within it the power to fulfil God's promises. All it needs is fertile, deep, rich, open, cooperative soil. It's never a case of God's part, then our part following; we do this together all the way or it doesn't happen.

The Bible and our own experiences confirm that the first sin that nullifies the promises, power and manifest presence of God in our experience, but not in reality, is the sin of unbelief.

> *Praise be to the God and Father of our Lord Jesus Christ, who has blessed us in the heavenly realms with every spiritual blessing in Christ. (Ephesians 1:3)*

If you are a believer, you now have everything in Christ, but if you don't act on that belief, you will never experience it. The next verse tells us the most important blessing of all:

> *For he chose us in him before the creation of the world to be holy and blameless in his sight. (Ephesians 1:4)*

He has already done that. Any attempt on our part to become holy in His sight is sin, and we need to repent of that sin of unbelief. Unbelief gives rise to every other sin in life, from the Garden of Eden till now. Why do believers still covet, steal, commit adultery or lie? It is because they don't believe they already have everything in Christ. You don't need to strive for acceptance in Christ or try to attain God's holiness by your religious performance. You don't need drugs to find peace. You don't need to manipulate people into liking you, because you are loved by God.

Unbelief is the first sin. All other sin that we feel bad about is our futile attempt to earn the things that God has already freely given us. God said to Adam and Eve, 'I give you everything in abundance. It is all good.' Then the serpent said, 'God is withholding something from you. If you really want to live, then in addition to all that God has given you, you need to take this forbidden fruit.' Taking the fruit was not Adam and Eve's first sin. Not believing what God had told them was their first sin. The sin of unbelief is where the fall began.

> *In love he predestined us to be adopted as his sons and daughters through Jesus Christ, in accordance with his pleasure and will – to the praise of his glorious grace, which he has freely given us in the One he loves. (Ephesians 1:4–6)*

There is no more that we need. We just believe what we are told and step out and act as if it were true. We have everything that we need for life in Jesus Christ – *all* we need for godliness, *all* we need for happiness, *all* we need for an authentic life, *all* we need for our church to look like the church Christ promised to build. If we have prepared good, rich, open, receptive soil, if we meditate on the fact that we have everything in Christ and act as if that fact is true, we will begin to experience what God promises to us. If we don't, we won't – it's that simple.

Our lives are full of all kinds of sins, and we tend to put them in different categories. We repent of them as we feel convicted, but until we repent of the first sin of unbelief, our lives will never work, and we will go on committing many other sins which flow from our unbelief. God told Abraham that he and Sarah would have a son. Abraham's unbelief caused him to try to help out by having a son with Hagar. He then had to repent of his second sin as well as the sin of unbelief.

So far in this book I have endeavoured in many ways to explain and demonstrate your complete freedom in Christ, that you are okay with God, that His life is given to you freely and you never have to earn it. Why have I done that? Why has this seemed like a cracked record? There are a number of reasons:

Firstly, it's New Testament truth that we all need to hear it often. Secondly, I love you as a brother or sister in Christ and I want you to become increasingly more free, full of joy and confidence, experiencing more and more of the abundant life which is yours in Christ. The third reason is that if you really believe and act on what I have been unfolding here, sin won't be an issue. Romans 6 says we are no longer slaves to sin. Hebrews 10 tells us that we have been made holy and presented to God, perfect in Christ. Paul sums it up well here:

It was not through the law that Abraham and his offspring received the promise that he would be heir of the world, but through the righteousness that comes by faith. For if those who depend on the law are heirs, faith means nothing and the promise is worthless, because law brings wrath. And where there is no law there is no transgression. Therefore, the promise comes by faith, so that it may be by grace … Romans 4:13–16)

The promise comes by faith so that it may be in accordance with grace. Grace means you don't have to work for it – you get it free. If it's by faith, anyone can do it. Religion says: 'You reach God's highest purposes if you are a good pray-er. You need to live a life of holiness and purity to reach spiritual maturity. You will only stand in the end-times army of God if you clean up your act.' No, no, no! You get it by faith, by believing what God has told you and acting on that, according to grace. Anybody can believe, you don't need super-intelligence; you don't need the right connections; you don't need to be wealthy or good-looking. Anybody can believe God's Word and then act on it.

Jesus' disciples asked Him, 'What must we do to do the works God requires (John 6:28–29)?' Jesus told them, 'The work of God is this: to believe in the One he sent.' This is our primary work – to believe in Jesus. If you want to work hard for God, let that belief be translated into action: become the person you already are in Christ. Belief without action is not belief at all.

Abraham believed God's promise to him, and a son was born. Naaman washed himself in a muddy river and his skin was healed. Paul expressed his wonderfully developed view of God's liberating and all-encompassing grace as he travelled all over, preaching and establishing the church and writing his teaching down which has been preserved for us. All three were given promises which would never have borne fruit if they hadn't participated with God by faith. Part of that work of faith is repenting of those things in which we are trying to achieve for ourselves what God has already given us.

That is why it is so crucial that we understand the full implications of God's grace and all we have in Christ. We need to know deep in our hearts that we are okay because Jesus made us okay, and therefore, 'Jesus plus nothing' is our salvation and our life. That is the only solid foundation for building the church. God will remove any other because anything built on a wrong foundation cannot last.

In the final analysis, if our life is not working, if we are struggling, hurting, suffering physically, emotionally or spiritually, it's not because of our mother or father or anyone else's sin against us. It's not even ultimately because of the secondary sins in our own life. Our problems arise from the primary sin of unbelief. When we know that we are totally, unconditionally loved, accepted and made holy before God and empowered by His free grace as given us in Christ, we are no longer intimidated by anything, either from without or within – even our own sins and shortcomings. We can hand them over to God once and for all.

The Bible is the account of men and women's experiences with God. It is His story, more than ours. God is the central character, the Creator, Author, Hero and Finisher of this long narrative, and as the story unfolds, so does the revelation about Him. From the beginning, He is a God of grace, choosing people and making promises to them, blessing them and keeping His promises despite their failure. Such is His love that He always treats His people with dignity and respect, allowing them to respond to Him by their own choice. Those commended by God in Hebrews 11 are the ones who chose to believe God, take part in His plans, and see the fruit emerge in their lives.

Therefore, since we are surrounded by such a great cloud of witnesses, let us throw off everything that hinders and the sin that so easily entangles. And let us run with perseverance the race marked out for us, fixing our eyes on Jesus, the pioneer and perfector of faith. For the joy set before him he endured the cross, scorning its shame, and sat down at the right hand of the throne of God. Consider him who endured such opposition from sinners, so that you will not grow weary and lose heart. (Hebrews 12:1–3)

Believe, act and receive – it really is that simple.

CHAPTER SEVENTEEN
Grace Permeates our Whole Life

Grace is not a static, passive or abstract concept. Grace is the dynamic, real presence of God that saves you, heals you and empowers you to be all that you were created to be and to do all that God has called you to do. So, in this study we have not just been exploring grace from different angles but discovering ways of participating in that grace and experiencing it personally, and that's important because everybody wants life! The apostle Paul understood this better than anyone:

> But because of his great love for us, God, who is rich in mercy, made us alive with Christ even when we were dead in transgressions – it is by grace you have been saved. And God raised us up with Christ and seated us with him in the heavenly realms in Christ Jesus, in order that in the coming ages he might show the incomparable riches of his grace, expressed in his kindness to us in Christ Jesus. For it is by grace you have been saved, through faith – and this not from yourselves, it is the gift of God – not by works, so that no one can boast. For we are God's handiwork, created in Christ Jesus [and empowered] to do good works, which God prepared in advance for us to do. (Ephesians 2:4–10)

God has created good works for us to do as we experience His empowering presence and become all that we can become and to do all that we can do now as we participate in His grace. When we discern what those good works are which God has prepared for us to do and then, by faith and with courage, step into them, that is when we find we have the power to do exactly what God has called us to in Christ, through Christ and for Christ.

When I look around in the Christian world, I see many people who are perpetually frustrated because they are trying to do something that they apparently don't have any gifting or power to do, or there's no market for it. I see others passively just waiting for something to happen; they're going to be there a long time! But I also see people who have moved gracefully, prayerfully, thoughtfully, intelligently and discerningly into the good works that God has prepared for them and then they have found the grace, the power, to do more! They are truly experiencing the abundant Christian life.

If I were to ask you, when were you saved, how would you respond? Well, there are at least three ways that you could answer which would be correct biblically. You could say, 'I was saved over two thousand years ago on the cross of Christ and it was in the heart of God to save me before the beginning of time. My salvation was conceived and accomplished by God single-handedly. I was saved by grace before I was even born.' That would be a correct answer.

> *So do not be ashamed of the testimony about our Lord or of me his prisoner. Rather, join with me in suffering for the gospel, by the power of God. He has saved us and called us to a holy life – not because of anything we have done but because of his own purpose and grace. This grace was given us in Christ Jesus before the beginning of time ... (2 Timothy 1:8–9)*

Or you could say, 'Well, yes, I was saved a long time ago, but I do not yet fully experience my salvation.' That answer is right also. There is a 'now but not yet' reality as we journey through the kingdom of this world and embrace the kingdom of God more fully.

> *Therefore, with minds that are alert and fully sober, set your hope on the grace to be brought to you when Jesus Christ is revealed at his coming. (1 Peter 1:13)*

You have been saved by grace, but you will not receive the full measure of that saving grace until Jesus returns or you are called home to glory. Salvation is not just the act of getting us into God's kingdom; it is the repairing and healing of everything that is wrong with us. But even that is only partial; we are all going to die. The final healing, the final salvation, comes when Jesus appears at the end of the age.

Or you could say, 'Yes, I have been saved by grace in the past and yes, I will be totally saved when the grace of God is fully revealed at the end, but it's also true that in an ongoing way I am being saved every day.'

> *For the grace of God has appeared that offers salvation to all people. It teaches us to say "No" to ungodliness and worldly passions, and to live self-controlled, upright and godly lives in this present age, while we wait for the blessed hope – the appearing of the glory of our great God and Saviour, Jesus Christ ... (Titus 2:11–13)*

The grace of God teaches us (present tense) to say no to death and yes to life. So, the saving grace of God is also a present reality and it improves the quality of our life day by day as we learn to participate in it. It is present and personal – the power of God in our lives, by the Holy Spirit.

> *Since we have now been justified by his blood, how much more shall we be saved from God's wrath [present continuous tense] through him! For if, when we were God's enemies, we were reconciled to him through the death*

of his Son, how much more, having been reconciled, shall we be saved [present continuous tense, i.e. ongoing] through his life! (Romans 5:9–10)

We were reconciled by His death; we are now constantly (present tense) being saved by His life. Salvation by grace is something that is ongoing. All of life is a grace, and if we respond favourably to that gift and live in an attitude of gratitude, our lives will work. If we don't, they won't, and it really doesn't have a lot to do with circumstances. Let's look at one of Jesus' most confronting parables.

For the kingdom of heaven is like a landowner who went out early in the morning to hire workers for his vineyard. He agreed to pay them a denarius [about a day's wage for a good day's work] for the day and sent them into his vineyard.

About nine in the morning he went out and saw others standing in the marketplace doing nothing. He told them, 'You also go and work in my vineyard, and I will pay you whatever is right. So they went.

He went out again about noon and about three in the afternoon and did the same thing. About five in the afternoon he went out and found still others standing around. He asked them, 'Why have you been standing here all day long doing nothing?'

'Because no one has hired us,' they answered.

"He said to them, 'You also go and work in my vineyard.'

When evening came, the owner of the vineyard said to his foreman, 'Call the workers and pay them their wages, beginning with the last ones hired and going on to the first.'

The workers who were hired about five in the afternoon came and each received a denarius. So when those came who were hired first, they expected to receive more. But each one of them also received a denarius. When they received it, they began to grumble against the landowner 'These who were hired last worked only one hour,' they said, 'and you have made them equal to us who have borne the burden of the work and the heat of the day.'

[13] *"But he answered one of them, 'I am not being unfair to you, friend. Didn't you agree to work for a denarius? Take your pay and go. I want to give the one who was hired last the same as I gave you. Don't I have the right to do what I want with my own money? Or are you envious because I am generous?'*

So the last will be first, and the first will be last. (Matthew 20:1–16)

Now this parable is not about labour and management. This is a parable about the kingdom of God. The landowner is God, and the employees are the rest of us. Let's begin by putting ourselves in the position of the workers he hired first. You set your alarm clock for 4 am (the best time of the day!) so you can be down at the marketplace in time to get a job for the day. You are conscientious, hardworking and industrious. Some days you stand there all day and don't get hired – but you are always back there again the next morning. This day, however, you get hired first thing in the morning and you are grateful for this grace of work. Nobody is obliged to hire you, there is no welfare system, so if you don't work, you don't eat. You're happy that at the end of the day you can go to the market and pick up some food for your family that evening.

You work hard all day and notice that other workers are joining you throughout the day. You probably don't think much about it until pay time. Then the boss does something interesting. He begins by paying the people who turned up last, not the early morning shift workers. However, the real shock comes when you discover that they are getting a full day's wages for only an hour's work! You think, 'Wow! This guy is generous, or he's won lotto, or he's a lousy businessman!'

Who cares? This is great; if he pays that much to those who came last, obviously the all-day workers will get even more. But then the foreman comes around and gives you exactly what you agreed to work for – one day's pay. You're angry, because at that point you compare your lot to someone else's, and on that basis, you determine what is fair or not. So, you protest. 'You've made these men who worked for only one hour, equal to us. It's not fair!'

The boss responds by answering, 'I am not being unfair to you. Didn't you agree to work for exactly what I paid you? Take your money and go – and be grateful. I want to give the man who was hired last the same as I gave you. Don't I have the right to do what I want with my own money? Or are you envious because I am generous?'

'It's not fair!' That is our typical fallen human response when we see other people getting more than we think they deserve and us getting less than we think we deserve. This is a very real part of our sinful nature, this sense of fairness. How many times do parents hear their children say, 'It's not fair?' We don't have to teach our children to stand up for their own rights, do we? They are born with this sense of 'fairness'. What we do have to teach them is to stand up for other people's rights. Watch what happens when you get one child to cut a cake but tell them that the others will choose their piece first. That child becomes extremely skilled in dividing the cake with mathematical precision, so that it's absolutely fair to him or her, the one who chooses last. The problem is, when we become adults, we don't seem to grow out of that desire for an equal lot. What God (the landowner) is saying in this parable is:

'You're saying it's not fair, but you all got a fair day's pay. In fact, work in the first place was a gift! I didn't have to hire you. Yet I did, and I have treated everybody fairly. Now, don't I have the right to do what I want with what is mine?'

Once everybody has been treated fairly, they can no longer demand their rights. The only person in the story who has any rights is God, the one with the resources. Everybody today knows their rights and everybody's an expert on what is fair and unfair as it relates to them. The idea that life itself in any form is a huge, undeserved gift is foreign to most modern minds, including those of many Christians.

The graciousness of God in allowing us to continue breathing each day ought to consume us with gratitude. If life happens to be kinder to one than another, it should not be an occasion for envy or bitterness or this evil sense of things being 'unfair'. This parable was told to make precisely that point. The problem arises because the king chooses to be especially gracious to some over others. Remember this is a story about the kingdom of God. God is treating some with more grace, more favour and more mercy than others.

What we need to learn is that God doesn't treat us all equally. If you think that, you're going to go through life frustrated and upset and wondering what in the world is going wrong. Understand this: *God treats everyone fairly – but not equally.*

That is what irritated the Pharisees so much about Jesus. He was a friend of sinners. Jesus treated the prostitutes, the criminals and the tax collectors as if they had gotten up at four in the morning and worked hard all day long and been good citizens, when in actual fact, they came in at the last hour and said, 'Hey Jesus, we've been really bad, but if it's okay, can we hang out with you?' They haven't 'earned' God's friendship, but Jesus gives it to them as a free gift. And that really gets up the Pharisees' noses – then and now!

That is what this parable of the workers is all about. We have to get this, or we are going to be miserable all our life. Grace is not earned, and it is never deserved. God shows mercy, favour and abundant grace towards some more than others, and many people see this as unfair. This goes against some deep sense of justice that the world instils in us. We try so hard to treat our children equally and fairly. Why doesn't God give it a try? I don't know. All I know is that the Bible reveals the ways of God, and this is the way God operates.

Jesus' mission involves healing the sick, binding up the broken hearted and releasing the captives from Satan's grasp. He has called us and empowered us to join Him in His mission because it is not God's will that any suffer physically or emotionally or spiritually because of the effects of sin. The victory that Christ had over sin He also had over the effects of sin. When we start taking that fact seriously, we'll see God in action in some very special ways.

However, regardless of the movement of God powerfully in all kinds of ways, your height, the colour of your eyes, your ethnic heritage etc. is the way God intended to make you. Your basic IQ is pretty much what God intended for you. God hasn't treated us all equally. He's made some more attractive (by human standards) than others. He's made some much more intelligent than others. He's allowed for certain life chances to be given to some but not to others. That's just the way life is. That's just the way God is. Those early workers were happy until they saw the grace which was shown to someone else. I have prayed for years that my children will grow out of the childish and destructive idea which says, 'It's not fair! I haven't been treated equally to someone else.'

Sadly, many adults have not matured past that childish perception. This attitude is potentially present in every one of us. It's called envy or jealousy, and it's evil and destructive. Those who allow such an attitude to rest in their hearts for any length of time will be consumed by it and I know of no stronger barrier to our experience of the real presence and power of God than this 'it's not fair' attitude.

If the enemy of God can keep us comparing ourselves to those who seem to be more blessed than us, then Satan will effectively blind us to those who have so much less. We need to ask God to break that bondage as we choose to turn the other way towards the millions of people in this world who have far less than us.

Next time we start losing sleep over our financial problems, we need to think of the thousands of people who maim their own children just so they can beg for money and stay alive. Next time we start complaining about our job, we should sit outside an employment agency to see the despair of those who cannot find work. As we think about those who have so much less, we should say, 'But for the grace of God, there go I.'

What about in the church? You might see people who have been given gifts that you envy. You might see people moving into leadership positions ahead of you. You might see people being given favour or responsibilities that you would like. You might see people forming relationships with others whom you desire to be close to but from whom you have no response.

Instead of thinking about the 'fairness' of all that, you should compare yourself to those outside the kingdom, not inside, then fall to your knees and worship the One Who rescued you and reconciled you, and be thankful you are even here in the first place. Anything else is a bonus from God, by His grace! We will never stop those comparisons coming to our attention – Satan has a steady supply for us; however, we do have a choice in how to respond. Don't let the 'it's not fair' thought even enter your mind. Don't let the blessings of others cause envy, jealousy, bitterness or resentment in you. God treats us all fairly, but not equally.

In Exodus 33:19, God says, 'I will show mercy to whom I will show mercy.' He created and bestowed life on us in the first place and He is free to give us as much or as little of life's blessing that He chooses. That's His right. You might be thinking that this sounds like fatalism. It sounds like God decided all this at the beginning of the world and there's nothing we can do to change it. Please don't let that thought stay in your mind because it isn't true. God does not sit in heaven at the beginning of the week and say, 'Okay, now, this week everybody with surnames beginning with A to L are going receive my blessings.' There's nothing arbitrary or fatalistic about God's blessings.

God gives to whom He chooses whatever He chooses, but He often chooses those who influence His choice. The first way that you can influence God's free grace and mercy towards you and those you love is profoundly simple: you ask for it. In Luke 11, we are told by Jesus to keep on seeking, keep on knocking, keep on asking. He reminds us that our heavenly Father is good, and He knows how to give good gifts to His children. Jesus said, '… my Father will give you whatever you ask in my name (John 16:23).' We exercise faith by persistent asking. James says in his letter, 'You have not because you ask not (James 4:2).' That's one reason why your life may not be working as it should: you have not asked God persistently and faithfully.

Secondly, God often shows mercy to those who are responsible with it. You find throughout the Bible statements like, 'To him who has little, more will be given. To the one who is faithful with a little, more is given.'

That's the positive side of it. The negative side is that love suffers long –
but it doesn't suffer forever. We see in the Old Testament where Israel
abused God's grace and blessings. He sent them prophets and judges, and
they experienced warnings and renewals. His love suffered long, but
sooner or later, because of their habitual irresponsibility with His grace,
He withdrew His protection and they found themselves in exile. While
we now live under the New Covenant where the judgement of God fell
on Jesus, the principle is still valid. God shows mercy towards whom He
chooses to show mercy, but He tends to show more mercy to those who
are responsible with it.

Thirdly, God also shows mercy to those who pass it on. There are
many dear children of God who desperately desire to experience the grace
and mercy of God in their lives in a richer and fuller way, but who block
that from happening by being so full of self-pity. When we are no longer
grateful for the life we have (no matter how that compares to someone
else's life), we can shut off God's mercy and grace (in our experience) and
become bitter in our soul and unhappy in our spirit. It is the most effective
and sure way of closing our heart to God and ensuring that we can no
longer hear from the Holy Spirit. Self-pity is often triggered by envy; that
is, comparing your lot in life to someone else's and concluding 'it's not
fair!' Such attitudes are deadly in our daily experience of God's grace.
They don't change how He feels about us, but they sure change how we
feel about Him and about ourselves and others.

These attitudes are also contagious. We teach our children and others
by our example to compare and complain, which leads us to doubt God
and envy others. Our very life's breath is a grace, a gift, and God delights
in showing mercy to those who pass it on to others. Those people who are
always sharing the abundant grace of God in their lives with others, who
are building one another up and spurring each other on to love and good
works, these are the people who invariably experience more and more of
God's grace in their own lives. There is an observable reality in the world:
if you become a channel for God's blessing, He entrusts you with more. If
you shut that off towards your neighbour or your family or your church,
it will dry up in you also.

We see many examples of this in the world today. Joni Eareckson-
Tada, crippled in a diving accident as a young person, had a choice. She
could have compared herself with the millions of people who seemed to
have a better life than her, but she chose to thank God that she had a life
at all. As a result, she became a channel of blessing to others and found
more and more of God's grace and mercy filling her and flowing through

her. She has had an enormous impact on millions of people around the world because she was able move past 'it's not fair' and embrace God's gift of life.

Sadly, there are countless Christians who have so much of life's blessings and freedom, who are abundantly rich by comparison to the majority of the world's population, yet they have become bitter because of some struggle or lack in their life. Whether physical or emotional illness, material or financial need, they see life as unfair and get angry with God for giving them such a raw deal. A lot of us never grow out of feeling that life is unfair. How must God feel when we dare even question what He has given us in life, let alone withdraw from Him or accuse Him or feel that He has robbed us in some way. But for the grace of God, we'd all be lost. Our very breath is a gift of God's grace. Some of us need a regular dose of Romans 9:20: 'But who are you, O man, to talk back to God? Shall what is formed say to him who formed it, "Why did you make me like this?"'

I am not saying you should accept disease or pain and struggles without crying out to God for healing. I am talking about your *attitude* in those situations. Are you consumed by self-pity, bitterness or resentment, thinking that life (or God) is unfair because of what you are enduring? Are you praying for God to heal you or bless you because it's your right, because you deserve it? Or are you just incredibly grateful that God, in His infinite love and mercy, chose to call you into His kingdom and give you the gift of eternal life? Does your heart and mind rejoice as you try to comprehend that He has seated you at His right hand in the heavenly places and He loves you with the same everlasting love that He poured out upon His own Son? Are you so overwhelmed by His grace that He even allows you to live so rich and so free compared to millions of your fellow pilgrims on this planet? Do you see every new day as a fresh gift of God's grace, a privilege, and never a right?

We each have a choice how we feel in this life. We can cry 'unfair' and let envy, jealousy, bitterness, resentment, doubt and fear grip our hearts, or we can allow the Spirit of God to enable us to see our life as it is, struggles and all, as a gift of God's amazing grace regardless of our circumstances. I pray that God would open up your heart and unburden you of anything that resembles self-pity, anything that is making you ungrateful, envious or bitter in any way, so that you can experience what it is to receive life as a grace from God – every day, all day.

The grace of God teaches us to say no to death and yes to life. All of life is a grace to us. Our response of thankfulness and praise to God, frees us from the self-focused, 'it's not fair' attitude of comparison and complaint. We are happy to agree that grace is neither earned nor deserved when we are the recipients of some special grace, but our hearts are tested in how we respond to the grace shown to someone else. When we make comparisons or become absorbed by self-pity, we are in effect judging God and what He chooses to do. Nothing will block our experience of the grace and presence of God more quickly.

We should all take a fresh look at Who God is, all that He has done for us and all that He has blessed us with, and we will be overwhelmed by gratitude and released in praise and worship. Our lives will then become fountains of grace, mercy and blessing to others. Then, just maybe, Jesus will finally be able to build His church through us.

CHAPTER EIGHTEEN
How Then Shall We Live?

If our salvation and eternal life is based on what Jesus did and does - not on what we do – the obvious question which must arise at some point in time is, why work if it's free? If the workers in the parable we looked at in the last chapter can arrive at the end of the day and receive the same wage as those who started work at first light, what is the point of getting up early and working hard all day? Why should we pick up our cross and follow Jesus? Why should we respond to the many exhortations and pleas in the New Testament to walk in holiness and purity? Why work out our salvation in fear and trembling? Why strive to live up to a standard that has already been achieved for us in Jesus and credited to us by God's amazing grace?

The apostle Paul gives us one answer in his first letter to the Corinthians. I have mentioned these verses many times already in this book, but they are important enough to examine again in light of the question before us. I believe this is perhaps the key statement from the Bible in our whole understanding of grace.

> *For I am the least of the apostles and do not even deserve to be called an apostle, because I persecuted the church of God. (1 Corinthians 15:9)*

He knows that if he had to be good enough for God, then he was out of the race!

> *But by the grace of God I am what I am … (1 Corinthians 15:10a)*

He didn't do anything to deserve this. He is an apostle by the grace of God …

> *… and his grace to me was not without effect. No, I worked harder than all of them – yet not I, but the grace of God that was with me. (1 Corinthians 15:10b)*

God's grace had its effect in him. Paul seems to suggest that a deeper appreciation of grace inspires hard work and empowers us to pick up our cross and follow Jesus and take the ministry of Jesus into the world. Grace causes that work to be a joyous, free offering. It makes the giving of our money such a joy – a liberating experience of gratitude. In fact, grace impacts every area of our life – or at least, it should. This is not surprising if we understand grace to be 'the empowering presence of God'. It stands to reason that the presence of God in us will have an effect. With that understanding as a backdrop, let's look at this very reasonable question: Why work, if it's free?

Firstly, because you love the person who has loved you. This is as profound as it is simple. God loved us to the bitter end, and love begets love. You will do things you never dreamed of before when the love of God really hits home deep within your heart. Fear of punishment or expectations placed upon you can never have that effect. We want to freely respond in love and service when we are impacted by God's love. I believe one reason many people don't love God more is that they have not yet comprehended the height, width, breadth and depth of God's love for them, as Paul prayed we would in Ephesians 3. It is not that we are bad people with no love to give, but the magnitude of God's love has not yet taken root in our hearts or minds. When it does, it will change every area of our life – that's a promise!

… God's kindness is intended to lead you to repentance. (Romans 2:4)

The threat of law and punishment has never worked and never will work. It will never make people good or willingly obedient. It will never make them love God more.

Preaching law simply cannot and does not produce joy, gratitude and hard work in people. To make God's free grace conditional may make people work harder and do more for God and for the church for a while, but it's not the good news of Jesus Christ – it's not the gospel! Like it or not, God has declared that it's free and when you understand grace in all its truth, you'll be so free that no one will be able to manipulate you or intimidate you again. Your response to God will be a free response.

The second reason why we should work hard in the kingdom of God is because it's enjoyable. I know that sounds a bit simple and 'unspiritual', but it's one of the major reasons why I do what I do. For me, the ministry of Jesus Christ is beyond compare. It's not easy – don't ever let anyone tell you it is – but it's enjoyable. There is nothing more satisfying than seeing the power of God's love change a human life right in front of your eyes. When you get to see God work in people around you, it is the most incredible experience known in this life.

The third reason why we should work hard for God and give freely of our time, talent and resources is for the rewards of doing so. I'm not talking about acceptance; we cannot work for acceptance. That's given to us freely in Jesus Christ. However, the Bible does say that we can, and will, work for rewards.

By the grace God has given me, I laid a foundation as a wise builder, and someone else is building on it. But each one should build with care. For no one can lay a foundation other than the one already laid, which is Christ Jesus. (1 Corinthians 3:10–11)

You cannot work for your salvation. You cannot build your own foundation in the kingdom of God. Your foundation is Jesus Christ, and you can't lose that. (You can now breathe a sigh of relief and praise God!) But if you build on that foundation, you're not adding to your acceptance, but you are leaving the imprint of your own personality on the work of Christ. Look at the next verses:

If anyone builds on this foundation using gold, silver, costly stones, wood, hay or straw, their work will be shown for what it is, because the Day will bring it to light. It will be revealed with fire, and the fire will test the quality of each person's work. If what has been built survives, the builder will receive a reward. If it is burned up, the builder will suffer loss [the loss of their reward], but yet will be saved – even though only as one escaping through the flames. (1 Corinthians 3:12–15)

He will be saved, but with the smell of smoke on him. It's entirely up to us whether we build on that foundation that Jesus has laid in our lives. Don't we want to work hard to bring Him something? Will we have anything to lay at His feet? Will there be any blessing with which we can honour Him? Some scars on our bodies or on our hearts for having served Him? Some work which says, 'I know this doesn't buy me acceptance, but this is my love offering of gratitude to you. It cost me, but who cares! My salvation cost You so much more.'?

Our good works don't need to be heroic. Jesus said, 'If you give a cup of water in My name you shall not lose your reward.' Concerning the widow who gave those two insignificant little coins, Jesus said, 'This is great, this will be remembered, this deserves a reward.' It doesn't have to be significant in other people's eyes. If it's done for Jesus, from the heart, it's precious.

Paul said, 'I am the least of all the apostles, I am what I am by the grace of God', but in the end, he said, 'I have fought the good fight, I have run the race; I have kept the faith (2 Timothy 4:7). I've done a really great job of preaching the gospel. My churches are standing all over Asia as a crown for me. There is a crown laid up for me'(2 Timothy 4:8).'

When the going gets tough, the rewards can often keep us going. Even though this ministry is the most enjoyable thing in the world, the going still gets tough! There is a real live enemy out there who is seeking to devour us and drag us down and away from God. Listen to Paul again:

Therefore, we do not lose heart. Though outwardly we are wasting away, yet inwardly we are being renewed day by day. (2 Corinthians 4:16)

This is a man who was shipwrecked and beaten and jailed and had many attempts on his life and was finally tortured to death.

For our light and momentary troubles are achieving for us an eternal glory that far outweighs them all. So, we fix our eyes not on what is seen, but on what [reward] is unseen, since what is seen is temporary, but what is unseen [reward] is eternal. (2 Corinthians 4:17–18)

Paul was motivated by the eternal rewards on the horizon. If you have problems with that, then let me tell you that Jesus did exactly the same thing in the garden of Gethsemane. Jesus looked beyond the suffering, the humiliation, the alienation from His Father and death itself. He looked beyond the pain of ministry to the reward of faithful ministry. We read about it in Hebrews:

… fixing our eyes on Jesus, the pioneer and perfecter of faith. For the joy set before him he endured the cross, scorning its shame, and sat down at the right hand of the throne of God. Consider him who endured such opposition from sinners, so that you will not grow weary and lose heart. (Hebrews 12:2–3)

For the joy set before Him, Jesus endured the cross. If you don't think that Jesus was rewarded for His ministry by the Father, then you need to think again. If your ministry or your work for the Lord isn't inspired by an overwhelming sense of God's love for you, or if your work for the Lord isn't inspired because it's enjoyable, then look to the rewards – it's entirely biblical and right.

A lot of the 'Christian' or 'spiritual' work that is done in the church today is not prompted by these motives. Sadly, too much of what is done can be prompted by something that is left over from the law and punishment of the Old Covenant. It is motivated by what people, or even God, might think of us if we don't do what is expected. I am doing everything I can to take that pressure off you in this book so that anything and everything you do will be a free response to God's love. If your good works for Him is not motivated by a positive reason, the Bible calls them dead works.

For example, most Christians would agree that Bible reading and prayer are important components of the Christian faith, but they have become a kind of 'law' for so many people. There are lots of good reasons why we should pray and study the Bible. However, we should never, ever, do anything, especially those two things, in order to get even with our tortured conscience or to be accepted by God or others! Jesus already prayed enough for you with respect to your relationship with God. His prayers and His knowledge of the Word have been credited to you when you believed; they are part of the free gift of God's grace.

Your standing in Christ, your relationship with God is not, and cannot, be affected by how much or how little you read the Bible or pray. Your quality of life and your intimacy with God will be greatly impacted by those things, but never your position in Christ, before God. Of course, behind this whole world of manipulation and dead works is the devil himself.

Then war broke out in heaven. Michael and his angels fought against the dragon, and the dragon and his angels fought back. But he was not strong enough, and they lost their place in heaven. The great dragon was hurled down – that ancient serpent called the devil, or Satan, who leads the whole world astray [one of Satan's key ministries is leading people astray by deception]. He was hurled to the earth, and his angels with him.

Then I heard a loud voice in heaven say:

"Now have come the salvation and the power and the kingdom of our God, and the authority of his Messiah.

For the accuser of our brothers and sisters, who accuses them before our God, day and night, has been hurled down." (Revelation 12:7–10)

Satan's primary ministry is accusation and the way he does that is through your conscience. Your conscience will never be fully converted in this life. It's the part of you that is wedded permanently to the Old Covenant. Satan uses it to punish you for breaking the law. Your conscience isn't evil, not at all; it just happens to be the place where the enemy of God does his best work!

The devil can't get at us theologically if we know the truth. We know that there is no condemnation for those who are in Christ Jesus, so he gets at us through our conscience at the 'feeling' and emotional level, through accusation. We may know that truth but not experience it. If we don't know how to deal with our conscience, we will suffer no matter what we believe about grace. As a result, we will launch, more often than not, into dead religious works.

The real problem with dead works is that they lead to dead ends. You can't do enough to get even with your conscience because there will always be something wrong with your motives. If you do manage to do something well, the devil accuses you of pride and drags you down again. You're damned if you do, and you're damned if you don't. That's why the only remedy for a sick church and a sick society is the unedited, pure gospel of God's free grace. The answer to the Accuser and your accusing conscience is the blood of Christ.

> They triumphed over him by the blood of the Lamb and by the word of their testimony … (Revelation 12:11)

We overcome the accuser by the blood of the Lamb. Put simply: in the Bible, blood always means death. The blood of a sacrificial lamb is death on behalf of guilty parties the lamb died for. That's true in the Old Covenant and that's true in the New Covenant. So, for you, as someone under the New Covenant, the blood of Jesus, shed for you, silences the accuser. The accuser will say, 'You have sinned. You have not obeyed the law of God. You must be punished.' Your conscience says yes, and up to that point you can agree with your conscience. Remember, there is nothing you can do to get even with your conscience. You can't feel bad enough or sorry enough for your sins. God hates sin! All of God's wrath was poured out on His Son, and the blood that flowed from the wounds of Jesus demonstrates that all the accusations that come against you are null and void. Those sins have already been punished. You can now deal with your conscience by speaking truth to it: 'The blood of Christ cleanses me from all sin and there is now no condemnation. Therefore, no accusation is going to take root in me.'

Now you may believe in your heart that the grace and power of God is free, but you will need to constantly apply that truth to your conscience. Let's look at Hebrews again:

> But when Christ came as high priest of the good things that are now already here, he went through the greater and more perfect tabernacle that is not made with human hands, that is to say, is not a part of this creation. He did not enter by means of the blood of goats and calves; but he entered the Most Holy Place once for all by his own blood, having obtained eternal redemption. The blood of goats and bulls and the ashes of a heifer sprinkled on those who are ceremonially unclean sanctify them so that they are outwardly clean. How much more, then, will the blood of Christ, who through the eternal Spirit offered himself unblemished to God, cleanse our consciences from acts that lead to death, so that we may serve the living God! (Hebrews 9:11–14)

Our consciences will be cleansed from dead works; the compulsion to work to get even with our conscience will be gone. Let's skip to the next chapter:

Therefore, brothers and sisters, since we have confidence to enter the Most Holy Place by the blood of Jesus, by a new and living way opened for us through the curtain, that is, his body, and since we have a great priest over the house of God, let us draw near to God with a sincere heart and with the full assurance that faith brings, having our hearts sprinkled to cleanse us from a guilty conscience .... (Hebrews 10:19–22a)

You cannot believe hard enough, or study hard enough, or memorise well enough to give you assurance, because your conscience will undermine your assurance. Your conscience works at the emotional level, out of reach of sound theology.

... and having our bodies washed with pure water. Let us hold unswervingly to the hope we profess, for he who promised is faithful. And let us consider how we may spur one another on towards love and good deeds ... (Hebrews 10: 22b–24)

We've come full circle. Now you're free and your conscience is free. You no longer do things to earn the acceptance of God or man. You now do things freely. So, let's spur one another on to love and good works. Now that we are completely cleansed, let's get to work. Why work if it's free? Paul said, 'By the grace of God I am what I am, and his grace to me was not without effect. No, I worked harder than all of them - yet not I, but the grace of God that was with me.'

God sets us so free that we do not have to respond to Him in any way at all. Paul experienced that amazing free gift of God at work in his heart, so he was thrilled to be where God was and to be doing what God was doing. He was inspired and overjoyed to be a part of broadcasting the news of God's amazing grace to everyone. Love for God overflows and expresses itself in every part of life. When we open ourselves up to experience His overwhelming love and His amazing grace, we will be changed.

There are many great reasons to work hard in the kingdom of God. God calls us into His joy. He wants us to be in relationship with Him and to enjoy His presence in everything we do. He also tells us that He rewards us for kingdom work. but He never, ever wants us to feel obligated to perform to any standard to win favour with Him, to ease our conscience or to please other people. Grace will have its effect on any heart that is prepared to freely accept all that God gives to us freely.

CHAPTER NINETEEN
Effective Grace

In Galatians 5:1, the apostle Paul reminds us that it is for freedom that Christ has set us free and so we must learn how to trust the Holy Spirit and operate within the freedom that God has given us in Christ. Throughout this book, I have been encouraging you to respond to God's love by loving Him back in all ways, but without the shame, the guilt, without obligation or any manipulation. There are great reasons for allowing God's grace to have an effect in us and for working hard: it glorifies God and releases abundant life in us.

In this chapter, I want to examine this further as we look at one of Jesus' most challenging parables. This is the classic 'guilt and manipulation' parable (as preached by many) but an understanding of God's grace in all its truth will set us free from any fear or shame that we may have associated with this story. We have called this story 'the parable of the talents', and this is Matthew's version in the RSV translation:

> For it will be as when a man going on a journey called his servants and entrusted to them his property; to one he gave five talents, to another two, to another one, to each according to his ability. Then he went away. He who had received the five talents went at once and traded with them; and he made five talents more. So also, he who had the two talents made two talents more. But he who had received the one talent went and dug in the ground and hid his master's money.

> Now after a long time the master of those servants came and settled accounts with them. And he who had received the five talents came forward, bringing five talents more, saying, 'Master, you delivered to me five talents; here I have made five talents more.' His master said to him, 'Well done, good and faithful servant; you have been faithful over a little, I will set you over much; enter into the joy of your master.' (Matthew 25:14–23)

That is what all true believers live for. If you have been touched by the love of the Father and you have received so much that the only response is sheer gratitude, then to hear Him say, 'Well done, good and faithful servant' is the goal and purpose of life and the final reward you long for.

> And he also who had the two talents came forward, saying, 'Master, you delivered to me two talents; here I have made two talents more.' His master said to him, 'Well done, good and faithful servant; you have been faithful

over a little, I will set you over much; enter into the joy of your master.' He also who had received the one talent came forward, saying, 'Master, I knew you to be a hard man, reaping where you did not sow, and gathering where you did not winnow; so I was afraid, and I went and hid your talent in the ground. Here you have what is yours.' But his master answered him, 'You wicked and slothful servant! You knew that I reap where I have not sowed, and gather where I have not winnowed? Then you ought to have invested my money with the bankers, and at my coming I should have received what was my own with interest. So take the talent from him, and give it to him who has the ten talents. For to everyone who has will more be given, and he will have abundance; but from him who has not, even what he has will be taken away.' (Matthew 25:23–29)

This is a very clear warning against apathy, slothfulness and laziness in the church, among Christians. This is a sharp rebuke to those who squander and hide God's grace, or who would put it out of reach of somebody else. On the surface we see a good news/bad news story about three servants. Two of them perform well and get a raise and one of them performs poorly and gets fired. That's on the surface. If you dig deeper, you will find this story is really about what God's grace does in you once you receive it; or rather, how you respond to God's grace once it is given. It demonstrates that receiving God's grace can be exciting or it can be dangerous, but it will never be passive; it affects you. God's grace pulls you more vitally into the joy and happiness of the Master, or it pushes you out of it altogether.

This parable is about how we enter into the fullness of God's joy and participate more in His grace. We are made happy and freer by embracing God's grace more fully. The world says, 'If you ride, then you have to pay.' The kingdom of God says, 'You get to ride free, and if you like it , you get to do it all over again.' Let's unpack this passage a little more.

Again, it will be like a man going on a journey, who called his servants and entrusted his property to them. To one he gave five talents of money, to another two talents, and to another one talent, each according to his ability. Then he went on his journey. (Matthew 25:14–15)

The master entrusted his property to his servants. He gave gifts – they hadn't earned them. He trusted them and paid them the highest compliment He could have. He said, 'Here's my property; you take the initiative with it.' He treated them with respect, and according to their ability.

The man who had received the five talents went at once and put his money to work and gained five more. So also, the one with the two talents gained two more. But the man who had received the one talent went off, dug a hole in the ground and hid his master's money. (Matthew 25:16–18)

So, one man is given five talents, and he immediately goes to work. The New Testament translators don't do justice to the original text at times. The Greek word which has been translated here as 'at once' actually means 'immediately lunged'. It is the image of a runner down on his hands waiting for the starter's gun. The attitude that is conveyed here is that this guy was ready to go for it even before he got the money. Perhaps that's why he got five talents. So, too, the man with two talents. The same word is not used in the Greek, but it does say that he did what the first guy did, so it's strongly implied that he also 'immediately lunged' into his new investment. The power of grace has its own effect. It multiplies simply because that's what grace does.

This is the heart of this story. God lavishly pours out His estate on us. He freely gives grace to all of us according to our ability to handle it and most people say, 'Let's go for it!' But some receive God's grace, freedom and gifts yet they don't trust Him. They receive God's grace; they dig a hole and bury it where they can't enjoy it and where nobody else can either. God's grace is ours, free, and He expects us to do something with it.

After a long time [sometimes this stuff isn't decided overnight and you've got to be willing day in and day out to work with God's grace] the master of those servants returned and settled accounts with them. The man who had received the five talents brought the other five. 'Master,' he said, 'you entrusted me with five talents. See, I have gained five more.' His master replied, 'Well done, good and faithful servant! You have been faithful with a few things; I will put you in charge of many things. Come and share your master's happiness!' (Matthew 25:19–21)

The same thing happened with the man with two talents. They both said, 'You entrusted me. You gave me this grace. I gained more.' Now some may think this is not a very humble attitude. Some may think a real servant would never take credit for anything. But who ultimately takes the credit here, the master or the servant? Let's look again.

Here we have the first servant paying tribute to the grace of the Master. '*You* entrusted *me*. Thank you. I am so glad that you gave me the dignity and the joy of trusting me with Your precious heritage. It was all yours and you gave it to me.' Then he goes right on in the same breath to say, 'and I multiplied it! I made it grow. I invested it and I have a whole lot more to bring back to you.'

So, who did it? The answer is both. The point is that we do it together. Jesus is not sitting in heaven thinking, 'Gee, I wonder if they're going to steal my glory. I'd better shut that down!' He is not stupid, neurotic or insecure. He says, 'Well done! You good and faithful servant, you did a great job with that. Here, have some more!'

In Luke's account of this parable, the servant says, 'Master, your talent has gained five more.' The language behind this is in what they call the 'middle voice'. We don't have it in the English language, so we lose the true meaning. The middle voice is not just something I do (active) and it's not something that is done to me or through me (passive); rather, it is something that God initiates and that I take hold of with my personality and run with it and make it a reality in my life and others. It's the middle voice of participation and partnership. Now guess what? The whole kingdom of God is in the middle voice! God initiates stuff and then asks us to get in there, get involved and put our personal stamp on His work. It's wonderful, it's amazing that He would do that –but that's why we call this 'good news'! What really glorifies God is men and women fully alive. He longs to say, 'Well done!', because that glorifies Him, and it blesses the children He loves.

This is the crazy thing about following Jesus and enjoying His grace. If you like it, if you put it to work and enjoy it and pass it on, you get more! The reward for good work is not retirement; it's more work to do. The work is also fun; it's a joy. It's the most fulfilling work known to us. The work is its own reward. That's what the parable says. 'I'll put you in charge of more and more, and your joy will increase!'

So, the point of this parable is this: if you like life and participate in it, you'll get more life. One of the reasons I will never push people into ministries or try to get people to do things in the church is because the work is its own reward and the workers to whom God says, 'Well done' are those who willingly respond to His call, not peer pressure or a sense of obligation. They freely accept God's invitation to partner with Him in His mission and ministry.

Now let me say this to everyone in the church who is currently involved in a ministry of some kind: you can knock yourself out in that ministry. You can do whatever you like – lose sleep over it if you like – but at the end of the day, the church won't owe you anything. Do it for Jesus, or don't do it at all.

The man with the two talents also came. 'Master,' he said, 'you entrusted me with two talents, see, I have gained two more.' His master replied, 'Well done, good and faithful servant! You have been faithful with a few things; I will put you in charge of many things. Come and share in your master's happiness.' (Matthew 25:22–23)

Whether you're a big star in the eyes of the church, a little star or no star at all, the reward is the same: you get to see God look you right in the eyes and say, 'Well done!' All you've got to do is pass on what you have.

Then the man who had received the one talent came. 'Master,' he said, 'I knew that you were a hard man, harvesting where you have not sown and gathering where you have not scattered seed. So, I was afraid and went out and hid your talent in the ground. See, here is what belongs to you.' His master replied, 'You wicked, lazy servant! So, you knew that I harvest where I have not sown and gather where I have not scattered seed? Well then, you should have put my money on deposit with the bankers, so that when I returned, I would have received it back with interest.' (Matthew 25:24–26)

He didn't even have to work! All he had to do was get it into circulation, but spitefully and fearfully he stuck it in the ground. If you've been to the Middle East, you know that the ground is ninety per cent rock. To dig a hole in the ground requires some work! There was a determined effort to hide that talent – that gift – to take grace out of circulation where nobody could get it. So, the Master says, 'Take the talent away from him and give it to the man who has ten.' The one who had the most ended up with even more! The dangerous thing about the grace of God is that if you hide it, if you suppress it, it will end up exposing you.

Your concept of God will run your life. That servant saw the master as a bad, mean–spirited person (which of course, he wasn't), and what you think of God will determine the quality of your life. You will never find a clearer example of that than here in this parable. This man had a misunderstanding of who God is. He was a Pharisee, or had been abused by Pharisees, and so he saw the master as a judge, an oppressor, one who ties up heavy burdens and puts them on his back and doesn't lift a finger to help. He wasn't about to risk losing the talent, so down it went, underground where it was safe and sound. But the New Testament is very clear about this: if you receive, you are supposed to pass it on. We are called to be channels, not reservoirs.

If you receive forgiveness, like the servant in Matthew 18 that was forgiven a huge debt, then you need to pass it on to others. If you receive a little joy, then smile at someone; make their life a little happier. If you receive some freedom, get off someone else's back for a while. If you've been blessed financially, help someone with it. And if you do, you'll get more! The Bible is very clear - if you sow sparingly, you will reap sparingly.

169

Now you don't do all of this in order to get more; you do it because you love Jesus (no other reason is valid), and He responds by giving you more. I believe you can have all that you want of anything, provided you don't keep it. When you give it away, you keep getting more – so you can give that away too! If you read what the text says, you can't even get guilt, shame or manipulation out of one of the strongest parables Jesus uttered. What the text actually says is, 'If you like life, you get more. If you don't like life, you don't get it. It's that simple. It's not whether you win or lose, get five per cent or a hundred per cent return; it's your attitude towards God's grace and gifts that determines whether you are a good and faithful servant or not . If your attitude is, 'Let's go for it!', prepare to enter more and more into the joy of the Lord.

The parable of the talents talks about what we do with what we have been given. God treats us with dignity and great honour as He gives us responsibility with His treasures. He gives according to His grace and generosity and in accordance with who He has created us to be. His gifting always comes with His enabling. Our eager and passionate response to His grace delights Him. He is glorified when we take Him at His word and throw ourselves unreservedly into the life He gives us. This is our highest purpose – mature fullness of relationship with God.

When we understand and accept grace in all its truth, we won't ask whether we have to work. We will be good and faithful servants without even noticing it! We will just be having the best time of our lives!

CHAPTER TWENTY
Grace and the Mission of Christ

In an earlier chapter, I suggested that there are two things which all people want in life more than anything else. This applies to everybody, those outside or inside the church. The first is acceptance. You want to be accepted as you are and for who you are. You don't want to have to jump through anybody's hoops or meet anyone's expectations to be accepted. Everyone wants this unconditional acceptance. We all want somebody to know us and affirm us as we are. Jesus Christ Himself gives you that; that is good news.

The second thing, paradoxically, is that you don't want to stay the way you are. You want to change; you want to grow and improve; you want to mature. We have already spent a bit of time on this concept, but I want to explore how this acceptance changes us and makes us more like the people we want to be, and the people God created us to be. God's acceptance works a gracious change in us. It's not something that is forced upon us or something that we have to strain to make happen. It's a change that comes from our very essence.

By responding to God's acceptance of us, we are changed from the inside out. The love and grace of God revealed to us in Christ has its own transforming power. The apostle Paul embraced this life-changing power and when he did, he couldn't help sharing it with people. Let's see what he wrote to the believers in the Ephesus:

> I became a servant of this gospel by the gift of God's grace given me through the working of his power. Although I am less than the least of all the Lord's people, this grace was given me: to preach to the Gentiles the boundless riches of Christ, and to make plain to everyone the administration of this mystery, which for ages past was kept hidden in God, who created all things. His intent was that now, through the church, the manifold wisdom of God should be made known to the rulers and authorities in the heavenly realms, according to his eternal purpose which he accomplished in Christ Jesus our Lord. In him and through faith in him we may approach God with freedom and confidence. (Ephesians 3:7–12)

Paul says this heavy burden to preach the gospel with all his might came to him as a gift of God's grace. God was gracious in giving Paul the opportunity to share this good news with even the Gentiles. Paul realised that this good news, this loving acceptance of God through His only Son

Jesus, is for *everyone*. He was called to make it plain to everyone. Now, can you imagine an orthodox Jew getting excited about sharing the good news with the Gentiles? This would have come as a big surprise to a man who was raised in a community that said, 'We are in and everybody else is out.'

Paul got excited firstly because God accepted him. Even though he had persecuted the church, he was loved and accepted by God and that grace impacted Paul and changed Him. So, he couldn't wait to tell everybody else! Paul discovered that the accepting grace of God was not just for him but for the whole world. This good news doesn't come written in the sky or on a banner from heaven or in a voice booming through the heart of the earth; it comes through Jesus Christ and the church that bears His name.

The good news, which was mysteriously hidden for all the preceding ages, was revealed by the grace of God as a joyous, spontaneous expression of life. You know that grace is doing its work in you when you accept and rejoice in God's unconditional love for you, and you find that you want to pass it on to somebody else.

That is real evangelism, and I will never exhort anyone to get out there and give away something that has not first impacted their life. I will never intimidate someone into performing some evangelistic duty. If the love and grace of God does not impact someone's life sufficiently that they are compelled from within to share this incredible news with others, then they need to read this book! They need to keep listening, keep asking, seeking and knocking, keep doing whatever it takes until they get it! Because their witnessing will not be effective, and it will not be honouring to God unless it comes from a deep, personal reality and experience of His grace.

We overcome the enemy by the blood of Jesus and the word of our testimony – not someone else's. Paul tells us that 'the love of God constrains us' to speak the truth. It comes from a reality within us. It's not a task we perform out of duty. John says a similar thing in his first letter.

> *Dear friends, let us love one another, for love comes from God. Everyone who loves has been born of God and knows God. Whoever does not love does not know God, because God is love. (1 John 4:7–8)*

Whoever does not love does not know God. God is love and if you've been loved by God, you know God and you know that you've been loved by God if you love others. Do you understand that logic? In other words, if you feel a joy and an impulse in your heart to tell someone the good news, that is the fruit of the loving acceptance of God in your heart. The grace of God has begun to do its work in you. Telling somebody the good news is no longer a case of 'I've got to' but rather 'I get to'. To know God is to know love, and when touched by that kind of love, the desire is birthed in us to express that love to others – that's just the way it works.

> *This is how God showed his love among us: He sent his one and only Son into the world that we might live through him. This is love: not that we loved God, but that he loved us and sent his Son as an atoning sacrifice for our sins. Dear friends, since God so loved us, we also ought to love one another. No one has ever seen God; but if we love one another, God lives in us and his love is made complete in us. (1 John 4:9–12)*

We don't start out with some theory which says God is love. The Bible says you don't know who God is until He reveals Himself. John tells us that God has revealed Himself through His Son, Jesus Christ. This is how we know who God is: because He first loved us, now we love Him. God loves us, and we know that we have experienced that love because we love Him back, and part of the way we do that is by loving others. When you see that happening in your life, you know that the love of God is at work within you, because you can't do that in your own fallen condition. Husbands and wives who love each other don't get up in the morning and spend time meditating about their spouse and working up love in their heads; it comes out spontaneously or it doesn't come at all.

The purpose of the church and the purpose of all my teaching is to expose us to the love and grace of God in worship, in ministry, in teaching, in everything we do, because that love and grace will do its own work; it will change us from the inside out. It will produce love and acceptance in us for others, and then evangelism and church growth will become the natural consequence of a healthy church, not a particular ministry that a few gifted people might feel called to.

In stepping out to give away the love and grace of God, it's essential to realise that God loves others as much as He loves us. The love of God that you are experiencing has no boundaries. It is not just for the church, not just for those who repent, not just for those who believe. The love of God is for *everybody*, and it is unconditional. The love and grace of God came to you free; you didn't earn it and you deserved only death. That same love and grace goes out from God to all people everywhere, regardless of their behaviour, lifestyle or their knowledge of that love.

Let's look at those two terms a little more: 'boundless' and 'unconditional'. First of all, God's love knows no boundaries; it has no limitation. His love is for everybody. John said it very clearly:

That which was from the beginning, which we have heard, which we have seen with our eyes, which we have looked at and our hands have touched - this we proclaim concerning the Word of life. The life appeared; we have seen it and testify to it, and we proclaim to you the eternal life, which was with the Father and has appeared to us. (1 John 1:1–2)

God loves the whole world. He gave His Son to live and die for the whole world. I can't make it more direct than that. The most quoted verse in the Bible (John 3:16) has told us this a million times over: 'For God so loved the world that He have His only son …' Jesus didn't live and die for a few, for the elect, for the Christians, for a chosen generation. His love and His grace reaches out to the whole world, to everybody, and here's the best news of all: we get to tell people that anytime we like!

When you look at evangelism in the church over the years, what has been preached to so many people outside the kingdom of God is, 'You are going to hell because of your sins and if you don't repent and change your ways, you will be lost for eternity.' Strictly speaking, that may be the truth. However, the truth can be painted in such a light that it communicates an emphasis which betrays that very truth or, at the very least, distorts it. To say 'You are going to hell without Christ and unless you repent and believe, God's judgement will fall on you' communicates a motive for repentance and turning to God which is not the central thrust of the Gospel, it is not the emphasis of the teaching of Jesus and Paul, and it is not the overall message you get from the New Testament. 'Turn or burn' is not the good news of the gospel and it doesn't work for most people.

The true gospel, the real gospel, the whole gospel happens to be the most compelling, beautiful, wonderful story that anyone could ever hear, and it simply must be told. Once the message of the gospel grabs hold of you and burns into you, you just can't help telling people. It bubbles up and out before you know it because the true gospel flows from a well of inexpressible and glorious joy. That's why they call it the 'good news'. We tell people about a good restaurant we went to or a good movie we saw because we want them to share our good experience. Any positive experience we have as human beings impacts us to the point where we want to tell someone.

What does that say about the experience of those Christians who never speak about their faith to anyone, or the ones who only speak about it in terms of judgement or criticism or condemnation of those who fail to live up to their high and holy standards? If you were to survey a thousand people on the streets across our nation this coming week who have nothing at all to do with the church and ask them what they thought the central message of the church was, what would most of them say?

Would they say: 'The church? Those lovely, positive Christians? That's easy: their central message is love. They claim to have met God in some personal way and have been transformed by that encounter. They just can't stop talking about this God of love. And you can see it in their attitude to life. They're always positive and seem to handle the pressures of life better than the rest of us.'

Or would they say: 'Let me think … the church? I would say the central thrust of their message is that they live the right way and the rest of us live the wrong way and are going to hell because of it. They are the self-appointed judges who tell us what we shouldn't do all the time. And yet I know some of these people and they are just as screwed up as the rest of us!'

Or would they say: 'I haven't got a clue what their message is. I have worked with a guy for eight years who I know goes to church every Sunday and to church meetings during the week and I couldn't tell you what he believes because he has never said a word about it the whole time I've known him. Maybe it's a secret or maybe it's just not important enough for him to talk about.'

The primary motivation for sharing the gospel is that it's good news – it's the best news anybody on this planet could ever hear – but that good news will never come out of you until it has first gone into you and transformed you. There are tens of thousands of people sitting in church buildings across this nation right now who have still not received the good news, the true gospel. How do I know that? Simple. No special discernment is needed; I just look at their faces when they leave church each Sunday, and I listen to what they talk about at work and in the community and post online (and what they don't talk about or post).

The heart and soul of the gospel of the Lord Jesus Christ is this: God loves you and accepts you unconditionally, just as you are now, in spite of your sin. He wants to give you the gift of eternal life, enjoying His presence and the power of His love, a love that will transform you over time into the image of His Son, our Lord Jesus Christ. When you accept the truth of this good news, in faith, it will become your experience.

When that is understood, love and grace will have an effect in any life and repentance and a changing character will be the first fruits of that grace encounter. 'You're going to hell. Repent and be saved from the wrath of God' is not what I would describe as good news. In fact, I believe that distorted motivation for turning to God is one of the greatest deceptions that Satan has perpetrated for more than two thousand years. Millions of people have turned to God because they don't want to miss out in eternity; they don't want this wrathful God to punish them. However, if 'fire insurance' is your motivation for turning to God, if the fear of judgement from a high and holy God is what got you interested in the church, you will never really experience the abundant Christian life unless someone is brave enough and loves you enough to challenge you with the undiluted amazing grace of God. Then, and only then, will you have heard the true gospel.

Thankfully, many Christians are confronted with the true gospel at some stage after their conversion. Sadly, many are not. Worse still, millions of people come under the sound of what we call the 'gospel' and walk away. There are thousands of people in our own community who have been connected to a Christian church at some point in their lives but have not stayed connected.

Why is that? I believe it's because they heard something other than the gospel. They may have heard some theologically precise sermons, they may have heard things that are supported by Scripture, but did they ever sit there on the edge of their seat and say, 'Wow! What a story! Is God really like that? Is that how God really feels about me? I had no idea! I always thought He was angry at me. I think I'll stick around this place and get to know God some more! This stuff is life-changing!'

If they had really heard the good news, most of them would have stayed. Let me tell you, friends, that if all the people who used to be part of the church across this nation came back next week, we would not have room to fit them all in. Every worship centre in the nation would be overflowing! The apostle Paul said that the gospel is the power of God that brings salvation (Romans 1:16), and when the true gospel is preached, people will respond. Grace will have its effect and the mission of Christ will be fulfilled.

Over the past few decades, I have been asked a few times when I am going to get off this 'grace' hobbyhorse and preach about sin and repentance. Paul was asked the same question and attracted the same criticism. He was constantly attacked verbally and even physically because his message of God's grace was an offence to the pharisaic mind, as it still is today. Religious people walked away from Jesus and Paul and criticised them because they made people feel good about themselves instead of forcing them on their knees to grovel in the dirt before a holy, angry God.

Religious people have walked away from me too over the last forty years, and they will do that with anyone who preaches the gospel of God's amazing grace. That's why Jesus locked horns with the Pharisees so often. The grace of God is an offence to those still under the bondage of religion. If focusing on sin and repentance when preaching to the lost served to advance the kingdom of God, I would do nothing else. But it doesn't, it never has, and it never will. Read your Old Testament. It is literally full of 'turn or burn' sermons. Did they work? No! The very fact that we have a *New* Covenant is clear evidence that preaching against sin didn't change the people – certainly not over the long haul. Paul actually said it made them worse!

If those 'turn or burn' prophetic sermons could have worked, Jesus would not have come and there would have been no need for His atoning death and glorious resurrection. Look at church history and many of the evangelistic rallies in the latter part of the twentieth century where many thousands of people responded to the 'save yourself from the wrath of God' sermons and see how many of those hellfire and damnation messages led to genuine, lasting repentance and changed lives.

I'm not talking about the people who are frightened into the church for a year or two and then leave. I'm not talking about the people who are frightened into the church and stay bound by religion for the rest of their lives. I'm talking about people who are genuinely saved and brought into the love and grace of God through that kind of preaching and who remain there and bear fruit. It just doesn't happen. That's why Paul said in Romans 2:4 that it's God's kindness that leads us to repentance. It's the overwhelming realisation that God loves us in spite of our sin and that He gives us the power to repent of our sin and change. That is what brings the fruit of repentance and holiness and allows sin to come out into the open and be exposed to the light of God's grace.

'You're going to hell, repent or die' sets up a win-lose proposition. The only way that you can win, and they can win, is for them to say yes to your invitation to follow Jesus. If they say no, the conversation comes to an end. The only way they can go on being your friend is for them to say yes. You put yourself on one side and them on the other. 'You're lost. I'm found. Repent and believe and come over and join me.' The seductive thing about this is that in a technical sense that statement has some truth in it, but it's not helpful and it is rarely effective.

The good news, the gospel of Jesus Christ, is always a win-win story. The proper way to tell this gospel story is something like this:

God loves you whether you believe it or not. God loves you whether you love Him back or not. God's love is boundless. You can't keep Him from loving you. How you feel about God is totally irrelevant to how He feels about you. You don't make God mad or stop His love for you because you sin. You might break His heart and grieve His Spirit, but His love for you is total, it's irrepressible, it's unconditional, it's unstoppable, it has no limits! You may not believe in God but God believes in you! God does not let anybody in the world determine His attitude towards them because of their attitude towards Him. God doesn't love you because of anything in you – good or bad. God does not stop loving you because of anything in you – good or bad. He loves you because of what's in Him. He loves you because He is love. He loves you whether you repent or not. God so loved the world before the world did anything.

Now *that* is good news. That is the most wonderful story known to mankind. You can tell that story anywhere, anytime. Don't leave home without it! And you can't find anybody that isn't better off after you tell them that story. It's a win–win situation. If they don't accept that God loves them, you can simply say, 'That's okay, I'll be back tomorrow to tell you again.' You maintain the relationship. You do not demand anything from them. You do not ask them to change in any way. You are giving them something they desperately need – acceptance – and that acceptance, especially as it flows through you from God's heart, is what will open their hearts to the gospel. Once you say, 'Repent, turn or burn', you get one shot and you either win or lose. Our experience tells us we usually lose, and that person is pushed further away from God and the church.

Do you think that the prostitutes, tax collectors and other drop-kicks with whom Jesus spent so much of His time actually responded to the gospel the first time they met Him? I doubt it. I have no Scripture to prove that, but I seriously doubt it. I think it's more likely that Jesus would have been building a relationship with these people by loving them unconditionally, sharing fellowship and meals with them and it was that acceptance of them as people which melted any barriers and brought the fruit of repentance. If He had said 'turn or burn' the first time He laid eyes on them, He would not have seen many of them again.

I've discovered that not only is this story good for people who don't yet believe it; in a way, it's even better for people who think they believe it, but who don't experience it yet. In many ways the people who need evangelising more than any other people in the world are the people in the church! They just need to really believe what they say they believe.

They need to experience what they have been told. They need to live what they sing about – that God loves them.

I get to tell this story almost every day of my life, and I get to see it literally change people's lives. It's the greatest thrill in the world. When I move out of this role and look back, I will see some really hard times and remember the intensity of the pain and heartache from being in the front line of ministry, but that will never cancel the joy of telling the story of Jesus over and over again.

God's way of producing the energy for us to engage with the mission of Christ is to fill us so full of His love and unconditional acceptance that it simply oozes out and overflows into those around us. When you realise that you can't lose no matter what you do, your motivation to get out there and do something is going to skyrocket. This story is so boundless that everybody, especially people in the church, need to hear it every day. It is never wasted on anybody.

There are people that you need to tell this story to today. Some kind of encouragement or blessing or expression of love is your way of saying to someone, 'You're accepted here, you're loved here and a little bit of that massive love that God has for you has come through me.' A smile, a hug, an offer to help – the wonderful thing is that it never falls to the ground, it never returns void. The grace of God that equips the church for Christ's mission is, first of all, unlimited, without boundaries, and secondly, it is unconditional.

Do you remember the story of Zacchaeus in Luke 19? Jesus was walking through the town of Jericho and saw Zac the tax collector up in a tree. He said, 'Zacchaeus, come down right now.' Now suppose that God woke you up in the middle of the night and said, 'This is God. Get up out of bed. I have words to say to you.' How would you feel? Just a little bit nervous, I would guess! 'Oops, I'm in trouble now!' We find it hard to get the policeman image of God out of our heads. I'm pretty sure Zacchaeus, given his life choices at that time, would have been expecting something from Jesus like, 'Zac, you're in deep trouble. You're a cheat, you're an extortionist, you're a turncoat. You're heading for hell. You need to repent, you need to believe, you need to make restitution to the people that you have cheated, and you need to do it now.'

Zac might have expected that from Jesus, because in one sense it was all true. But the Pharisees, the established church leaders, the senior pastors in town, had been telling Zac that for years and it hadn't done any good at all. Highlighting his sin and need for repentance had not changed Zac's heart in any way.

Zac climbs down and braces himself for another barrage of criticism and a good old-fashioned 'turn or burn' sermon. However, what he gets is so radically different, so unexpected and so out of character compared to what religion has dished out to him for years. What he gets is the spotless, sinless Son of the living God Himself saying, 'Hey Zac, I like you – and I am dining at your house today' (or words to that effect). Zac is shocked to say the least.

To share table fellowship with someone in that culture was an intimate thing, something that communicated strong acceptance of that person. Zacchaeus (and everyone around him) could not believe that Jesus would want to share that kind of intimacy with a low-life scumbag like Zac.

But he is not about to refuse this grace, so he leads Jesus off to his house and sits down and is on his best behaviour. He brings out the food, and he's just waiting for Jesus to say, 'Now, Zac, let me tell you why I'm really here. I want your pledge card and a tenth of all you earn and a promise that you'll be a good boy from now on.' But he didn't get the lecture he expected. Jesus just said, 'Pass the bread, Zac, I'm hungry.' Zac waits and waits and can't believe it when Jesus gets up to leave without preaching to him about his sin. 'Hey Jesus, is that it? Is that all you're going to say to me?'

Yes, that's it. Jesus just wanted to enjoy Zac's company and his home and have a meal with him. He wanted to identify personally with Zacchaeus. He wanted His grace towards Zacchaeus to be His message. Jesus loved Zacchaeus unconditionally. All the others are outside saying, 'He's eating with sinners!' Jesus' reputation was now shot! His credibility as a teacher in that part of town was now destroyed, yet He says, 'This is why I came – to eat with the sinners. I came for those who are sick and know they are sick ,not the ones who are sick and think they're not.' Zac is overwhelmed. 'You mean, you love me the way I am? You haven't asked me to repent or give any money back or change or conform in any way. Wow, I can't believe it.'

Now, listen, in Jesus' name, please get this – what is this man's reaction to the unconditional love and acceptance of Jesus? Repentance followed naturally. When grace came to Zac's house, he said, 'I promise to give half of what I own to the poor and if I've cheated anybody, I promise to pay back four times what I cheated.' And Jesus said, 'Today salvation has come to this home.' He didn't once mention sin or repentance or judgment, and yet the result was conviction of sin, repentance and a changed life.

Can you see the incredible power behind this story of Zacchaeus with regard to evangelism? It's mind-blowing. This is the unconditional love, acceptance and grace of God at work. That's why Paul said the gospel is '... the power of God for *salvation*.' Jesus came to seek and to save the lost, the sinners. As you look outside the church, you need to know that the Spirit of Jesus is hovering around those people seeking to save them. Whoever you talk to, you know that Jesus has already been there.

You don't change in order to be accepted. Acceptance empowers you to change. That is grace. That is the gospel. If you have even the slightest doubt whether you are totally, unconditionally accepted by God, please do whatever you have to do until you believe that, because your life will not work, and you will not become who God created you to become until you get this straight.

One of the changes will be that you will find joy in telling this story to someone else. You won't be witnessing under the weight of obligation, afraid to offend or lose friends; you will experience an inexpressible and glorious joy which compels you to tell this story to everyone in the world. When that happens, you've got the gospel; you've discovered the power of God's amazing grace.

If you have never felt relaxed and comfortable witnessing in the past, maybe it's because you were telling the wrong story or you were telling someone else's story because it was not your own experience. When God's grace is understood and embraced, it will well up inside you and you'll speak out what is in your heart. The more you do it, the more it works. The more you respond to those little inclinations to tell somebody the good news, the more joy you have in doing it.

The most rewarding and fulfilling thing for me in my forty-plus years in ministry is to see people's lives changed by the love and acceptance of God. To see someone's eyes sparkle as the reality of the grace and love of God hits home and to see that person change in character and personality before my eyes is more exciting and fulfilling than watching a leg grow when I am praying for it. Believe me, I've seen both, and I can tell you that the bigger miracle of God for me is to see how simple words about God's love, and the Spirit of God in people confirming that, changes them and empowers them to go out and to tell others so this thing spreads and grows and takes on a life of its own. That is the real wonder and miracle and joy of ministry for me.

Repentance and a changed life are not conditions for salvation; they are the first fruits of salvation, and if we would only believe that truth and act upon it, our church and our community would be turned on its head for Jesus Christ! When the people in our community hear that God loves them unconditionally, and that in spite of their lifestyle and morality and sinfulness, while they were lost in that sin, God sent His only Son, our Lord Jesus Christ, to die for them and take the punishment for all that sin and more so they can have a relationship with Him again, they are going to hear the real gospel, perhaps for the very first time.

When those people find in you and in me the same unconditional love and acceptance that they would find in Jesus, when they don't hear us or feel us judging their behaviour or telling them what they have to give up before we'll accept them, when we can look past the cigarette smoke, the smell of liquor, the immorality, and the foul language – without condoning it – and look straight into the eyes of their heart, like Jesus did with Zacchaeus and say, 'I love you and accept you as you are because God loves you and accepts you as you are', then, and only then, our community and our whole nation will see revival. I am confident of that because I know the power of God's accepting love and God's amazing grace.

The powerful testimony of the early church is that coming into contact with Jesus and accepting the grace of God through Him changes people from the inside out. God delights to use ordinary people to do extraordinary things. When we receive blessings or good news, we can't wait to tell others. That is how the gospel spread in those early days – people had to tell their neighbours about the good things they had found in God. That is the mission of Christ and engaging in that mission is the purpose of the church. The life and love that He has given us will have an effect in the world around us. People will be drawn to God through the church when they see His love and acceptance and experience that from His children, the church. We have good news to tell: God doesn't want anyone to be lost. He wants them to be found by Him.

Understanding and receiving God's amazing grace has to be our highest priority across the body of Christ because our nation will never see the light and life and glory of God until His people, who are called by His name, connect with His truth. Then we will be changed and empowered to spread that truth as fast as the wind of the Spirit can blow.

CHAPTER TWENTY-ONE
The New Way of the Spirit

The apostle Paul preached about God's amazing grace often and intensely. He repeatedly said that we are loved and accepted and given the power of God without the works of the law and that it all came to us freely through Christ Jesus. There was no other message for Paul, and he preached that message tirelessly wherever he went.

His letter to the church at Philippi shows Paul rejoicing with these believers who stood with him in sharing the work of the gospel. It is Paul's most intimate and joyful letter, as he recounts his own journey of living under grace. Then he concludes:

Further, my brothers and sisters, rejoice in the Lord. (Philippians 3:1a)

Maybe he meant to stop there because that sums it up – the Christian life is meant to be one of power and joy and fruitfulness – but he couldn't stop there. He went on and said:

It is no trouble for me to write the same things to you again, and it is a safeguard for you. (Philippians 3:1b)

He explains his single-mindedness: 'It's a safeguard for you that I keep preaching this and reinforcing how much God loves you, how freely He accepts you, and how that can never be taken away from you.' He says it's not a bother for him to say this over and over again. Paul's attitude regarding the gospel and what is a safeguard is somewhat different to many in the church today. Teachers of religion say that it is unsafe to emphasise the free, radical grace of God without the works of the law. Of them, Paul says this:

Watch out for those dogs, those evildoers, those mutilators of the flesh. For it is we who are the circumcision, we who serve God by his Spirit, who boast in Christ Jesus, and who put no confidence in the flesh. (Philippians 3:2–3)

Paul says, 'You are what you are by a gift from God, not any work of the flesh. Now, act like it.' The church will be renewed the day we truly believe who we really are. We are already law-keepers before God in Christ; we are already perfect before God in Christ. When that truth hits home, we will see transformation in our community. The power of God will creatively communicate what we are, and the message of who Christ is, to those who don't know it. Grace is the heart and soul of the gospel.

People will be attracted to us and to the church like never before when we are living in the victory, the freedom and the power that is already ours.

As we have already discussed here, the law is the tool that Satan uses to attack us and drag us away from God and each other. We see in Colossians 2 that Satan needs the law in order to accuse us, and in that same beautiful passage, we see that God disarmed the devil by nailing the law to the cross. We keep the devil disarmed by preaching grace over and over and over and over again.

That's why Paul says, 'It's no trouble for me to keep telling you and reminding you of God's love and acceptance and empowering through grace. It's no trouble for me and it's a safeguard for you, because it keeps the devil disarmed.'

Many have grown up in the church with the idea that our greatest struggle in life is between doing good and doing bad. The truth is you are accepted freely by grace regardless of your good deeds or bad deeds. When you lose sight of that truth, you expose your heart and your life to the enemy of God. Any lie, but especially a religious lie, is dangerous because it becomes the fertile soil where the 'father of lies', the devil, plants his seed and grows his evil crops.

There are lots of great reasons for doing good. We know that we reap what we sow. If you choose to do good, whether you are a Christian or not, your life will work a lot better, all things considered. If you choose to do evil, whether you are a Christian or not, the chances are pretty high that your life will be impacted negatively. So, choose to do good; it's good for you, and it's good for those around you. Sin does not glorify God and it hurts you and those around you, so don't do it. It's that simple.

However, sinning or not sinning has nothing to do with our relationship with God, because that relationship was established for us in Christ and given to us as a free gift. The big personal conflict facing us all is not choosing between good and evil but choosing between the Spirit and the flesh. We worship by the Spirit and put no confidence in the flesh. There is always conflict between Spirit and flesh.

What does it mean to be in the Spirit? Does that refer to a vision or special revelation, or to be in the presence of God in a truly powerful way in worship, or when you say or do something that really blesses someone else, or when you pray in tongues? All of those things may well be spiritual, but that's not what Paul is talking about. Being in the Spirit, according to Paul, is to glory in Christ, rather than putting confidence in the flesh.

A person is not a Jew if he is only one outwardly, nor is circumcision merely outward and physical. No, a person is a Jew if he is one inwardly; and circumcision is circumcision of the heart, by the Spirit, not by the written code. Such a person's praise is not from other people, but from God. (Romans 2:28–29)

When we're righteous according to the written code, we get our praise from each other. But we get praise from God by believing that He has given us everything freely. It really is that simple. If you feel less inclined to work for the kingdom because you realise that God isn't going to pay you for it with His blessings or power, nor praise you for it either, then your motivation was wrong. Paul contrasts the Spirit with the written code.

We identify some things by looking at their opposite. Living by the Spirit, by grace, putting confidence in Christ alone is the opposite of living and relating to God through the law, through religious behaviour and rule keeping.

One of the reasons that preaching law doesn't work is because the law has absolutely no value in restraining sinful behaviour. Sinful passions are aroused by the law! Being under the law didn't work. We all tried and failed and tried and failed and tried again. People will tell you that is the normal Christian life. No, it's not! That's the abnormal Christian life. It's trying to live the Christian life under the law, and the two don't mix! The new way is by the Spirit, the old way is by the law.

For when we were in the realm of the flesh, the sinful passions aroused by the law were at work in us, so that we bore fruit for death. But now, by dying to what once bound us, we have been released from the law so that we serve in the new way of the Spirit, and not in the old way of the written code. (Romans 7:5–6)

Now, back to Philippians:

For it is we who are the circumcision, we who serve God by his Spirit, who boast in Christ Jesus, and who put no confidence in the flesh – though I myself have reasons for such confidence. If someone else thinks they have reasons to put confidence in the flesh, I have more … (Philippians 3:3–4)

The new way is by glorifying Christ. Paul says, 'I don't just put some confidence in the flesh; I put *no* confidence in the flesh.' Being in the flesh, according to Paul, is putting confidence in our own ability to gain favour with God by the works of the law; in layman's terms, trying to please God by our performance.

Being in the flesh is being in yourself rather than in Christ. When operating in the flesh, our relative worth and acceptance is dependent upon our performance. Flesh is self-righteousness. When 'holiness preachers' tell us that the church is full of flesh, they're right, but not in the way they think. When they rave against the sin in the church, they are not referring to the flesh, even though they think they are. There's more flesh in what they're preaching than in those they're preaching to! They are encouraging a breed of self-righteous Christians who judge their relative worth in the kingdom of God and in His church by what they do and how well they do it. That is the flesh! Let's see how Paul defines it:

> *If someone else thinks they have reasons to put confidence in the flesh, I have more: circumcised on the eighth day, of the people of Israel, of the tribe of Benjamin, a Hebrew of Hebrews; in regard to the law, a Pharisee; as for zeal, persecuting the church; as for righteousness based on the law, faultless. (Philippians 3:4–6)*

Flesh is being a good, holy, right person and being proud of it. We have the choice of being in the Spirit (having confidence in Jesus and allowing the Spirit to communicate with us and to establish a relationship between us and God) or being in the flesh (thinking the law can mediate our relationship with God). Paul says we cannot and do not rely on our own effort in any way, shape or form. So those who say that a little law is needed to balance grace are, in essence, saying that a little flesh is needed to balance Spirit. But Paul says he puts no confidence in the flesh whatsoever:

> *But whatever were gains to me [with all this law keeping and legalistic righteousness; after all, I am a perfect Pharisee] I now consider everything a loss because of the surpassing worth of knowing Christ Jesus my Lord, for whose sake I have lost all things. I consider them garbage [the Greek is much stronger than that!], that I may gain Christ and be found in him, not having a righteousness of my own that comes from the law, but that which is through faith in Christ – the righteousness that comes from God on the basis of faith.*

> *I want to know Christ – yes, to know the power of his resurrection and participation in his sufferings, becoming like him in his death ... (Philippians 3:7–10)*

We think that our good deeds are at least some gain before God, but Paul says forget it; they are rubbish before God. We think that obedience and sacrifice and being good gets us closer to God; Paul says that's garbage! If anyone could have done that, it would have been Paul.

Instead, he says he had a revelation of God's grace in Christ, through the Holy Spirit, and so he now counts all that hard work and obedience as loss. He puts no confidence in that whatsoever. Paul's profound and compelling reason to put absolutely no confidence in the flesh is so he may know Christ. Paul learned the one thing that matters above all others – to actually know Christ and to know His power. This was his prayer for all believers:

> I keep asking that the God of our Lord Jesus Christ, the glorious Father, may give you the Spirit of wisdom and revelation, so that you may know him better. I pray also that the eyes of your heart may be enlightened in order that you may know the hope to which he has called you, the riches of his glorious inheritance in the saints, and his incomparably great power for us who believe. (Ephesians 1:17–19)

Paul wanted to know God in an intimate way, and he wanted the power of God in His life and ministry. He says we can all get that, not by doing more and trying harder through the law, but by receiving the Spirit of wisdom and revelation. The Spirit ministers God's total, free acceptance of us in Christ and His unconditional love for us because of the blood sacrifice of Christ. That is how we know God as our Saviour. God wants to be known as He really is. That is why He sent Jesus Christ and why Jesus said:

> Anyone who has seen me has seen the Father. (John 14:9)

Some of you have a hunger and longing to know God and at times that hunger triggers impatience and frustration. You need to remember that fruit doesn't just pop out the minute the seed is planted; it takes time. The Lord is able and willing to give you immeasurably more than all you ask or imagine, but He won't give you everything tomorrow. Just like a fruit tree, when the seed has grown and been nurtured with the right food, the fruit will show at the right time, but that season of fruit bearing is preceded by years of growth and maturing.

So too with your relationship with God. Be hungry and thirsty for more of His presence, His blessings and His empowering for ministry – He gave you that hunger, it's good – but recognise that it takes time. There will be instant change in some areas, as people are set free from spiritual bondage and legalistic oppression, but other things will be slowly transformed and dealt with over the long haul. It will happen as you grow in the Lord, and often, slow change is the most profound of all. But let me say this – the speed at which you travel on this road with God, and the size and nature of the blessings and ministry and opportunity, will depend largely on how much you really want this. 'You have not because you ask not ...' (James 4:3). Many of us are fearful of asking for more from God because we don't think we are worthy of it, or we don't think we will be able to handle it when it comes. Both are lies from the enemy.

God's bidding is God's enabling and if we have the humility, He will give us the ability. He gives us the strength, the power and the wisdom, as and when required, for the fruit that He desires to bring. However, to a significant degree, we determine how much we want from God. As far as I'm concerned, let's have the lot! Back up your truck to heaven and ask God to dump everything. Let Him worry about whether you can handle it or whether you deserve it; that's His problem. He just told us to ask for it. Now the key to fruit-bearing is remaining in Jesus, not keeping the law. So, what does 'remaining in Jesus' mean? Jesus told us:

> *You are already clean because of the word I have spoken to you. Remain in me, as I also remain in you. No branch can bear fruit by itself; it must remain in the vine. Neither can you bear fruit unless you remain in me.*

> *I am the vine; you are the branches. If you remain in me and I in you, you will bear much fruit; apart from me you can do nothing. If you do not remain in me, you are like a branch that is thrown away and withers; such branches are picked up, thrown into the fire and burned. If you remain in me and my words remain in you, ask whatever you wish, and it will be done for you. This is to my Father's glory, that you bear much fruit, showing yourselves to be my disciples.*

> *As the Father has loved me, so have I loved you. Now remain in my love. If you keep my commands, you will remain in my love, just as I have kept my Father's commands and remain in his love. I have told you this so that my joy may be in you and that your joy may be complete. (John 15:3–11)*

The two components of remaining in Christ, or maintaining intimacy with Him, are attending to His word and obeying His commands. Sadly, religion takes these very things and turns them into oppressive law and legalistic duties.

I have seen so people transformed and given new life and joy and meaning because of the words that have come from this teaching. It's a mystery, but it's an observable fact. There is a new kind of life, a new kind of expectation, a new thing happening in those who know they have been hearing the words of Jesus, interpreted by His Holy Spirit and lodged in their heart as seeds.

Reading the Bible is a great way of sowing those seeds. His Word is life. If you let it in, meditate on it, protect it and let it dwell richly in you, it will of its own accord produce life and fruit in abundance. Seeds look very ordinary – tiny and lifeless; they show no sign of the amazing life potential inside them. Words are common, but if they contain the life-changing Word of God and you take them in, they find fertile soil that the Holy Spirit has prepared, and they germinate. When the time is right, life explodes from that seed, intermixed with excitement and joy.

I remember when this happened for the first time for me many years. I was thinking, 'Something is breaking up through the ground. The stony walls of my heart are coming down! The seeds are destroying the foundations of my legalism! My entire perspective of God, of myself and of others is changing!' One tiny life-impregnated seed can split a huge lifeless rock, because life always overcomes death. Light always dispels darkness. We remain in Jesus by attending to His Word. Each time you take it in, you are impacted by something different. That's the power of the Word of God.

The second way we remain in Jesus is by doing what He says. Again, we are so close to religion here. If we turn just half a notch on this dial, the devil turns this into legalistic, life-destroying religion. Doing what Jesus says is entirely different to obeying the law. The law is written on paper, on stone; it is objective, it doesn't care about your circumstances. The instructions of Jesus come from a person to a person, and they come with character and personality. They come in the context of a relationship, and we can never have a personal relationship with an impersonal law.

A cold, abstract law does not inspire motivation, but when a person whom you love and respect and want to please calls you to live in a certain way, everything changes. Jesus pleads with us as dearly loved children. He says, 'Your lives will work and you will be so blessed and joyful and fulfilled and happy. That's what I want for you, and that will happen if you do what I say.' Commands in the New Testament are spoken against a very different backdrop to those commands under the old covenant law. In fact, I would be happier personally if we referred to them as exhortations, for in effect that is what they are.

The New Testament calls people like me shepherds but understand this: shepherds do not feed sheep. Shepherds lead the sheep to food and the sheep decide to eat it or not. I cannot force people to take in what they need, or to change or to do anything. I care greatly when I see people in the church struggling under the load of guilt or rejection or pain, and I could lose sleep and energy over the sheep who don't want to eat, but I realise that I can never change that. It's not my job to feed anyone; that's their responsibility. I cannot take responsibility for your life or anybody else's life.

I don't want you to believe anything or do anything I suggest in this book because it's in this book. I want only one thing, and I want it with all my heart – I want you to know Jesus Christ. Everything I have written here is designed to make that connection – a personal intimacy with your Creator and Redeemer! Just love Him. Develop a personal face-to-face relationship with Jesus.

Many people find that statement difficult. Some people have been going to church and living as a Christian for years, but still don't know what that really means. Trust me, there is more, a whole lot more. In fact, if you don't get to know Jesus in a personal, vibrant, intimate way, you really have nothing. Don't let the devil deceive you and keep you locked in some kind of 'intellectual faith', which is really a contradiction in terms. You can know Jesus personally. Jesus is alive! If you have welcomed Him into your life, then He is alive in you. He will speak to you, He will stimulate your emotions and give you courage and joy. He will alter your life in such a way that you will know that He's alive and you can experience Him walking with you – and you will settle for nothing less than that. You will experience Him as the Holy Spirit releases the presence and power and ministry of Jesus in your church, in your community and across your whole nation.

Allow me to take away one last opportunity for legalism and say this: if you just can't get your mind around the free grace of God or cannot accept it at this point, don't worry about it. You are not outside of God's grace just because you don't understand it. As long as you're seeking, you're seeking, and if you can't believe this in your heart, then I will believe it for you for a while – maybe a long while – because we're all in this together. Ultimately, Jesus wants you to know Him as He knows you. There will never be a time in your life when you are not going to need a Saviour to love you; you're never going to outgrow the need for God as He really is. You will know God and will experience His love, His power, His compassion and His mercy, when you understand His grace in all its truth, by revelation from the Holy Spirit.

The primary purpose of this book has been to prepare us to participate with Jesus Christ in His mission, for that is the only mission we have. The church doesn't have a mission. Christ has a mission, and that mission has a church. It has been my goal in this teaching to strip away all religious baggage by exposing some of the ways in which it comes into our lives and the lies that perpetuate it. Jesus paid the price to free us from religion once and for all time, and that freedom is experienced as we walk in intimacy with Him.

To know Jesus at all is to know Him as a free gift. To participate in His mission and to experience fellowship with one another and minister to one another, we have to understand God's amazing grace. We need to receive love from God and love from others, and never try to earn it. We also need to learn to give God love freely in worship, obedience and service, and freely give love to each other in acceptance and kindness. We've been accepted and loved freely. When that reality hits home, we are empowered to accept and love others freely. Revival, renewal and reformation will come when the grace of God is preached and understood in all its truth. I share Paul's conviction as recorded in the book of Acts, and I can think of no better words than his to express my heart's desire as I finish.

> *… I consider my life worth nothing to me; my only aim is to finish the race and complete the task the Lord has given me – the task of testifying to the good news of God's grace. (Acts 20:24)*

www.ingramcontent.com/pod-product-compliance
Lightning Source LLC
Chambersburg PA
CBHW072131020426
42334CB00018B/1750